CELEBRATION

A World of Art and Ritual

Office of Folklife Programs
and
Renwick Gallery
of the
National Museum of American Art

Smithsonian Institution Press, Washington, D.C., 1982

Published on the occasion of an exhibition
cosponsored by the
Smithsonian Institution's Office of Folklife Programs
and
Renwick Gallery
of the
National Museum of American Art
Washington, D.C.
and presented at the Renwick Gallery
March 17, 1982–June 26, 1983

This publication has been made possible
by a generous grant from the
James Smithson Society.

Library of Congress Catalog
Card Number: 81-23999

ISBN 0-87474-433-4

Cover: 159a.
Groom's Headdress, before 1960;
Bengal, India. NMNH 399628.

Contents

Foreword

Celebration: A World of Art and Ritual gathers objects from all of the Smithsonian museums that depict or play a role in human celebrations. To celebrate is human—all societies collectively honor the past, rejoice in increase, and mourn loss. The objects in the exhibition speak in unison of the commonalities of human celebratory expressions—the occasions, motivations, and modalities. They also sing in a many-voiced harmony of the multitude of ceremonies and symbols through which people in different epochs, climes, and conditions have ordered and intensified their lives.

As Emile Durkheim, Victor Turner, and others have shown us, celebrations of seeds planted or crops harvested, of battles won or lost, of births or deaths, are, in a sense, celebrations of community—a group feeling shared by people with similar moral values, cultural identities, and aesthetic styles. It seems especially fitting that the national museum of the United States house such an exhibition, for we are an institution that from its inception in 1846 has studied, presented, and celebrated the cultures and aesthetics of American peoples. In the past, we have concentrated almost exclusively on tribal cultures and, hence, the preponderence of items in the exhibition are from these societies. Lately we have turned our attention to folk societies, cultural groups that exist within larger, encompassing social structures. The number of folk objects in our collections is still relatively small, and folk cultures—especially from Europe and America—are underrepresented in the exhibition. We have tried to redress this lack with photographs of American celebrations in each of the galleries and with the staging of living celebrations by American folk groups as part of the exhibition. Through them we may learn something of America's celebratory heritage and experience the effervescence of communal feeling.

The catalogue for *Celebration: A World of Art and Ritual*, like the exhibition itself, was shaped by the guiding intellect of the guest curator, Victor Turner. The descriptions of objects, based upon the work of a team of researchers, emphasize, where possible, the meanings given to the objects by the people who use them. The objects of celebration herein, their meanings and the heritage of the people who created them, are explained and presented in a catalogue that can be pleasurably browsed through and profitably read. Both catalogue and exhibition, like many of the objects themselves, celebrate shared feelings of community in traditional societies.

S. Dillon Ripley
Secretary, Smithsonian Institution

About the Exhibition

When the Secretary of the Smithsonian Institution appointed a Folklife Advisory Council in 1976, it was charged with the responsibility of exploring both the more contemporary idea of folklife and its place in the Smithsonian's ongoing programs. At an early meeting, one of the council's members suggested that what the Smithsonian really needed was a folklife museum. Although the idea was far more grand than the council had been established to consider, it did lead to the idea of using the Renwick Gallery's temporary exhibition spaces to mount a major exhibition that would reveal the Smithsonian's long interest in studying and collecting objects from folk and traditional cultures. Ralph Rinzler, director of the Office of Folklife Programs, and I, as director of the Renwick Gallery, were appointed co-directors for the project.

What would be in such an exhibition? How might it be focused? Who would select it? Given the Renwick Gallery's experience since 1972 in presenting temporary exhibitions, it was quickly agreed that this museum would be responsible for the exhibition's presentation and the Office of Folklife Programs, with its knowledgeability about folklore and traditional culture, for research leading to the exhibition and for its scholarly content. Suggested by Folklife Programs, the celebration theme was warmly endorsed by members of the Folklife Advisory Council. The eminent anthropologist Victor Turner, William R. Kenan Professor of Anthropology at the University of Virginia, was invited to serve as guest curator.

Elaine Eff, experienced folklorist and research coordinator for the initial phase of the project, began in 1978 to examine and photograph objects in the collections of thirteen Smithsonian museums. Aided by his wife and colleague Edith, Dr. Turner helped first to reduce the volume of photographs to two thousand objects and eventually to refine the selection to approximately six hundred objects associated with the celebrations of some sixty-two cultures around the world. The final selections were drawn from nine of the Smithsonian's museums.

Many of the objects chosen had not been examined or studied since they were collected by scientists or explorers in the last century. Further, most had never been exhibited and—even when available—information on their cultural origins and uses was scanty. It became clear very quickly that the work involved in identifying many of the ethnological objects correctly and interpreting them in the context of their specific use in celebrations required more time than the Smithsonian's museum scientists and historians could reasonably spare from their ongoing research. Consequently, seventeen specialists in the specific cultural areas represented by selected objects were employed to conduct research under the supervision of staff ethnologists, and a second team of writers was employed to prepare informative labels from the factual data that had been gathered.

Kristine E. Miller became project manager for the production phase of the exhibition to oversee its myriad details and to work closely with the Renwick's curator, Michael W. Monroe, who took the challenge of designing the installation. I have thought at times that an exhibition like *Celebration*, with so many contributors to its completion, is rather like a quilt made of many pieces composed to create a whole. That this exhibition has come together with the order of a log cabin pattern rather than as a crazy quilt is largely due to Kristie Miller.

The decision to print an inexpensive guide to the exhibition that visitors could use while viewing it came late, as a solution to providing more information about the objects than labels in the cases could accommodate. Three other publications related to the show were also in progress—a book of scholarly essays on celebrations, a guidebook to Washington-area celebrations, and a handbook for teachers. The decision to publish this more fully illustrated exhibition catalogue was a natural corollary to these other publication projects.

The scope of *Celebration: A World of Art and Ritual* exceeds every exhibition the Renwick Gallery has presented in its ten years of existence. We can only hope that in viewing it, reading the publications prepared to augment the visual power of the objects themselves, and reflecting upon the diversity and beauty of the world's celebrations, each visitor to *Celebration* will look again at the world we know and realize that our folkways are but a single response to the universal phenomenon of life in celebration.

Lloyd E. Herman
Director, Renwick Gallery, and
Codirector, *Celebration: A World
of Art and Ritual*

Celebration: A World of Art and Ritual, one of the largest pan-institutional exhibitions in the Smithsonian's history, has grown from the deliberations of the Secretary's Folklife Advisory Council. Just before Christmas 1977, the council decided that an exhibition should be mounted to show the extent of the Smithsonian's historic involvement with folklife studies. The exhibition project has been at once familiar and strange to our program, which plans and produces the Festival of American Folklife, an annual presentation of living practitioners of traditional culture. The project has been familiar in the theme, in the involvement of living performers, and in the guidance of Victor Turner, whose ideas have influenced our approach to traditional cultures for several years now.

The symbolism, style, and elements involved in staging celebrations have held theoretical and practical interest for the Folklife Program since 1967, when the first Festival of American Folklore was mounted. Our goal is to present living traditional cultures authentically, understandably, and respectfully and as often as possible to recreate traditional forms of celebration. This has of necessity brought us face to face with the problems of the dynamics and semantics of festivity. The Folklife Program's collections are limited almost solely to recorded sounds and images of traditional cultures (the few objects acquired by us for this exhibition will find a permanent home in the Smithsonian museum collections). Material culture has, however, been a central theme in our activities—from a conference held in 1967 concomitant with the first festival to the publications of monographs and films on the manufacture, use, and meaning of traditional material forms.

These predilections account for our acceptance of the offer to conceive and plan a museum exhibition. We were immediately struck by the difference between presenting traditional culture on the one hand through its living practitioners in a festival setting and on the other hand through objects in a museum setting. The basic difference, of course, is that people can be encouraged to speak for themselves while objects—even celebratory objects—cannot. Or rather, to quote Victor Turner, "objects speak," but in a symbolic language audible only to the people who make and use them. In *Celebration: A World of Art and Ritual,* the persons who have enabled us to hear what the objects say about traditional cultures are the researchers, who documented objects with information from their own ethnographic field research and gleanings from the published and unpublished work of others. Although the objects had sometimes lain virtually undocumented in Smithsonian collections since they were accessioned, the researchers have brought to light knowledge that enables us to hear what the objects say with understanding, respect, and some inkling of the historical conditions under which they were created.

Ultimately the exhibition is a tribute to the genius of countless unnamed craftsmen and celebrants whose hand and eye captured the essence of communal and societal values, thus yielding these richly handsome, meaning-laden objects.

Ralph Rinzler
Director, Office of Folklife Programs, and
Codirector, *Celebration: A World of
Art and Ritual*

Acknowledgments

One of the most comprehensive exhibitions in the history of the Smithsonian Institution has required the coordinated efforts of many individuals. Each person involved in research, exhibition design, conservation, and installation has performed with high professional standards to create an exhibition that is both unique in concept and exacting in execution. The number of persons responsible for the final product reaches the hundreds, from the processers of procurement forms to installers of objects into the Renwick Gallery. Although it is impossible to mention and thank all those who have assisted in this extensive project, the staffs of the Renwick Gallery, the Office of Folklife Programs, and the exhibition staff for *Celebration: A World of Art and Ritual* acknowledge and appreciate the contributions made by all who participated in the project.

The concept for *Celebration* developed from the deliberations at the Folklife Advisory Council chaired by Wilcomb E. Washburn. The guidance and support of Dr. Washburn, Charles A. Blitzer, Dean W. Anderson, and other members of the council made the ideal concept of celebration a museum reality.

Kristine E. Miller, project manager for the exhibition's production phase, discharged her responsibilities with a vivacity and diplomacy as dependable as her ability to cope calmly and efficiently with problems that others might have considered to be of near-crisis proportions. Her enthusiasm for *Celebration* kept the project buoyant, whether she was sorting out disparate terminology for objects in label and catalogue text with the editor or updating the budget with the latest prices for wallboard.

Michael W. Monroe, curator of the Renwick Gallery and designer of the exhibition, directed his energies to the challenge of exhibiting the objects in an aesthetic as well as a culturally authentic and environmentally safe display. Ellen Myette, associate curator of the Renwick Gallery, organized the shipment of objects to, and storage in, the gallery. In this task she received capable assistance from Philip C. Wright and Claudine Weatherford. Frank Caldwell, exhibition production manager of the Renwick, offered major assistance in attending to innumerable logistical details related to the project, especially in the mounting and preparation of objects for exhibition to the public.

Special credit is due Elaine Eff, who served as project manager during the initial research and object selection phase. Her painstaking survey of the collections and suggestions on installation provided a strong foundation for the construction and production of the exhibition.

Peter Seitel, senior folklorist of the Office of Folklife Programs, served as consultant to the project. A team of label writers, Priscilla Rachun Linn, Mei-Su Teng, and Jill Vexler, transformed the research data submitted into the catalogue's text.

Carroll S. Clark, editor-in-chief at the National Museum of American Art, tackled the enormous job of bringing consistency and clarity to the descriptions of objects and celebrations with which she had, for the most part, little or no familiarity, and of devising appropriate formats for the labels used in the display cases and the sizable catalogue and checklist prepared for the exhibition. Expert supplementary editing was provided by Kathleen Preciado of the Smithsonian Institution Press.

Other persons whose particular services must not remain unmentioned are, most notably, the exhibition staff for *Celebration*, Elizabeth V. Hantzes and Carol Foster. Together they provided invaluable assistance in major areas of the preparatory work entailed by the exhibition. With commendable diligence Elizabeth Hantzes pursued the rights and research for photographs and films included in the exhibition to show the contexts within which the objects were used. Her unfamiliarity with her diverse subject matter did not affect her ability to complete a major goal of the exhibition. Carol Foster tackled the enormous task of coordinating the research through the appropriate curatorial channels of the Smithsonian Institution. Her meticulous manner of keeping information flowing throughout the Smithsonian and back to the *Celebration* office provided an indispensable service to the overall completeness and correctness of the data used in the labels and publications.

A substantial debt of gratitude for research and documentation is owed to Stanley Walens, who provided supplementary symbolic data on North American Indians, and to the following, whose areas of specialization are indicated after their names: Leon Siroto, Africa; William H. Crocker, Brazilian Canela Indians; Grace Grossman, Judaica, Chang Su Houchins, Japan and Korea, and Elizabeth Stockton, other parts of Asia; Priscilla Rachun Linn, Latin America, United States, and other areas; Jane Walsh, Mexican masks; Yvonne Lange, New Mexican Santo figures; Ira Jacknis, North American Indians; David Penney and Maryanne George, Oceania; Paula Johnson, United States and eastern Europe, and Anne Schaffer, eastern Europe. Allegra Fuller Snyder developed a script for a video presentation on the element of dance in celebration, Martha Foster screened and recommended ethnographic films for inclusion in the exhibition's audio-visual components, and Shirley L. Green and Diane Hamilton provided research for still photography.

The numerous and complex routing procedures for objects and research were facilitated at the National Museum of Natural History by Dr. Douglas Ubelaker, chairman, and U. Vincent Wilcox and Linda L. Eisenhart, of the Department of Anthropology; at the National Museum of American History by Douglas E. Evelyn, deputy director, and Mary Newbold, research assistant, and the curators of the Department of Cultural History; and at the Museum of African Art by Lee Williams and Bryna Fryer, curatorial assistants.

Under the direction of Curator Barbara Shissler, the Department of Education at the National Museum of American Art developed a unique educational program for elementary and secondary school children in the Washington, D.C., area. This program was funded in part by a grant from the Office of the Assistant Secretary for Public Service. Appreciation for valuable assistance in preparing the program is extended to Nora M. Panzer; Marjorie L. Share; Elizabeth Rees Gilbert; and Susan Nichols, author of *Let's Celebrate!*, a teachers' handbook prepared for the program. Allen B. Bassing, assistant curator for education at the Renwick Gallery, has developed a series of imaginative performances and public programs related to the exhibition theme.

The staffs of the Renwick Gallery and the Office of Folklife Programs contributed daily assistance and special attention to the project. Elizabeth C. Beuck, administrative officer of the Office of Folklife Programs, oversaw many of the myriad details and budgetary matters for the exhibition and was always available to the staff as an administrator, a staunch supporter, and a friend. Richard Derbyshire, photography archivist of the same office, through his expertise provided essential services in photographic reproduction and video.

Many exhibitions and museum projects depend upon the invaluable aid of interns and volunteers. Renwick interns Amy Bernhardt, Stephen Hamp, Walter E. Hill, Kate A. Nearpass, Lea Nickless, and Rebecca Waning and volunteers Kitty Coiner, Annie S. Curet, and Ann Elise Hoffman provided the leg work and support services so desperately needed for the timely production of many aspects of the exhibition and related public programs.

The support provided by the Smithsonian Institution Press is indicated by its endorsement and publication of all five of the exhibition manuscripts. Stepen Kraft, senior designer, and Carol Hare, who designed this catalogue, deserve special recognition. The Press's reinforcement of the concept of celebration brought meaning and promise to the project.

Film clips to supplement the visual display and provide a fuller context for the use of the objects were supplied by the following companies and individuals: Appalshop Films; Audio Brandon; Australian Institute for Aboriginal Studies; Barr Films; BFA Educational Media; Brigham Young University in cooperation with the Polynesian Cultural Center and Institution for Polynesian Studies, Brigham Young University, Hawaii Campus; CBS, Trust Estate of Edward R. Murrow; Coronet Films; Dr. William H. Crocker and Dr. Gordon Gibson of the Smithsonian Institution; Eliot Elisofon Archives, National Museum of African Art; Encyclopaedia Britannica Educational Corporation; Encyclopedia Cinematographica; Global Village; Cherel Ito; National Film of Canada; Cinémathèque Pacifique; Phoenix Films; Rod Thompson/Films North; and University of Washington Press.

Numerous individuals and companies contributed to the education programs related to the exhibition. Thanks go to the Office of Printing and Photographic Services, Smithsonian Institution; Carroll Matheson Connell; Robert Hort, Enterprise

Press, Inc., New York; and the James Smithson Society for their generous support of the project.

Each contributor to the exhibition's progress has provided a welcome service to the Smithsonian Institution and to its first pan-institutional project by bringing objects from within its collections together for a time. This is an occasion for celebration.

L.E.H. and R.R.

Introduction to the Exhibition

All human societies celebrate. They mark with ceremony and ritual, in places and times separated from everyday routine, their triumphs, joys, and even sorrows. Religious and political groups commemorate their founders, saints, martyrs, and heroes with feasts and fasts. The turning agriculture year is punctuated with festivals of planting, first fruits, and harvest. Hunting and fishing cultures celebrate exceptional kills and catches. Individual lives are seldom neglected as sources of celebration: birth, puberty, marriage, elderhood, and death provide occasions for rites of passage.

During celebrations people think and feel more deeply than in everyday life. They express the meanings and values of their societies in special, often vivid ways. Among these is the creation of beautiful or striking objects, which exist only because humankind celebrates its own existence.

The museums of the Smithsonian Institution contain many objects used in celebration. This exhibition is a selection made by anthropologists and folklorists from among the Smithsonian's rich, often randomly collected holdings. Naturally, no exhibition of this type can be fully representative or inclusive; there must be obvious gaps and omissions. Indeed, no museum has systematically collected celebratory objects on a worldwide cross-cultural scale. The objects in the exhibition have mostly been collected since the beginning of the last century by travelers in America or abroad and have found their way, by gift or purchase, to the Smithsonian Institution. The purpose of the exhibition is simply to bring before the public a sample of what women and men anywhere can do when they are moved to celebrate.

Victor Turner
Guest Curator for the Exhibition

Colorplates

Identified by catalogue number.

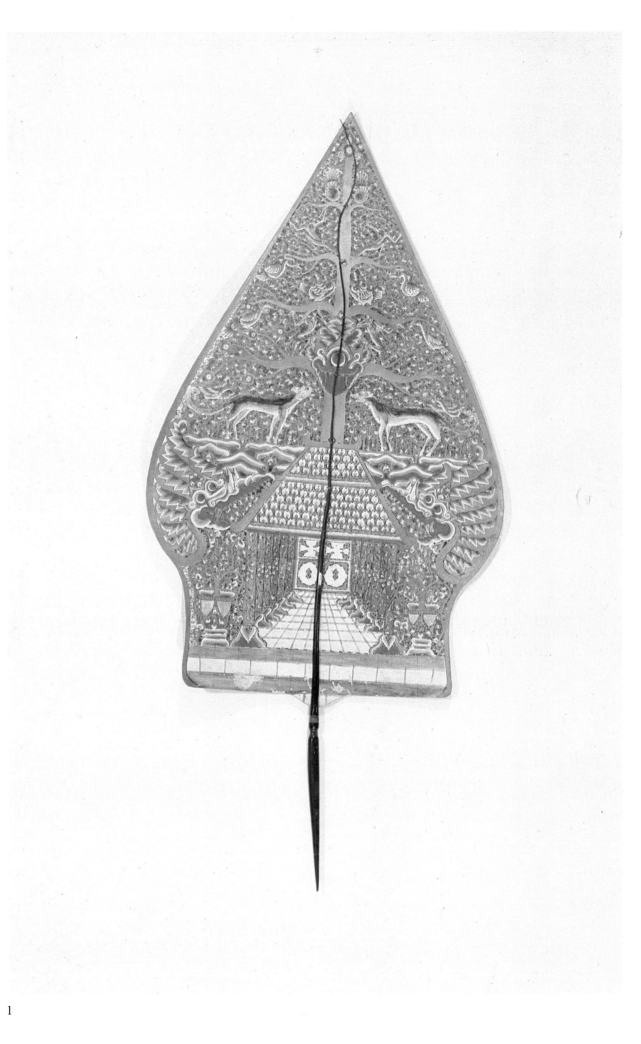

11 a, b, c,

12

19

27 b

Dancer wearing Mwaash A Mbooy mask performs for village, Kuba people; Muentshi, Zaire, 1972. Courtesy, Eliot Elisofon Archives, National Museum of African Art, Smithsonian Institution (see no. 27 b).

28 b

28 e

32

34

22

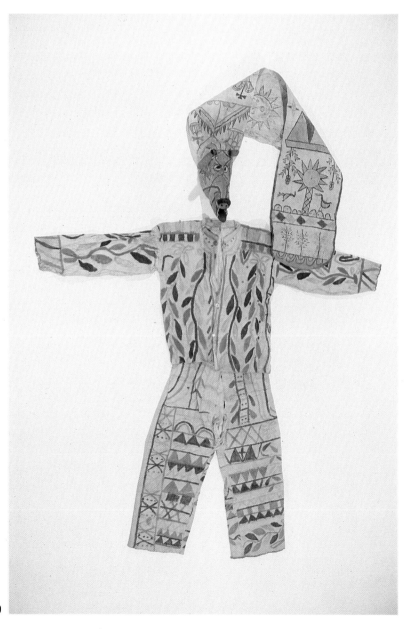

40

56 b

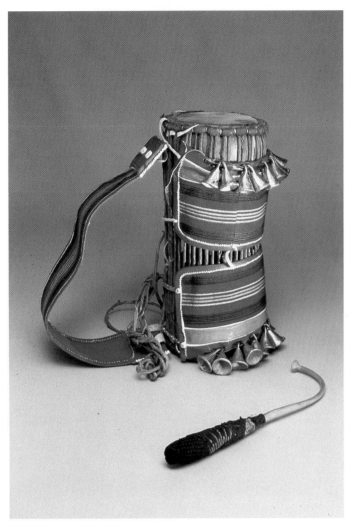

60

64

74

23

84

86

88

100 f

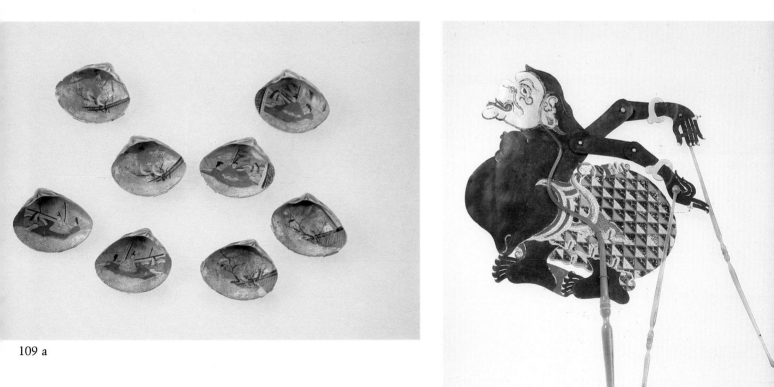

109 a

101 c

25

111 a, b, c

111 d

115 c

122

124

128

Decorated for a Ramkokamekra-Canela kêêtúwayê ritual, several boys too young to perform are carried on the shoulders of "ceremonial friends"; Canela, Brazil, 1978. Courtesy, William H. Crocker (see no. 131).

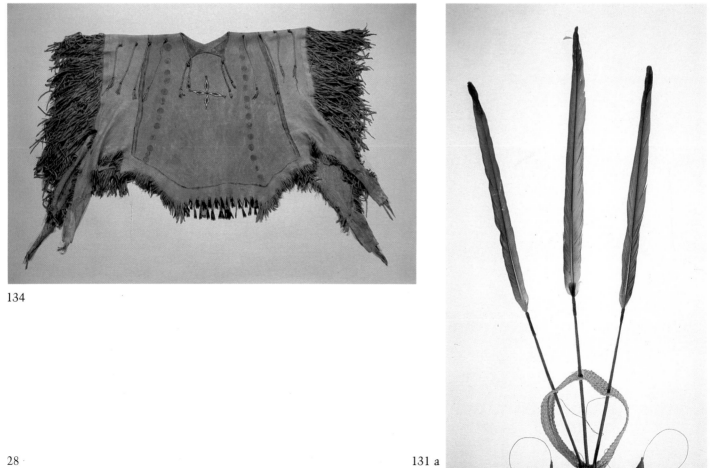

134

131 a

141

140

143

A Ndebele woman wearing a wife's beaded apron (mapoto) stands before the brightly colored murals of her house; Northern Transvaal, South Africa, 1977. Courtesy, Suzanne Priebatsch and Natalie Knight (see no. 143).

145

146

148

155 a

163

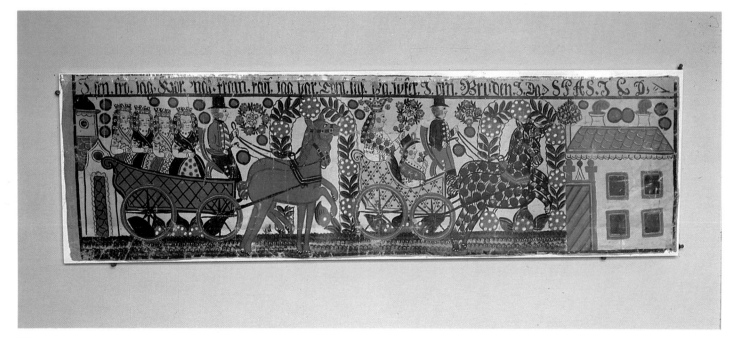

170

173 (two gourd whistles)

174

Day of the Dead Altar; Oaxaca city, Oaxaca, Mexico, November 1970. Courtesy, Jill Vexler (see no. 182).

185

190

A procession of three great chariots carrying statues of Jagannatha, Lord of the Universe, and his brother and sister at the great annual **ratha** jatra *(car festival) held at Puri in the state of Orissa, eastern India. Courtesy, Harry Miller, © National Geographic Society* (see no. 198).

198 b

200 j

203 a

204 a

Ancestral altar in the palace compound of King Oba Akenzue II with brass heads of the king's grandfather (back) and father (front); Benin City, Nigeria, 1970. Courtesy, Eliot Elisofon Archives, National Museum of African Art, Smithsonian Institution (see no. 207).

214 a

211 i

218 d

223 a

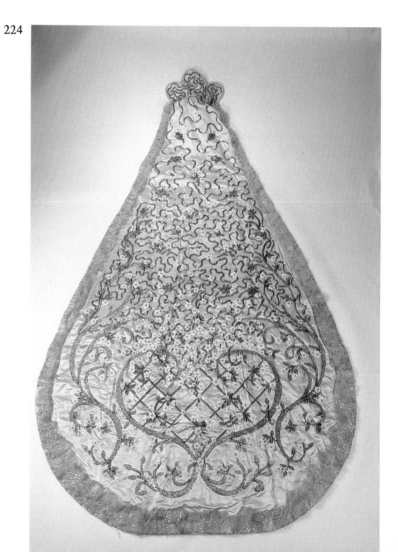

224

230 a

Prancing Ramkokamekra-Canela men in beastlike masks perform humorous antics to entertain the women gathered in the village plaza. A specialist in chanting holds a gourd rattle as she prompts the women to sing; Canela, Brazil, 1970. Courtesy, William H. Crocker (see no. 231 a).

233 e

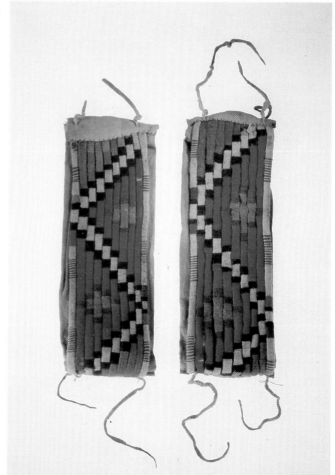

233 f

234

236 a

236 b

238 d

240 b

242 a

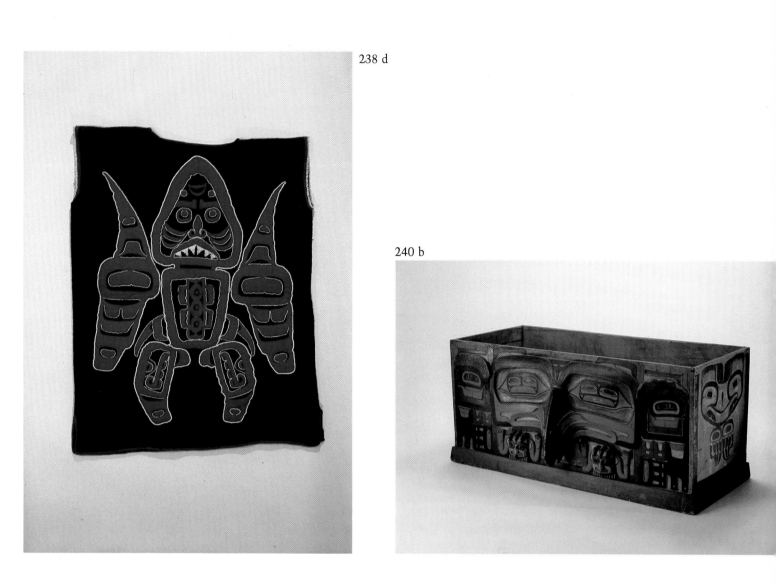

252

243 a

246

253

254 b (hide kilt)

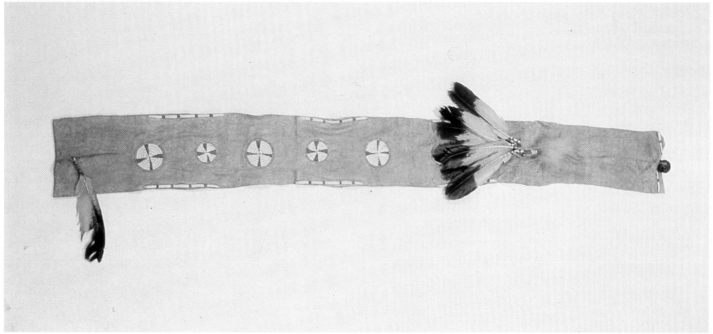

254 c

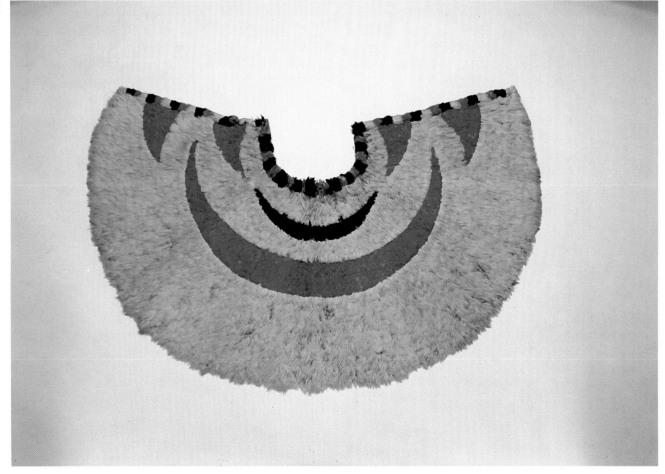

257

270

Catalogue of the Exhibition

The dimensions of the objects are in inches,
followed in parentheses by centimeters.
Height precedes width and depth.
Unless otherwise indicated, all objects are from
the collections of museums and offices of
the Smithsonian Institution, which are identified
by the following abbreviations:

AfA   National Museum of African Art

C-H   Cooper-Hewitt Museum

FP   Office of Folklife Programs

HM&SG   Hirshhorn Museum and Sculpture Garden

NASM   National Air and Space Museum

NGA   National Gallery of Art

NMAA   National Museum of American Art

NMAH   National Museum of American History

NMNH   National Museum of Natural History

NMNH-NAA National Museum of Natural History,
          National Anthropological Archives

OH   Office of Horticulture

SI   Smithsonian Institution Building

1.
Shadow Puppet (*kajon; kekayon; gunungan*), before 1981
Java, Indonesia
horn, bone, water-buffalo hide, paint
36 × 18¾ × ¾ (91.4 × 47.6 × 1.8)
NMNH 421866
Illustrated in color, p. 17

In Javanese shadow-puppet plays, this figure signals the beginning and end of performances. It stands as a visual threshold between the everyday world and the world of heightened imagination created within the play. With it, we welcome you to *Celebration: A World of Art and Ritual*.

The translucent leather figure shown here represents a mountain on which the tree of life grows. In its branches are birds and monkeys that symbolize the vanities of life. The roots of the tree are concealed by doors flanked by giant guardians—here mythical birds of great strength and speed. The two large, wolflike dogs are a reminder that power and force uncontrolled are a menace to peace. More shadow puppets are displayed in the "Retelling Myth and History" component of the Elements of Celebration Gallery and are discussed in number 101.

Objects Speak

The objects shown here, whether beautiful or bizarre, are themselves a kind of speech, eloquent in their very silence. They come from various cultures, some literate and complex, others simple and preliterate. In their original settings some related to celebrations of joy, others to mourning; some were sacred, others secular. Several are beautiful in the eyes of any beholder, others strike the attention of strangers but remain, unless decoded, baffling and mysterious. One task of this exhibition is to decode them and thus make them speak to us, for these objects are all *symbols*, things that stand for other things. Each object is much more than it seems to be. The key to its meaning is in what those who made it said about it, how they used it, and how together they behaved toward it.

What we think strange another culture thinks familiar, and of course the reverse is also true. Celebratory objects of our own, such as the Christmas tree, are perhaps of all things most familiar to us. Yet another society's important objects of celebration may impress us as being among the most peculiar of its cultural expressions. A rich diversity of outward forms both conceals and reveals the common humanity of all societies as they celebrate.

2.
Christmas Tree, "Homespun Treasures," 1979
USA
synthetic Christmas tree decorations: variously sized ornaments, wood, fabric, yarn, paint, bread dough, porcelain, and other media
height: 72 (182.9)
diameter: 48 (121.9)
OH; Created for OH by the Northern Virginia Handcrafters' Guild, Inc.

Decorating an evergreen tree at Christmas time is a northern European custom that came to the United States with German immigrants. A Christmas tree is the focus of the secular, family-centered celebration of Christmas. Family members gather to decorate the tree on Christmas Eve. Each person constructs or hangs an ornament. Under the tree are gifts to be opened on Christmas Day.

The work of almost two hundred craftsmen is represented on the tree shown here. Woodworking, sewing, crocheting, painting, and the use of bread dough, porcelain, ceramics, pewter, and brass are just a few of the many crafts and materials represented in the decorations.

In the diversity of their modes of construction, materials, and forms, they reflect America's many ethnic traditions.

3.
Chasuble, probably mid-18th century
Spain or Mexico
cloth, thread, pigment
46 × 21 (116.8 × 53.3)
NMAH 467

The chasuble is the outermost garment and visible sign to Roman Catholics that an ordained priest has earned the right to celebrate Mass or other services connected with the Mass.

Chasubles are cut in several forms today. This chasuble has a fiddle-shaped front that indicates a Hispanic origin. It was probably made in the mid-eighteenth century, with repairs, including the addition of materials, made later. Different colors associated with chasubles symbolize different liturgical seasons, feasts, or rites. A red chasuble such as this one (now faded to pink) may be worn on Passion Sunday, the Wednesday of Holy Week, Good Friday, and Pentecost. Red represents the sacrifice of life for the love of God.

4.
Trapunto Quilt, 1856
Logan County, Kentucky
cotton
94 × 96½ (238.8 × 245.1)
NMAH T10269; Gift of Miss Lillian V. Lewis

After attending the Logan County fair near Russellville, Kentucky, in 1856, Virginia M. Ivey went home and created from memory this quilted representation of the event. In it she portrayed horses and riders, carriages, livestock, and visitors to the fair, paying close attention to detail to capture the spirit of the occasion.

Trapunto, or stuffed quilting, gives more dimension to designs than is afforded by regular quilting. After outlining the designs with quilting stitches, the quilter stuffs bits of wool or cotton into certain details through the loose weave of the backing fabric. With the stuffing she may give more volume to a woman's skirt here or more contour to an animal's haunch there. The high relief of stuffed quilting is specially effective in all-white quilts, such as Miss Ivey's.

4

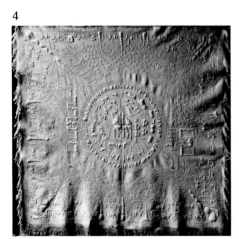

4 (detail)

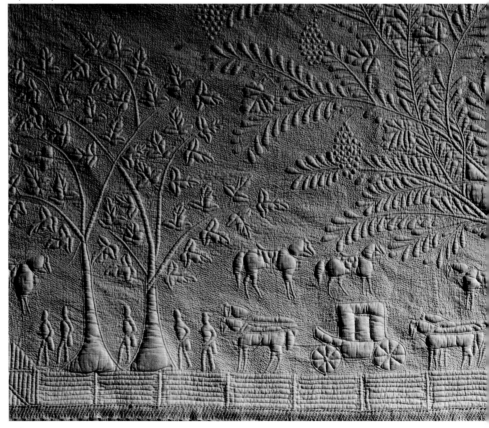

5.
Bull-Roarer (*aije*), 1850–1900
Bororo Indians; Mato Grosso, Brazil
wood, pigment, native twine
28¾ × 5½ × 1 (73 × 14 × 2.5)
NMNH 210833

When swung overhead in a circle, the bull-roarer re-creates for the Bororo people the cry of a dangerous mythical river beast. Bororo men sound the instrument—as many as sixteen at once—during the last phase of funerary rites. Mourners wrestle with and symbolically triumph over death by controlling the great beast heard in the bull-roarer's noise.

The bull-roarer symbolizes life as well as death. The initiation of boys into manhood forms a part of Bororo funerary rites. For youths coming of age, the final mystery is to see the bull-roarer. This moment signifies that they are sexually ready to take wives. The bull-roarer's symbolic procreative force is said to be so potent that Bororo women are not permitted to lay eyes on it lest they die from supernatural pregnancies that end in exploding bellies.

6 b

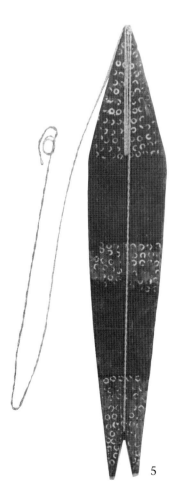

5

6.
SERVING SPOON AND BOWL. In the Dan villages of Liberia and the Ivory Coast, wealthy men give large feasts for their friends and neighbors to enhance their status or make amends for some wrong they have committed. At such a feast, a village woman noted for her hospitality assists the host by serving great quantities of rice with her personal wooden serving spoon and bowl, which symbolize her generosity. These implements are given by mothers to their daughters and are proudly displayed in the homes of the owners.

a.
Serving Spoon (*wa ke mia; wunkirmian*), 1900–1950
probably Dan people; Liberia and Ivory Coast
wood
24¼ × 6⁷⁄₁₆ × 3⅛ (61.6 × 16.3 × 8.1)
AfA 69-8-23

Personalized large serving spoons such as this one are emblems of the favored position of their owners as well as dwelling places of spirits who help them to maintain their status as persons of notable hospitality and generosity. The shape of this implement is suggestive of female anatomy and fecundity. Another example of a Dan serving spoon is displayed in the "Feasting and Drinking" component of the Elements of Celebration Gallery and is discussed in number 94.

b.
Serving Bowl, 1900–1950
Dan or We people; Liberia and Ivory Coast
wood
4⅝ × 10⅜ × 9⅞ (11.8 × 26.3 × 30)
AfA 68-4-14

This bowl is a small version of those used to carry cooked rice to a feast. The woman in charge of serving rice scoops it from the bowl with her spoon and distributes it to the guests.

6 a

7

8.
Expiatory Straw Effigy (*cheyong;
cheung; ch'ŏyong*), ca. 1885
Korea
rice straw
3½ × 28 × 11½ (8.9 × 71.1 ×
29.2)
NMNH 315465; Gift of Miss Eliza
Ruhamah Scidmore

When bad luck is portended for Ko-
reans who rely on astrology, they
may attempt to avert such predic-
tions with a straw figure similar to
the one shown here. On the night
of January 14, those who have received ominous forecasts place
cash and rice in various parts of
such an effigy. Then they throw
the straw figure on the side of a
road or under a bridge in the hope
that someone will tear it to pieces
to find its contents. In this way a
bearer of ill fortune transfers bad
luck either to the straw figure or to
the finder—especially if the original owner's name, birthdate, and
astrological sign are enclosed in the
effigy.
   When atoning for misdeeds, sinners may purchase similar straw
figures from Buddhist priests. Re-
penters fill the effigy with a large

sum of money. After they have cast
the image aside, they hope that a
poor person will tear it apart for
the cash—an act that will relieve
them of their guilt.

9.
Two Shinto Bird Charms (*uso; uso-
kae; uso-gae*), before 1963
Dazaifu-machi (city), Fukuoka
prefecture, Japan
pine, paint
largest: 5⅞ × 5⅞ × 4 (14.8 × 14.8
× 10.2)
NMNH 402420, 404321

In Japan, Shinto worshipers observe *uso-matsuri*, or the festival of
uso, each January. In the Japanese
language *uso* is a homonym, the
word both for bullfinch and for
falsehood. During the festival *uso*
bird charms are distributed and
sold at shrines. Visitors may exchange their *uso* for those of
others, an act that symbolically replaces past falsehood or bad luck
with truth or good luck for the new
year. Among the charms given out
by a shrine, one is believed to be
the luckiest because it is made of
gold.

7
Ancestral Board (*gopi*), before 1965
Gibe people; Papua New Guinea
wood, pigment
46 × 11¾ × 2¾ (116.9 × 29.8 ×
6.9)
NMNH 403107; Gift of Morton
May

For Papuan Gulf peoples, many religious and social events centered
on *gopi* boards. Representing totemic or guardian spirits, such
boards linked the living with their
ancestors. A tablet such as this
could also ward off illness and evil
and, at its owner's request, could
cause misfortune for an enemy. Especially important during initiation
ceremonies for young men, the
gopi was a distillation of clan heritage and lore. Initiates performed
special songs and dances celebrating their new, adult identities and
reenacted myths of origin.

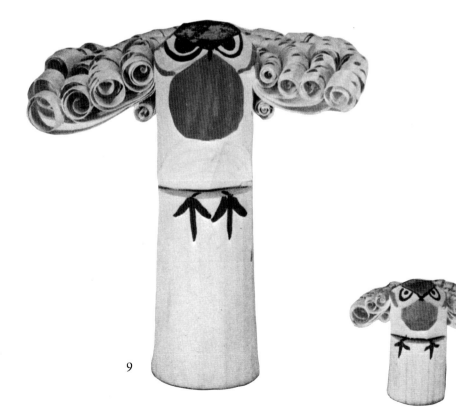

9

10.
Piñata, 1981
Mexico
papier-mâché, crepe paper
27 × 28 × 28 (68.6 × 71.1 × 71.1)
FP 1981.4

During the Christmas season, which in Mexico lasts from December 16 to December 24, friends and families gather in one another's homes for evening entertainments called posadas ("inns"), which recall the search by Joseph and Mary for shelter as they traveled to Bethlehem. Piñatas are traditionally used to enliven these festivities.

To create piñatas, Mexican artisans decorate clay pots holding candies, small toys, and coins with colorful papier-mâché and crepe paper. These decorations may take the shape of stars, lambs, burros, birds, horses, clowns, or other fancifully designed forms. A blindfolded child or adult vigorously swings a stick at the piñata, which is hung to dangle above the participants. Onlookers shout gleefully as someone moves the piñata so it will escape the first destructive blows. After it has been broken, children scramble wildly for its contents, pocketing all they can. Wry songs have been recorded that praise the piñata but show no mercy for its ultimate fate.

In Spain piñatas are cracked the first Sunday after Ash Wednesday. In the United States piñatas are often homemade and may be used for children's parties and birthdays as well as for Christmas festivities.

11.
FEATHERED BASKETS. Among the Pomo Indians, baskets of all kinds were essential to social life. From birth to death the Pomoans were surrounded by baskets, using them in every stage of food acquisition and processing—from hunting; fishing; and gathering the dietary staple, acorns; to storing, cooking, and serving.

The Pomoan groups reserved feather baskets for important occasions. During wedding ceremonies, the bride's family exchanged fine gifts with the groom's; among the Eastern Pomo, baskets covered with red-headed woodpecker feathers were considered to be the ideal gift from the bride's family. During funerary rites, mourners expressed their grief by covering the corpse with valuables, none more prized than feathered baskets. These were believed to attain to a glorious destiny when they were burned with the body.

The peoples called Pomoan actually spoke seven distinct though related languages. They were in no sense a unified group. Thus, the baskets called Pomoan are organized more by region than by nation.
Illustrated in color, p. 18

a.
Feathered Basket, ca. 1880–1920
Pomo Indians; California
willow rods, sedge weft, clamshell beads, abalone shell, native twine, feathers (meadowlark, mallard, quail)
1⅞ × 6½ (4.8 × 16.5)
NMNH 360607

b.
Feathered Basket, ca. 1880–96
Central Pomo Indians; Shiyéko, California
willow rods, sedge root, clamshell beads, native twine, feathers (red-headed woodpecker, meadowlark, mallard, quail, California jay)
2 × 5½ (5.1 × 13.9)
NMNH 203415; Collected 1896 by John W. Hudson

The feathers in this basket include those of the red-headed woodpecker, which figured in Pomoan mythology. Like the Pomoan peoples, the bird stored acorns and was regarded as a gambler. Its colors—red, black, and white—were the basic Pomoan ritual colors. When white clamshell beads and the black topknot of a quail were added to a red-feathered basket, the ceremonial triad of colors was formed.

c.
Feathered Basket, ca. 1885–92
Eastern and Northern Pomo Indians; Shinal, Bachelor Valley, California
willow rods, sedge root, white and blue glass beads, clamshell beads, native twine, feathers (mallard, meadowlark, quail)
2¼ × 5 (5.7 × 12.7)
NMNH 203483; Collected 1892 by John W. Hudson

d.
Feathered Basket, ca. 1890–1940
Pomo Indians; California
willow rods, sedge weft, clamshell beads, abalone shell, cord, feathers (mallard, red-headed woodpecker, meadowlark, quail)
1½ × 8¾ (3.8 × 22.2)
NMNH 418695 a

12.
Drums [of Peace] (*kanko*), probably late 18th or early 19th century
Japan
wood, fabric, gold paint, lacquer
largest: 25½ × 11 × 11 (64.8 × 28 × 28)
NMNH 154966
Illustrated in color, p. 18

In Japan the word *kanko* originally meant "drums of remonstrance." The drums stood before the magistrate's office so that any person who had been wronged could beat them in an appeal for redress. *Kanko* has now come to connote good government and peaceful society.

During Japan's Edo period (1615–1867), *kanko* drums appeared during important Shinto festivals. In celebrations of the two deities Sanno and Kanda Myojin, the drums were either placed atop portable shrines or used to set a stage on ritual ground. They were not played as musical instruments but were used for their symbolic value. The circular gold design was an emblem of creation and the gilt cocks represented peace and prosperity.

13.
Drum, Drape, and Sticks, before November 25, 1963
USA
wood, metal, cloth
drum: 23 × 18 (58.4 × 45.7)
NMAH 251343.01, .02, .03; Transfer from Department of Defense

Three days after the assassination of President John F. Kennedy on November 22, 1963, his body was buried. The muffled cadence of four leader drums set a solemn ceremonial pace befitting the death of a chief of state and commander of the armed forces. Master Sergeant Vincent Batista beat this drum as caisson, coffin, and mourners slowly made their way from the

13

White House to Saint Matthew's Cathedral, then to Arlington Cemetery.

In the procession a riderless horse with boots reversed in the stirrups and sword sheathed symbolized the slain warrior. At Arlington Cemetery salutes by Air Force planes, rifles, and cannons further signaled respect for a fallen president, while the traditional taps played at the burial echoed the sense of loss felt throughout the nation.

14.
Carp Streamers (*koi-nobori*), 1981
Japan
cotton, bamboo, paint
range (length): from 47 to 118
(119.4 to 299.7)
FP 1981.1

Every year in Japan on the fifth day of the fifth lunar month, carp streamers fill the sky. The occasion is the boy's day festival, a time to express thanks for healthy male children and offer prayers for their protection from harm. Reputed to be hardy fish, carp exhibit strength, courage, and persistence in swimming upstream. Japanese prize these attributes as essential for achievement.

The custom of flying banners in the early spring originated in the countryside. Farmers eager to drive away airborne pests hoisted brightly colored streamers and

fierce animal likenesses above their fields. During the seventeenth and eighteenth centuries, government authorities encouraged boy's day festivities to stimulate martial spirit.

15.
Totem Pole, ca. 1850–75
Tlingit Indians; Alaska
cedar, red and black paint
176 × 20 (447.0 × 50.8)
NMNH 54297; Probably collected
by James G. Swan

The word totem sometimes means an animal or plant species with which a particular social group is religiously or genealogically identified. Although Native Americans of the Northwest Coast link themselves to ancestors who were transformed animals or were helped by them, they do not believe the creatures to be sacred. Rather, they regard them as family emblems or logos—similar to medieval crests or western cattle brands. A totem serves to identify a kin group and its history.

The word pole has been applied to several kinds of carved uprights, from grave posts measuring three feet in height to memorial columns of fifteen to seventy feet. Most are connected with the burial or commemoration of the dead; all have animal crests and depict family history. House posts were also

traditionally carved with totemic emblems. Some stood outside to identify the owners of houses and others gave support to roof beams indoors.

In many ways the raising of a pole and the occasion of its dedication were more important than the pole itself. Northern groups, especially, restricted pole raising to memorial feasts and potlatches marking the succession of an heir. At these observances the story of a family and its rights to the crest figures on the pole commanded everyone's attention. Without the story, the exact meaning of the pole is unclear. The significance of the figures on this example is no longer known. The man at the top wears a clan hat with a series of basketry rings, one for each potlatch he has given. Below him are probably a bear and a frog. For additional information on potlatches, see numbers 238 through 241.

15

16

16.
Feather Headdress, 1900–1925
Sioux (?) Indians; Northern Plains,
USA
felt hat, trade cloth, satin, red flannel, eagle feathers, fur, horsehair
dyed pink, ermine tails, glass beads
17 × 30 × 30 (43.2 × 76.2 × 76.2)
NMNH 357452

Among the Indians of the Northern
Plains, the early feathered headdress was an object of sacred art.
Before about 1880 none but certain
high-ranking leaders could wear
such a headdress—and then only
on occasions of great ceremony.
Fabricated originally under strict
ritual regulation, the headdress
later attained broader usage as a
protective charm. Some warriors
sought invulnerability to bullets

and arrows by wearing a feathered
bonnet, while others feared that
the headdress would only serve to
give their enemy a better target.

By the turn of the century there
was little restriction on the use of
the feathered bonnet. To the rest of
the world, this headdress became
the symbol of the American Indian.
In response to this widely held image, many Indian nations adopted
the bonnet and wore it without the
earlier constraints.

17.
Ceremonial Spade, 1892
St. Louis Shovel Company, Missouri
paint, wood, steel, silver, brass
39¼ × 7⅝ × 3 (99.7 × 19.2 ×
7.6)
NMAH 1979.0803.19

In a ground-breaking ceremony on
July 12, 1892, this spade was used
to remove the first earth for the
construction of the Illinois and
Mississippi Canal, also known as
the Hennepin Canal. The inscription on the blade reads in part:
"presented to the United States as
a memento of the Great National
Work."

This public work, which was
under construction for fifteen
years, coincided with a period of
great agricultural and industrial
growth throughout the nation. At
the time, railroads could not meet
the urgent transportation needs of
Illinois's farmers, merchants, and
manufacturers. Charles Henry
Deere (1837–1907), whose name is
one of four photoetched on the

17

blade in brass, was an industrialist who supported the Hennepin Canal as a cheaper and more convenient alternative to railroads. Heir to and developer of the John Deere line of agricultural equipment, Charles Henry Deere died in 1907, the year the canal was completed.

Could he have known by then that this shovel initiated a project obsolete before it was finished? The channel on the Illinois and Mississippi Canal did not allow passage of the large vessels needed for efficient water transport. It never fulfilled its planners' expectations and soon fell into disuse except for fishing and drainage.

18.
Mask (*mbala*), 1900–1950
Yaka people; Zaire
wood, branches, raffia-cloth fibers, resin, pigments, shredded raffia
31 × 28 × 20 (78.7 × 71.2 × 50.8)
AfA 73-7-365

The Yaka people of Zaire make elaborate masks for initiation ceremonies of young men entering manhood. Of the two kinds of *nkanda* (initiation ceremonies) masks shown in the exhibition, the *mbala* mask is the most important. It is distinguished by a high pointed headdress with horizontal ascending brims. Another *mbala* mask and two *ndemba* masks, also used in Yaka initiation ceremonies, are displayed in the "Birth and Initiation" component of the Rites of Passage Gallery and are discussed in numbers 124 and 125.

Great drama surrounds the use of the *mbala*. First it is covered and brought before the gathering of initiates and adults and then unveiled. Only the best young dancer is allowed to wear this mask.

Each initiation ceremony is sponsored by a wealthy man in the village. He earns prestige through his generosity, which is extended to the local mask makers. These specialists frequently incorporate witty, shocking, or rarely discussed themes of village life into the front of the headdress.

The *nkanda* dances are a high point of village life. Each Yaka village takes pride in its dance troupe, which may be sent to other villages to perform. In this way, regional prestige is established and mem-

bers of the troupe are given the chance to find wives in neighboring villages.

19.
Statue of Jagannatha, ca. 1962
Puri, Orissa, India
wood, cloth, pigment
50¾ × 31¼ × 21¹⁵⁄₁₆ (128.9 × 79.4 × 55.8)
NMNH 401696 a
Illustrated in color, p. 19

Jagannatha, Lord of the Universe, is worshiped at the shrine of Puri in the state of Orissa. This image of him, made especially for the Smithsonian, duplicates the traditional one used in Hindu celebrations throughout the year.

The most famous festival in which Jagannatha appears is the *ratha jatra*, or car festival. After removing the statue from the shrine, celebrants place it on a huge cart and, with massive effort, pull it through the streets to Jagannatha's garden house. Traditionally, thousands of participants joined the procession, some taking turns at the ropes and others throwing themselves before the advancing wheels. In English, the corrupted form of Jagannatha's name, *juggernaut*, derives its meaning from the ponderous, inexorably advancing vehicle. Another statue of Jagannatha is displayed in the "Shrines and Altars" component of the Religious Celebrations Gallery on the second floor and is discussed in number 198d.

Elements of Celebration

A celebration is a public performance that marks an important event in the life of a person or a group. This event may be in the past or present. If it is joyous, the emphasis is on festivity. If it commemorates a hero's death, a martyrdom, or a glorious defeat, the stress is on solemnity. Celebrations usually have several stages and make publicly visible the social structure of the groups that sponsor them. But they also give vivid form to the shared values of the community. "We are truly one," they seem to say, "though seemingly divided by rank, class, status, role, gender, age, ethnicity, religion, or the like."

Celebrations are composed of elements that we have found to be of wide if not universal distribution. Each of these elements exists outside the frame of celebration, but never otherwise so artistically treated. They are *masks, costumes, sound and music, dancing, feasting and drinking, retelling myth and history,* and *games and sports.*

Masks

Masks do for the face what costume and body painting do for the body, but they do it more profoundly, for almost everywhere the face is regarded as the expressive part of the person that everyone knows. But masks are themselves faces. They are carved and painted in the likenesses of gods, demons, heroes, kings, queens, clowns, animals, and other powerful or strange characters. To put on a mask is to put on another personality, to become that which is represented by the mask. Masks are often regarded with awe and fear because they seem capable of transforming what seems to be most stable and enduring—one's self or individuality—into something wildly unlike it, of exalting or debasing a person almost in the twinkling of an eye. Masks abound in celebrations because celebrations are themselves powerful transformers of everyday life into something rich and strange.

20.
Mask of Rangda, ca. 1971
Bali, Indonesia
wood, cloth, cardboard, paint, bamboo, fiber
38 × 16 × 14 (96.5 × 40.6 × 35.6)
NMNH 416881; Gift of Dr. William Stockton
Illustrated in color, p. 19

In Bali, Rangda, a witch who cannot be killed, embodies evil, anger, and fear. In an annual temple festival, Rangda confronts another masked figure, Barong, who represents good. They battle over the souls of a group of celebrants whom Rangda has cast into a trance. Although her opponent is able to lift the spell he cannot conquer the witch, and it is clear that the two adversaries will regularly renew their struggle.

21.
Cornhusk Mask, ca. 1930–40
Seneca Iroquois Indians; Cold Spring Longhouse, Allegheny Reservation, New York
cornhusk, commercial cloth
13 × 11½ × 5 (33 × 29.2 × 12.7)
NMNH 380940

To the Seneca, cornhusk masks represent a mythological race, the Husk Faces. These mythical farmers live on the other side of the earth and appear at every new year, during the Midwinter Ceremony. As messengers of the Three Sisters—Corn, Beans, and Squash, the traditional crops—they ask to dance with those gathered in the ritual structure. Their presence is a sign of good fortune for the next growing season.

21

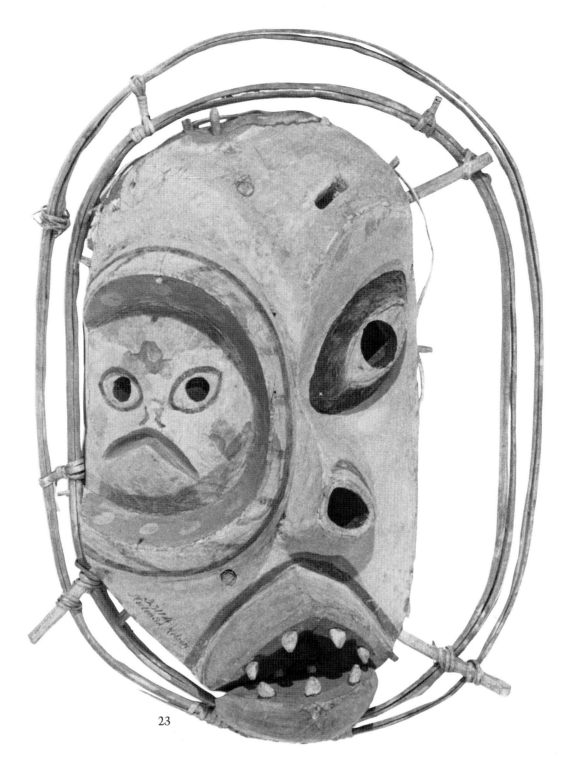

23

22.
Demon Mask (*oni no men; kimen*), date unknown
Japan
wood, gesso, pigments, hair (horse-hair?)
26 × 19½ × 9½ (66 × 49.4 × 24.1)
NMNH T499

Fierce enough to frighten devils, demon masks like this one appear in Buddhist ceremonies to drive away winter's evil spirits. They are also worn in dances that dramatize the confrontation of sinners and demons in hell. Sometimes *oni* masks preside atop tall poles during exorcism rites.

23.
Mask, ca. 1850–77
Eskimo; Norton Sound, Alaska
wood; wooden pegs; willow root; root lashings; black, blue, and red paint
20 × 14½ × 4¼ (50.8 × 36.8 × 10.8)
NMNH 33114

In Eskimo masks, a small face set within a larger one represents the *inua*, or spirit, of the larger creature. Such a mask was carved under the direction of a shaman, or perhaps by him, for use in religious festivals.

24.
Body Mask (*táwü*), ca. 1930–40
Tucano-speaking Indians (probably Cubeo); Brazil
tapa cloth, basketry, paint, unknown media
55 × 28 × 13½ (139.7 × 71.1 × 34.3)
NMNH 381485

During their mourning ceremony, the Cubeo look to the spirit world for assistance in expressing grief and then in banishing the dead. The spirits are represented by men wearing bark-cloth body masks. The wearers—always male—dance, sing, play musical instruments, and pantomime the behavior of animals

24

or supernatural beings. As the funerary rites progress, the "spirits" and others present become increasingly rowdy, changing the tone of the occasion from one of solemn grieving to one of lusty goodwill. After driving away the soul of the deceased, the mourners burn the bark-cloth masks.

25.
Mask (*ere gelede*), 1900–1950
Yoruba people; Nigeria and Republic of Benin
wood, pigments
8¾ × 11 × 11¾ (22.2 × 28 × 29.8)
AfA 67-25-4

Yoruba men in the *gelede* cult seek to appease the power of witchcraft in women by performing spectacular dances. Masks worn during these ceremonial dances portray various stereotypic personages, animals, and objects. This mask repre-

sents a Yoruba man wearing a traditional cap with its crown cut in an elaborate openwork pattern.

26.
Helmet Mask (*sowoi*), 1900–1950
probably Mende people; Sierra Leone
wood
17¼ × 10½ × 11½ (43.8 × 26.6 × 29.2)
NMNH 385719

Among the Mende, the guardian spirit of women was represented by this mask. It was worn by a woman—an extremely rare practice in traditional Africa—and the mask figure guided girls through their secluded rites of initiation into adulthood. The same masked figure also appeared in Mende villages to bring men to trial on charges of mistreating women.

27.
HELMET MASKS. During initiation ceremonies for Kuba youths in

Zaire, three maskers performed a dance acting out a love triangle. The maskers represented three of the main figures in Kuba mythology—Mwaash A Mbooy, an idealized king and son of a Kuba culture hero; Ngaady A Mwaash (not displayed), his sister and incestuous wife; and Bwoom, a pygmy and common villager. The dance of the three masks dramatized the rivalry between king and commoner for the love of the king's sister.

These masks might also have been mounted atop a wall in the initiation enclosure. There they would have presided over the instruction of youths in the Kuba system of politics and correct social behavior.

a.
Helmet Mask (represents Bwoom), ca. 1850–1900
Kuba people; Zaire
wood, copper sheet, ceramic and glass beads, string, iron wire, tree seeds, viverrine fur, brass, raffia cloth, cowrie shells, European cloth, laundry blueing
13⅝ × 9¾ × 12 (34.6 × 24.7 × 30.5)
NMNH 204462

b.
Helmet Mask (represents Mwaash A Mbooy), ca. 1900–1950
Kuba people; Zaire
wood, white metal, cane, string, raffia cloth, raffia fibers, feathers, cowrie shells, beads, pigments
20 × 17 × 15 (50.8 × 43.2 × 38.1)
AfA 73-7-440
Illustrated in color, p. 20
See also colorplate, p. 20

28.
MEXICAN MASKS. In pre-Hispanic Mexico, the tradition of using ceremonial masks was widespread. After the Spanish Conquest, this tradition was continued by many of the indigenous peoples of the country and passed on to their descendants, particularly those in isolated areas who managed to remain relatively aloof from the new European culture. As rural Mexico became more densely populated, cultural exchanges between its various peoples became frequent and the mask became a familiar element in rural Mexican folk culture. Today masked dancers and mimes play a prominent role in the tradi-

27 a

tional festivities and religious celebrations held in small towns throughout Mexico, and in many urban centers, as well.

a.

Umbrella-Man Mask (*paraguero*), 1965
Tlatempan area, Tlaxcala, Mexico
wood, plaster, clay, glass eyes, false eyelashes, spring mechanism, string
10¼ × 6½ (26 × 16.5)
NMNH 420030; Collected by Donald Cordry

Tlaxcala carnival masks share a distinctive style. Their fine paint and glass eyes with movable lids give them a finished, sophisticated look somewhat incongruous with

the small, provincial towns where they are used. Painted with oil and enamel, the masks are notable for their prevalence of gold teeth. Most represent city people. Maskers in the *paraguero*, or umbrella-man, dance carry umbrellas and wear frock coats, black trousers, dress shirts, and white gloves. They cut surprisingly cosmopolitan figures in village carnivals.

b.

Cowboy Mask (*vaquero*), ca. 1940
Nahua-speaking people; Tlapanec area, Axoxuca region, Guerrero, Mexico
wood, leather, paint, wire, ribbons
20 × 16 (50.8 × 40.6)
NMNH 420007; Collected by Donald Cordry
Illustrated in color, p. 21

The *vaquero*, or cowboy, dance is one of a number of occupational dances performed primarily in the Mexican states of Morelos, Puebla, and Guerrero. In a celebratory spirit, these dances give public recognition to people who work at particular jobs and stress their contribution to community life. They also instruct a community in the attitudes and skills needed for these jobs.

Despite regional variations in choreography or dramatic structure, one scene is common to all versions of the cowboy dance: the capture of a bull. Usually two groups of cowboy dancers engage in a dialogue of movement, eventually coming together to overpower the

28 f

animal. Today a dancer in bull mask and costume has replaced the live, snorting beast used in earlier times.

c.
La Malinche Dance Mask, ca. 1900–1910
Altamirano region, Guerrero, Mexico
copper, basketry hat, horsehair, deer antlers, ribbons, string, paint
11¾ × 8 (29.8 × 20.3)
NMNH 420017; Collected by Donald Cordry

An Indian woman, Malinche, who served as interpreter for Hernán Cortés, is regarded by some Mexicans to be a traitor whose uncontrolled lust—she was also Cortés's mistress—destroyed the Indian nations of Mexico. Many express a certain admiration, however, for Malinche's power over the Spaniards. This mask is worn in a special Dance of the Malinche.

d.
Mohammed Helmet Mask (*maoma*), ca. 1920–30
Nahua-speaking people; Pachivia region, Guerrero, Mexico
wood, paint
27 × 37¾ (68.6 × 95.9)
NMNH 419936; Collected by Donald Cordry

The Dance of the Moors and Christians has been interpreted as a dramatic confrontation between evil and good. Probably the first Christian dance introduced into Mexico, it is recorded as having been presented to Cortés in 1524. Today this dance—actually a complex of dances—is performed throughout New Mexico, Mexico, Central America, many countries in South America, and even the Philippines.

e.
Sad or Suffering Moor Mask (*moro de pasión*), ca. 1950
Nahua-speaking people; Ăcapetlahuayă, Guerrero, Mexico
wood, paint
11¼ × 7 (28.6 × 17.8)
NMNH 419853; Collected by Donald Cordry
Illustrated in color, p. 21

The mask of the sad or suffering Moor contains two traditional elements, the meanings of which have

30

been lost. One is the coiled nose, which the mask's collector interprets as a representation of a butterfly's proboscis (the butterfly was a common symbol for Xochiquetzal, the pre-Hispanic goddess of flowers and beauty). The other, which remains a mystery, is the gold protrusions above the brow and on either cheek.

f.
Dwarf Mask, ca. 1900
Nahua-speaking people; La Parota region, Guerrero, Mexico
wood, paint
36 × 13½ (91.4 × 34.3)
NMNH 419926; Collected by Donald Cordry

Small boys performed the Dance of the Dwarfs as a petition for rain. Rain gods, believed to be dwarfs themselves, lived in caves. At the beginning of each rainy season, twelve boys, each wearing a large mask like the one shown, acted the part of dwarfs and danced before the rain gods' dwelling. The blue-green eyes, rippling beard, and sinuous snakes of this mask create an unmistakable impression of water and its movement.

29.
Booger Mask, 1946
Eastern Cherokee Indians; North Carolina
wood, hide, red and black pigment
12 × 9 × 6 (30.4 × 22.8 × 15.2)
NMNH 403780

Boogers are the boogeymen or ghosts who appear in Cherokee dance-dramas. They do not speak Cherokee and their behavior is aggressive and obscene. They represent the diametric opposite of ideal conduct. The foreigners in their number include Frenchmen, Germans, Chinese, Blacks, and alien Indians. Even animals—in this case, a buffalo—are represented.

30.
Cannibal Crane Mask, ca. 1880–94
Nakwoktak Kwakiutl Indians; Fort Rupert, British Columbia, Canada
cedar; red, white, and black paint; shredded cedar bark; native cedar twine; iron plate and rivets
38½ × 61½ × 7 (97.8 × 156.2 × 17.9)
NMNH 169106; Collected by Franz Boas

The Kwakiutl saw myriad forces at work in the world, all needing to be balanced. Through ritual this balance was achieved.
   The cannibal crane was a mythical creature that preyed upon men, just as man preys upon other creatures for his food. During the long, complex winter ceremonials, these creatures appeared in the human world, threatening to bring destruction to the human social order. To allay them, humans reaffirmed through their rituals the acceptance of their own death and their responsibilities to the spirits.

The dance of the cannibal crane required a great deal of strength and agility. The masks are heavy and awkward, the dance steps difficult, and the beak of the mask must be opened and closed in time with drumbeats. The dancer made a symbolic sacrifice for other people, for he took upon his shoulders the weight of the responsibility for acknowledging their fears of destruction from the outside and from their own inner, uncontrolled desires as well.

31.
Mask and Gorget, ca. 1850–80
Eskimo; Point Barrow, Alaska
wood, braided cord, teeth, red and black paint, iron nails
mask: 9 × 5½ × 2½ (22.8 × 13.9 × 6.3)
gorget: 4⅞ × 19 × ½ (12.4 × 48.2 × 1.2)
NMNH 64230; Collected by Edward W. Nelson

In Point Barrow, masks such as this one were worn in a ceremony to mark the end of the whaling season. With the participation of the entire community, crewmen danced in masks and gorgets. The large figure depicted in the center of this gorget is the legendary Kikamigo, who controlled whales and other marine creatures.

Costumes

The term costumes here refers to the style of dress, including accessories, typical of the celebratory mood. It also includes body painting—the decoration of the skin itself. Both costume and painting transform nature's nakedness into a medium of cultural expression. Colors and patterns often stand for religious, mythical, and cosmological scenes, events, and personages. In wearing such costumes people become more than they ordinarily are; they become culture incarnate. Body painting has even more radical effects. The totemic clan designs on a tribesman's body place him outside ordinary time. He now lives the myth that the painting symbolizes, and by his symbolic actions in dance and mime brings the myth's generative power back into the failing world.

32.
Warrior's Costume, ca. 1875–99
Ojibwa Indians; Minnesota
wool, fur, leather, feathers, beads, yarn, cloths, buckskin, skunk skin, wood, ermine, slate
approximately 66 × 30 (167.6 × 76.2)
NMNH 201154
Illustrated in color, p. 22

Ceremonial outfits such as this one were worn at Ojibwa tribal gatherings and later at pan-tribal powwows. Ojibwa costumes, which were subject to influences from whites as well as from Sioux and other Indian groups, were in a continual state of development. In early days a man's basic costume consisted of breechclout, leggings, and moccasins, with a robe added in winter, all made of tanned buckskin. In the early 1820s a man might wear the outfit shown here: a blue broadcloth blanket folded around the shoulder, a calico shirt, red-cloth leggings, and beaded moccasins, with a belt, knife sheath, pouch, and feathered frontlet of skin around the forehead. Headgear varied greatly. Trade cloths such as velvet were used frequently, and beadwork, especially loom-woven beads, replaced porcupine quills as decoration. Despite its non-Indian, manufactured touches, a hide outfit of the sort displayed was rather traditional for its time among the Ojibwa.

33.
BODY PAINT. For the Arapaho and other Plains tribes, paint was a symbolic medium used for protection, personal decoration, and religious communication. Paint was used by the Arapaho for protection against heat and cold, for good luck, and to keep evil spirits away. Medicine men painted themselves and their patients for immunization against disease. To indicate a time of war, young women painted streaks on their cheeks, forehead, and nose. To signify peace, old women painted a spot on each cheekbone, one on the forehead, one between the eyes, and a line from the mouth to the chin. Discarding the colors of youth, old people used only red, a color having symbolic associations with red skin, red blood, and the red earth.

Both of these leather bags contain red paint.

a.
Paint Bag, ca. 1900–1930
Northern Arapaho Indians; Wyoming
hide, glass beads, pigment
½ × 4 × 10 (1.3 × 10.2 × 25.4)
NMNH 418490

b.
Paint Bag, ca. 1875–95
Northern Arapaho Indians; Wyoming
hide, glass beads, pigment
½ × 2½ × 8 (1.3 × 6.3 × 20.3)
NMNH 200666

34.
Tattooing Set, ca. 1850–1900
Osage Indians; Oklahoma
rushes, native twine, fibers, beads, wood, steel needles, brass bells, feathers, thread, commercial cloth
rush mat: 1 × 26 × 23⅙ (2.5 × 66 × 59.1)
NMNH 263122
Illustrated in color, p. 22

Body decoration changes and expands the identity of a ceremonial participant to a more public or cosmic level. Many Native American groups decorated their bodies with paints for particular ceremonies, but some groups used tattoos as a permanent sign of valor and achievement and of self-dedication to the proper moral and social paths.

The principal symbols tattooed on Osage men—the sacred pipe, ceremonial knife, and rays of the sun—represented their role as warriors and ritualists. Women were heavily tattooed with cosmological symbols such as stars and mountains and with important animal symbols, such as sacred turtles and spiders' webs. The latter symbolized the connection of all the world by gossamer threads of human responsibility.

Tattooing was a sacred act and the tattoo set shown here is similar to other Osage sacred bundles. As in many Plains Indian rituals, it was important for the participant

Wa-shin-ha (Fat on Skin) holding a peace pipe that relates to his tattoos; Osage Reservation, Oklahoma, around 1900. Courtesy, National Anthropological Archives, Smithsonian Institution (see no. 34).

35

not to cry out but to accept the burden of pain that the spirits have made part of human destiny.

35.
Coat (*atsushi*), before 1889
Ainu people; Japan
elm-bark fiber, cotton appliqué
46 × 50¼ × 2 (116.8 × 127.7 × 5.1)
NMNH 150661

The Ainu, the indigenous people of Japan, wore this coat on special occasions, such as a ceremonial dance march held to celebrate the return of a chief from a long sea journey, the annual spring bear feast, or the owl-worship ceremony.

36.
Headdress and Costume, 1850–1900
Zaparo Indians; Ecuador
hair, bird bones, shell, feathers, seeds, pods, bast fiber, twine, teeth
headdress: 21 × 14½ (53.3 × 36.8)
NMNH 164685 a–e, g

This elaborate headdress was worn by male participants in Zaparoan festivals. Its precise use is not known, but its elaborate construction and the known data about regional tribal festivals suggest that prestigious Zaparo tribesmen, who in daily life went nearly naked, wore elaborate costumes such as this to enhance their status at important feasts.

37.
Oil Container, 1850–1900
Peoples of the Middle Congo Basin
fruit of a forest vine (probably *Strychnos icaja*)
4¼ × 4¾ (10.8 × 12.1)
NMNH 323499

Peoples of the Congo basin extracted cosmetic oils from the fruits of both the oil palm and the raffia palm. Applied alone to make the body lustrous or mixed with barwood powder to impart a reddish tone, the oils were essential components in festivities. Richly carved seed capsules of this kind held the oils for these important occasions.

37

Their attractiveness to women was increased by the practice of decorating their upper torsos with these intricate designs. The color black usually symbolized informality, playful joking, and sexuality.

a.
Body Stamp (*me-ipihôc-tsä*), ca. 1966
Ramkokamekra-Canela Indians; Sardinha village, Maranhão, Brazil
palm pith, pigment of charcoal with latex binder from steppe tree
1½ × 5⁹⁄₁₆ × 1¹³⁄₁₆ (3.8 × 14.1 × 4.6)
NMNH 404988

b.
Body Stamp (*me-ipihôc-tsä*), ca. 1966
Ramkokamekra-Canela Indians; Sardinha village, Maranhão, Brazil
nutshell of babacu palm
1¾ × 2 × 2 (4.4 × 5.1 × 5.1)
NMNH 404985

c.
Body Stamp (*me-ipihôc-tsä*), ca. 1966
Ramkokamekra-Canela Indians; Sardinha village, Maranhão, Brazil
pith of burití palm
¾ × 3¾ × 1¹⁄₁₆ (1.9 × 9.5 × 2.7)
NMNH 404990

38.
Three Pieces of Barwood (*tool*), late 19th century
Kuba people; Zaire
heartwood of the padauk tree (*Pterocarpus soyauxii*)
each: ½ × 2½ × 1⅛ (1.2 × 6.4 × 2.9)
NMNH 204483

As part of their attire for festive occasions, Kuba men and women add color to their skins and dress in fine clothing. The main cosmetic is a red powder that they prepare from a rarely found local tree. Usually, women rub two blocks of the heartwood of this tree together to obtain the pigment in powdered form. It is a highly prized commodity and is traded widely throughout the region. For festivals, local cosmetic experts are employed to apply the intricate designs to the bodies of the participants. The color red symbolizes life, blood, and energy. The same barwood powder is also used as a dye for coloring foods and for painting textiles, masks, utensils, and statues.

39.
FOUR BODY STAMPS. These body stamps from the Brazilian state of Maranhão are contemporary representations of an ancient tradition of body ornamentation among the Canela Indians that has not been practiced extensively since the 1950s. Traditionally, a well-painted body was an important element of self-esteem among the men, whose wives and nieces stamped on the designs. The men decorated their bodies for daily singing and dancing in the village.

36

d.
Body Stamp (*me-ipihôc-tsä*), ca. 1966
Ramkokamekra-Canela Indians;
Sardinha village, Maranhão, Brazil
palm pith, pigment of charcoal
with latex binder from steppe tree
1½ × 3²⁷⁄₃₂ × 1⅜ (3.8 × 9.7 × 3.5)
NMNH 404989

40.
Bark-Cloth Mask, Trousers, Jacket (*cucuá*), 1833–1910
probably Panama
tree-bark cloth, leather, paint, basketry, teeth, pitch, jawbone, wood
55 × 22½ (139.9 × 57.1)
NMNH 164695, 248568, 248569
Illustrated in color, p. 22

Costumes such as this one were worn during the Feast of Corpus Christi in the central provinces of Panama by masked and costumed men performing the Danza Cucuá or Bark-Cloth Tree Dance. These dancers were *cholos*, men of Indian descent who lived in the rural, mountainous regions but came to town during this festival to cavort in the streets and beg for alcoholic drinks (*aguardiente*) from the spectators.

Townspeople liked to believe that these masked "devils" were part of the performers' Indian heritage, but the tradition of the dance stems, in fact, from Christian origins. The sun and the crowns on the mask's trailer may well relate to Christian symbolism.

A local poetess described the mask as follows:

Eyes of a tiger it had,
the nose of a bull, enlarged;
the ears of a hungry wolf,
a long red tongue;
the horns of a stag on the forehead,
strange fangs and snout,
the crowned head of a rhinoceros.
It was the face of a devil!
Martina Andrion of Coclé Province, Panama
(translated by Philip D. Young)

The mask shown here shows no sign of a stag or rhinoceros but incorporates the tiger's eyes, wolf's ears, and the long tongue, fangs, and snout.

41.
Mask and Costume (possibly *agbogho mmoo*), probably 1825–50
Ibo people; Nigeria
wood, pigments, cotton, string
79 × 36 × 19 (200.7 × 91.4 × 48.2)
AfA L80-5-16

The Ibo of the Nsukka region worship the goddess Ani, who rules the underworld and imparts fertility to the fields of her faithful. One of Ani's most important daughters is Ikorodo, who represents her mother at many public celebrations.

The members of Ikorodo's cult are young men of a certain age who dance out their representation of the sacred maiden to the accompaniment of a band made up of wooden drums, wooden bells, slit gongs, rattles, and side-blown horns. The masks and the bands represent villages and village sections. Dancing in a female style, the young celebrants compete with one another and also with women, who challenge them from the audience.

Sound and Music

Sounds of many sorts are associated with acts of celebration. A twenty-one gun salute, a chorus of voices, a ritual chant, an explosion of firecrackers—all instantly identify the event occurring.

Of all sounds, music is perhaps the most potent in creating celebratory atmospheres. It can create a magical aura outside mundane time, when rejoicing can become absolute and mourning pure beauty. Celebration is almost unthinkable without music. It can express and symbolize a whole community as well as the "still small voice" of the individual.

Instruments of every kind are pressed into the service of celebration: plaintive stringed instruments—lutes and harps—reeds and flutes, xylophones, as well as drums. Instruments used specifically for celebration are often given particular treatment. They may be made from a special material, carved and elaborately decorated, given names like people, even consecrated by special ritual (for example, Candomblé drums in Afro-Brazilian rites are "baptized"). The musicians of celebration who play the instruments may belong to a special caste or clan.

Although instruments most commonly accompany celebratory songs and actions, at times their functions may be essentially non-musical. Bells may be rung or horns blown to signal the turning points in a ceremony. Rattles may be shaken to establish communication with the gods or blades of wood whirled in the air to sound a tone imploring a change in weather.

42.
Midwinter Horn (*midwinterhoorn*), 1974
The Netherlands
wood
3½ × 12 (9 × 30.5)
NMAH 1981.0422.01

Midwinter horns are traditionally played during Advent by farmers in East Holland. They perform over their wells, which act as resonators to amplify the sound as a signal to neighbors that the farmers are well and alive. As with a bugle, only about five tones are possible. Nowadays, there are midwinter-horn contests of skill.

43.
Bull-Roarer, ca. 1850–75
Hopi Indians; Arizona
wood; white, green, and black paint; cotton string; stick
½ × 9 × 2⅝ (1.2 × 22.9 × 6.7)
NMNH 22982

The Hopi use the bull-roarer solely for religious observances. At the beginning of the outdoor ceremonies of the Snake and Antelope societies, a war priest whirls it briefly to bring summer rains. Apropos of this usage, the bull-roarer was often decorated with a lightning bolt and its sound was said to be like thunder.

44.
Panpipes (*pedu'ba*), 1875–1900
Cubeo Indians; Colombia
bamboo, bast fiber, paint
largest: ¾ × 12¾ × 4 (1.9 × 32.4 × 10.1)
NMNH 385560

Among the Cubeo, only young men play panpipes. They employ the instruments whenever there is drinking, feasting, or dancing and during celebrations of passage. During the festive phase of the mourning ceremony, when the participants turn from grief, panpipes are played to invoke the spirit of the vulture, which—so the Cubeo believe—hovers above their mourning rituals. Invoking the spirit of birds assures the people that the spirits of the animal world will join their celebrations. This participation promotes harmony between humans and the beneficial forces of nature.

45.
Rattle (*asson; baksor*), 1900–1950
Croix-des-Bouquets, Haiti
gourd, glass beads, snake vertebrae, cotton string
10¾ × 4½ (27.2 × 11.4)
NMNH 382580; Gift of Dr. A. Metraux

This *asson*, or gourd rattle, enables the priest or priestess who uses it to invoke and then communicate with capricious and formidable deities during Voodoo services. Mastery of the instrument is so central to Voodoo priesthood that attaining this office is called "taking the rattle." Much of the training for the priesthood involves learning the eloquent movements and nuances of gesture that make up the language of the rattle.

In Voodoo services, the sound of the rattle invokes deities to possess their worshipers. If the spirits become too violent or overstay their welcome, the correct manipulation of the rattle can control or dismiss them. Imbued with the power to speak to the gods, the rattle mediates between the divine and human worlds. Another example of a Voodoo rattle is displayed in the "Shrines and Altars" Gallery and is discussed in number 197i.

46.
Ram's Horn (*shofar*), 1981
Israel
ram's horn
4¼ × 8 × 9 (10.8 × 20.3 × 22.9)
FP 1981.3

The piercing blast of the ram's horn, or *shofar*, is heard many times during the Jewish New Year (Rosh Hashanah) service and once at the end of the Day of Atonement (Yom Kippur) to signal the end of the Jewish High Holy Day season. Used in ancient times to mark important events, the *shofar* arouses worshipers on Rosh Hashanah to their ethical and ritual responsibilities.

48

and cause a great clatter. When shaken in time, sistrums can transmit familiar messages or accompany songs.

49.
New Year's Eve Horn, ca. 1980
USA
paper, aluminum foil, plastic
16 × 1¾ (40.6 × 4.5)
FP R501

The New Year's Eve horn is, technically speaking, an inexpensive single-tone reed noise-making device. It is usually distributed on December 31, shortly before midnight, to party-goers at festive gatherings. At exactly midnight it is blown repeatedly for several minutes to signal the arrival of the new year and, by implication, a new start on life and a cleansing of the old year's sins. An expendable item requiring no expertise in performance, its lifespan rarely exceeds an hour.

50.
Gong (*kendo*), 1900–1950
Puna or adjacent people; Gabon and Congo
iron, wood, pigments
17¼ × 5⅜ × 4½ (43.8 × 13.6 × 11.4)
AfA 79-16-49

In western equatorial Africa, chiefs use iron gongs to announce their ceremonial approach and arrival, to communicate with the spirits of their forefathers, and to assemble their people. An iron gong is struck mornings by village clairvoyants to call their fellow villagers together for an interpretation of dreams. Gongs are also used during the rites of various initiatory groups and in rituals celebrating the birth of twins.

51.
KOREAN FARMERS' BAND MUSIC. *Nong'ak,* or farmers' music, has a long history in Korea. In ancient times farmers held festivals to celebrate the planting of crops in May and their harvesting in October. The singing and dancing of these observances gave rise to farmers' band music, which both inspires and relaxes farmers work-

47.
Side-Blown Horn, 1750–1850
probably Maninka or related people; western coast of Africa
African-elephant tusk
5 × 18 × 2½ (12.7 × 45.7 × 6.3)
NMNH 4793

Side-blown horns—especially those made of ivory—figured prominently in the pageantry of court life on the Guinea Coast. The instruments announced the arrival and reception of dignitaries, communicated with spirits on ritual occasions, and assembled the populace for important proclamations. They were also sounded in wartime.

Ownership of ivory horns, such as the one shown here, was usually regarded as the prerogative of chiefs and kings. Such men of wealth often maintained horn ensembles to entertain their subjects and associates; these public performances added to their prestige.

48.
Sistrum (*wasamba*), probably 1900–1925
Bamana people; possibly Bamako region, Mali
handle: wood
disks: rind of fruit of calabash tree
(*Crescentia cujete*)
12½ × 19¼ × 7¼ (31.7 × 48.8 × 18.4)
AfA 73-7-688

In the West African republic of Mali, Bamana youths retreat after circumcision to secluded initiation camps for recuperation and further rites of passage into adulthood. During this interlude they are believed to be in a vulnerable state; supernatural danger could befall them if they are seen by women or uninitiated boys. To avert undesirable encounters when taking exercise or foraging for food, the novices carry sistrums and play them loudly. Shaking the instrument makes the disks slide up and down

50

a.
Hourglass Drum with Stick
(*changgo; changgu*), before 1964
Korea
paulownia wood, skin, silk cord,
brass, pigment
25½ × 18½ (64.8 × 47.0)
NMNH 403168

An hourglass drum such as this
one often contributes to Korean
music. Its use ranges from farmers'
band music to traditional court
ceremonials. The drummer strikes
one head of the instrument with
his palm to produce a soft, low
beat and the other head with a
bamboo stick for a contrasting
high-pitched sound.

b.
Drum with Handle (*sogo*), before
1893
Korea
wood, rawhide, cloth, hemp cord,
brass
21½ × 12½ × 3 (54.5 × 31.7 ×
7.8)
NMNH 95622

In addition to being used in farmers' bands, single-handle drums
such as this one are used to accompany Korean folk dancing.

51 a (drum)

ing in the field. Rhythmical and
joyous, farmers' music is a compos-
ite of song, dance, and instrumen-
tation. The band consists of a small
and large gong; an hourglass, barrel,
and single-handle drum; and a dou-
ble-reed oboe.

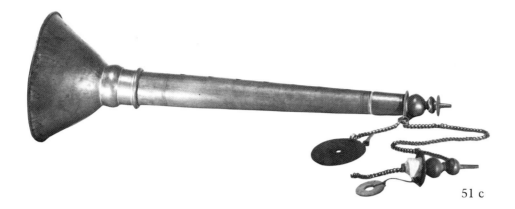

51 c

c.
Oboe (*t'aep'yongso; hojok; nlanari*),
before 1891
Korea
brass, grass stalk
15⁹⁄₁₆ × 4¹⁵⁄₁₆ (39.5 × 12.5)
NMNH 95212

The oboe carries the melody in
farmers' band music. Although its
range is narrow, its sound is loud
and piercing—ideal for outdoor performances. Traditionally the oboe
was played in military processions
and court ceremonies.

d.
Gong with Stick (*ching*), before
1964
Korea
brass, wood, fabric
gong: 18 × 14 × 4 (45.7 × 35.6 ×
10.2)
NMNH 403173 a, b

In farmers' band music, the small-
gong player is responsible for maintaining rhythm. The instrument is
also used in military marches and
various religious ceremonies.

52.
Long Trumpet (*kakaki*), 1965
Hausa people; Katsina city, Nigeria
tinned iron
96¾ × 3⅞ (245.6 × 9.9)
NMNH 407346

The Hausa associate the sound of a
kakaki trumpet with their chieftain, the emir, and other dignitaries. The horn is played in an ensemble with a special drum and an
oboe. The horn's two notes can be
modulated in melodies and
rhythms used exclusively for official music. Once a week the *kakaki* is sounded before the emir's
palace. Its music also accompanies
such special events as installations
of new leaders, state visits, the advent of war, military inspections,
and the funeral of an emir.

53.
Marimba (*marimba de tecomate*),
mid-19th century
Tactic Indians; Guatemala
wood, gourds, twine, native fiber,
beeswax
20 × 70 × 16 (50.8 × 177.8 ×
40.6)
NMNH 15248; Gift of Henry
Hague

African slaves brought the idea of
the gourd marimba with them to
the New World. Guatemalan Indians now associate the instrument
with their own ethnic heritage, especially in the performance of two
dances, the Dance of the Dead and
the Dance of Invitation. In these,
masked dancers re-create ancient
tales of the tribal past.

The marimba is also used at festive dances called *zarabandas*, held
by religious officials of the community.

54.
RASPS AND SCRAPERS. In Puerto
Rico, nearly all festivals—both sacred and secular—include music.
Before commercially recorded popular music reduced their numbers,
folk musicians provided all the in-
formal accompaniment to singing
and dancing at holiday celebrations. The musicians played gourd
or tin rasps with forked scrapers,
as well as guitars, accordions, and
rattles. During the Christmas season traditional music was especially esteemed, and carolers with

53

54 a

guitars, rattles, and rasps moved from house to house to entertain the people.

a.
Gourd Rasp with Scraper (*wis-guiro*), ca. 1850
Puerto Rico
gourd, wood, metal wire, cotton string
14⁵/₁₆ × 24½ × 2½ (36.4 × 62.2 × 6.3)
NMNH 201483 a, b

b.
Tin Rasp (*guiro*), ca. 1850–1910
Puerto Rico
tin
length: 15¾ (40)
diameter: 3½ (8.9)
NMNH 274806

55.
Gourd Rattle (*cu'tōy*), 1964
Ramkokamekra-Canela Indians;
Sardinha village, Maranhão, Brazil
gourd, wood, manufactured string,
red-seed beads, gold and silver glass beads
22¼ × 6 (54 × 15.2)
NMNH 404830

Song and dance are integral to life in Canela villages, not only during festivals but in daily routine as well. The precentor, or leader of singing and dancing, is an important person, and the gourd rattle is a symbol of his status. With it he summons villagers and enlivens

their celebrations. Whether rejoicing in an exceptional harvest or greeting a beautiful morning, villagers respond to the voice and vigor of the leader.

The Canela apparently do not attach conscious meaning or symbolism to the cross and curves etched into the gourd rattle.

56.
AKAN DRUMS. In Ghana, voluntary associations of musicians provide entertainment for Akan communities. Made up of village members, these groups perform on many festive occasions—weddings, installations of chiefs, military demonstrations, and various holidays. Their music usually welcomes an infant on its first venture out of doors. Good-natured rivalry among groups leads to striving for distinctive effects—visual as well as musical. Ornately carved and decorated drums like these are the result.

a.
Single-Membrane Drum, 1900–1950
unspecified Akan people; Ghana
wood (membrane lacking)
32¾ × 20 × 22¼ (83.1 × 50.8 × 56.5)
AfA 68-36-398

b.
Single-Head Drum on Supporting Human Figure, 1900–1950
unspecified Akan or Ewe people; Ghana
wood, hide, string, beads, pigments
33½ × 18 × 20 (85 × 45.7 × 50.8)
AfA 67-23-4
Illustrated in color, p. 23

55

57

Helping to direct puberty rites for Cuna Indian girls, a guardian of the cacao brazier (wearing a necklace of pelican bones, designed to clatter as he moves) leads a line of dancers; Rio Tigre, San Blas, Panama, 1970. Courtesy, James Howe (see no. 57).

57.
Flute Necklace *(korki-kala)*, 1875–1925
Cuna Indians; San Blas region, Panama
bones, cotton string, glass beads, pitch, pigment
¾ × 26⁹⁄₁₆ (1.9 × 67.5)
NMNH 327396

During girls' puberty rites among the Cuna Indians of San Blas, minor religious functionaries wear pelican-bone flute necklaces. Instead of playing the flutes, wearers of these necklaces enliven their dancing with the clatter of the instruments.

While it is possible that in the past the bones were played as flutes, they now function in ritual ceremonies principally as percussive instruments, as personal decorations, and as badges of office.

58.

Harp-Lute (bolon donso-nkoni ko),
1900–1950
Manding or Manding-influenced
people: Maninka, Bamana, Senufo,
Dan, Mano; Guinea Coast of Africa, Mali, Ivory Coast, Liberia
wood, hide, calabash, string, iron
14¼ × 37¾ × 10¼ (36.2 × 95.7
× 26)
AfA 68-19-17

The simple harp-lute appears to
have been used in the rites and ceremonies of hunters and warriors in
Manding and adjacent societies.
Professional musicians played harp-lutes to accompany hunters'
dances, epics, and songs of praise
for past and present heroes. In traditional groups, hunters were also
warriors. The harp-lute exhorted
them to war as well as to the hunt
and followed them in battle.

59.

Pressure Drum and Drumstick
(iya'lu dundun), possibly 1940s
Yoruba people; Ogbomosho city,
Nigeria
wood (Afzelia africana), leather,
cloth, brass
25 × 18 × 10 (63.5 × 47 × 25.4)
NMNH 407396 a, b

The iya'lu dundun is played only
by a master drummer. Through his
drumbeats he tells the Yoruba king
what is happening at the palace
gate and drums out praise for prestigious visitors as he recites their
names and personal histories.
When played in ensembles of pressure drums, the iya'lu serves as
lead or mother drum, improvising
and "talking" over the other drumbeats.

Yoruba musicians in Nigeria
hold these pressure drums between
their inner arms and the sides of
their chests. Pressure on the thongs
connecting the tops and bottoms of
the drums changes the pitch of
their notes and replicates the tonalities of Yoruba speech.

60.

Pressure Drum and Drumstick (akika dundun), possibly 1940s
Yoruba people; Ogbomosho city,
Nigeria
wood (Afzelia africana), leather,
cloth, brass
9 × 16½ × 8½ (22.8 × 41.9 ×
21.6)
NMNH 407395 a, b
Illustrated in color, p. 23

The akika, a special member of the
dundun set, resembles the iya'lu,
or mother, dundun (no. 59). In the
Ogbomosho region, the akika is associated exclusively with a cult
based on masks that honor ancestors and provide entertainment.
During performances by masked
cult members, the akika supplants
the iya'lu as leader of the dundun
set. Distinctive phrases and drumbeats reserved for the cult extoll its
members and recount their ancestry.

61.

Horn (hõ'hi), before July 8, 1966
Ramkokamekra-Canela Indians;
Sardinha village, Maranhão, Brazil
cow horn, bamboo, string, feathers,
plaiting fiber
17 × 28¾ × 4¾ (43.2 × 73 ×
12.2)
NMNH 404823

Any Canela male with strong lungs
and a desire to increase group participation in festival dancing may
sound the horn trumpet. Musicians
do not play these instruments in
unison nor seemingly in any particular rhythm. The sound emitted is
a one-tone blast with a little
rhythmic variation. The Canela
also use horn trumpets to give
warning, to call meetings in the
village, and while hunting.

62.

Midé Bark Rattle, ca. 1900
Ojibwa Indians; Red Lake, Minnesota
birchbark, wooden handle, wooden
pegs, rattle pellets, sinew ties
10½ × 3¾ (26.6 × 9.5)
NMNH 263230

The Midé, or Grand Medicine Society, was the central religious institution of the Ojibwa. Its members, both men and women, aimed
to promote health and long life. All
members met each spring for a general initiation ceremony and gathered in smaller groups throughout
the year for curing and rededication
to their faith. Each of the eight degrees or levels of membership in
the Midé had its own distinctive
rattle for use at these observances.
The degrees represented different

62

64.
Shell Rattle, ca. 1850–73
Clallam Coast Salish Indians; Port Townsend, Washington
spruce-root hoop, red and blue flannel, string, feathers, scallop shells
12⁹⁄₁₆ × 14½ × 6¾ (32 × 36.8 × 17.1)
NMNH 13117
Illustrated in color, p. 23

Scallop-shell rattles like this one were part of the ceremonial regalia of the *saihwe* dancers, a religious society among some of the Coast Salish peoples of the southern coast of British Columbia. The *saihwe* performed during ceremonial rites of passage and whenever an individual assumed a new status and guests received gifts. *Saihwe* danc-ers were four in number, each wearing a birdlike mask, a neck shield, rows of swan feathers, leggings of swansdown skin, and deer-hoof anklets. A dancer carried a cedar branch in his left hand to balance the scallop-shell rattle held in his right hand.

65.
Carved Wooden Rattle, ca. 1800–1840
Northwest Coast Indians; British Columbia, Canada, and Alaska
wood; sinew; black, red, and blue paint
16½ × 18¼ × 6½ (41.9 × 46.3 × 16.5)
NMNH 2668; Collected by the U.S. Exploring Expedition, 1841

stages of specialized knowledge within the society.

63.
Snapping-Turtle Rattle, ca. 1878
Seneca Iroquois Indians; Six Nations Reserve, Ontario, Canada
snapping-turtle shell, hickory splints, twine, sinew or gut, red ribbon, wild-cherry pits
15⁹⁄₁₆ × 6¹⁵⁄₁₆ × 2¾ (39.5 × 17.5 × 7)
NMNH 253672

The Iroquois conceived of the earth as floating in a huge sea on the back of a snapping turtle, and rattles made of this creature's shell are their most important musical instrument. The rattle is always sounded alone. Constructing one requires more parts and more painstaking care than are needed for other Iroquois instruments. Those who play the rattle to accompany singing and dancing always do so with great vigor, seeking to affect their listeners, both mortal and spiritual, through the rattle's many distinct sounds.

63

68

Although this object was originally identified as a water-fowl decoy, it is safe to assume that a chief used it for musical accompaniment on ceremonial occasions.

66.
Turtle Leg Rattle, ca. 1870–87
Eastern Cherokee Indians; North Carolina
box-turtle shells, groundhog skin, cloth, pebbles
12 × 8½ × 4²³⁄₃₂ (30.5 × 21.5 × 12)
NMNH 133008

Among the Cherokee and other southeastern tribes, women alone wear leg rattles made of turtle shells. With one strapped around each ankle, a skillful dancer is able to control her movements so that the rattle is heard only when appropriate. Accompanying male dancers who sing and sometimes play a gourd rattle, the women reinforce and punctuate the beat in the Green Corn and Friendship dances and in many animal dances. Nowadays the rattles are used in the popular "stomp" dances.

67.
Sistrum Rattle, 1880–1900
Pima Indians; Pe'-eptčilt, Arizona
wood, tin-can lids, iron wire, root lashing
6 × 9¾ × 1¾ (15.1 × 24.6 × 4.4)
NMNH 218066

The Pima used the sistrum rattle in their Navitco ceremonies. Navitco, a spirit who, according to legend, had introduced the cultivation of gourds to them, was honored every eight years or, if crops were especially good, every four years. But Navitco was also thought to be responsible for several ailments—swelling of the knees and inflammation of the eyes. Curing ceremonies for the afflicted were led by masked medicine men accompanied by the sistrum.

Although used and collected in a Pima village, this instrument was not native to the Pima. It was probably acquired through trade from the Yaqui, who had adopted both the disk sistrum and the violin from the Spanish.

68.
Dewclaw Rattle, ca. 1870–85
Hupa Indians; northwestern California
blacktail-deer dewclaws, white glass beads, twine, cloth belt
36½ × 6¾ × 1 (92.8 × 17.1 × 2.5)
NMNH 77190

Dewclaws are vestigial claws on the ankles of some animals, so called because they were said to reach only as far as the dew. Most Native Americans in California associate the rattle of dewclaws with girls' puberty rites, but the Hupa used them in gambling and in curing ceremonies. A long belt adorned with dewclaws, such as the one displayed here, could be tied around the waist, twisted around a stick, or swung from the fingertips.

69.
Peyote-Rite Gourd Rattle, ca. 1880–95
Southern Arapaho Indians; Oklahoma
gourd; green, white, red, blue, and orange glass beads; horsehair tuft; rawhide
30 × 4½ (76.2 × 11.4)
NMNH 175626

Decorated gourd rattles are used by Plains Indians in the rites of the peyote religion. The beads and star designs on this rattle represent hallucinatory images seen with the help of peyote. The figure on the gourd holds a peyote fan.

At the time that this rattle was collected, Arapaho peyote meetings consisted of nightlong fireside singing. After chewing peyote, participants took turns singing through the night, accompanying themselves with gourd rattles. At dawn they put aside the paraphernalia of the peyote rite and took food. During the day the participants rested in the shade, some occasionally singing to themselves with their rattles.

70.
Cow-Horn Rattle, ca. 1920–40
Seneca Iroquois Indians; Cold Spring Longhouse, Allegheny Reservation, New York
cow horn, wood, nails, shot
10½ × 2¾ (26.6 × 7)
NMNH 380929

Played to accompany singing and dancing, the cow-horn rattle is, with the snapping-turtle rattle and water drum, one of three major Iroquois musical instruments. It is featured in the New Year's midwinter ceremony and other calendrical rites. This rattle is sounded by being struck against the palm or thigh.

71.
Altar Bell, ca. 1950
USA
brass, bell metal
5¼ × 2⅜ × 2⅜ (13.3 × 6 × 6)
FP 1981.2

In some Christian churches altar bells alert the congregation to the most solemn parts of the service. Particularly among churches preaching transubstantiation, the bell is rung at the moment when, it is believed, the communion wafer becomes the body of Christ and the wine his blood.

72.
Marching-Band Bass Drum, before World War II
Eveleth, Minnesota
wood, metal, plastic, paint
16 × 29 (40.6 × 73.7)
Courtesy of John Berquest, Eveleth, Minnesota

This drum is used in the clown band of Eveleth, Minnesota, which performs once each year during the Fourth of July parade. The members of the band perform in a deliberately inverse and somewhat inebriated manner to contrast with the other bands in the parade. Instead of dressing in the same uniform, each "clown" devises his own costume to look as ridiculous as possible. Parody of women's clothing is a specialty. Rather than marching in straight parade fashion the clown band snakes around and even intermingles with the spectators. In place of the customary Sousa marches, the band's repertoire consists of polkas.

Ifuya *dancers with attendands; N'Gabe, Congo, circa 1945. Courtesy, Agency HOA-QUI, Paris, Michel Huet, photographer* (see no. 74).

Dancing

Although certain costumes and accessories—such as ballet tutus or the leg rattles of African dancers in initiation rites—are regularly associated with dance, we have chosen to represent this vital part of celebration by audio-visual means and by live performance. For dance is pure process; it is the essence of movement in time. Even more than objects, dance "speaks," though like objects it uses no words. For this reason, it can "say" things about secret thoughts, wishes, and feelings that can never be fully communicated by the spoken or written word. In a very real sense, the true meanings of celebration are "danced out, not thought out," as the anthropologist R. R. Marett once commented.

73.
Caiman Mask, ca. 1940
Nahua-speaking people; Totozintla region, Guerrero, Mexico
wood, barrel staves, paint
66 × 10¾ (167.6 × 27.2)
NMNH 419969; Collected by Donald Cordry

Often performed together, the fish dance and the caiman, or crocodile, dance help to insure a good catch for fishermen along Guerrero's rivers. To the accompaniment of drums, harp, or violin, maskers dance with wooden figures suspended from their waists. In some versions young boys wearing caiman figures like this one dance to elude the nets of persons masked as fishermen. Other Mexican masks are displayed in the "Masks" component of this gallery and are discussed in number 28.

74.
Head on Handle *(okamba),* 1900–1950
Kuyu and Mboshi peoples; Congo
wood, pigments
21⅝ × 6 × 6½ (54.8 × 15.2 × 16.4)

AfA 69-8-38
Illustrated in color, p. 23

The *ifuya* dance is a joyful, highly charged performance presented on special days. Dancers wear conical raffia cloaks surmounted by carved wooden heads like the one shown here. By holding the heads above themselves, at arm's length from within their costumes, the dancers turn themselves into towering, armless figures. The heads, decorated with plumes, usually represent beautiful or important persons. Dancers compete to the accompaniment of songs that describe the person represented.

Twirling to a drumbeat, the *ifuya* dancer crouches to make his cloak billow in a spinning hemisphere. Whoever can maintain this stance for the longest period while keeping the edge of his cloak uniformly distant from the ground is the acknowledged winner of the dance. Dancers from the same village compete among themselves but reserve their keenest rivalry for dancers from other communities.

Feasting and Drinking

Feasting and drinking not only express communal well being but also, in religious celebration, communion with gods and ancestors. The leaders and followers of the human group solemnly become one with the deities and the good dead, as in Christian communion and Polynesian kava festivals. Such communal vessels are holy for their users, and all are requested to regard them as such. Other vessels hold offerings, such as incense, for the gods themselves. Still others contain food and drink that promote a festive solidarity among the living.

75.
Two Ceremonial Cups, probably late 19th or early 20th century
Kuba people; Zaire
wood
largest: 8¾ × 4¾ × 5½ (22.2 × 12 × 13.9)
AfA 73-7-410, 73-7-413

Among the Kuba people, carved wooden cups such as these were used in the ceremonial sharing of palm wines on public and ceremonial occasions. The cup figured in the elaborate etiquette of these events and was an important item of personal display. Kuba leaders commissioned cups from master craftsmen, who vied with one another to produce original and distinctive forms. The origins of many of their designs are found on Kuba textiles and baskets.

75

76.
Double-Mouthed Cup (*kopa*), 1850–1950
probably Suku people; Zaire
wood
3⅜ × 3¹⁵⁄₁₆ × 2⁹⁄₁₆ (8.7 × 10 × 6.5)
AfA 73-7-417

The northern Suku consider the double-mouthed cup to be a symbol of formal leadership. The cup is inherited by one leader from another as an integral part of chiefly regalia. Its use is carefully guarded and only the leader currently in office may drink from it. The *kopa* is used in a special palm-wine-drinking ceremony, which is held before a leader's consultation with his council.

77.
Drinking Horn, probably 19th century
probably Luluwa people; Zaire
African-buffalo horn, cord
6⅛ × 12⅝ × 3 (15.5 × 32 × 7.8)
NMNH 174782

Peoples of the Congo River Basin valued the buffalo-horn drinking vessel because of its association with a powerful animal and also, perhaps, because of its capacity for palm wine. Palm-wine events were occasions for peaceful social discourse in all levels of society. In the Upper Kasai region of Zaire, these events took on ceremonial significance in which the quality of vessels used for drinking expressed the social status of participants. The prestigiousness and variety of buffalo-horn vessels are implied by the large number of skillful imitations made locally from wood.

78.
Two Double Cups (*ragal*), before 1962
Paiwan people; Taiwan wood
largest: 1⁹⁄₁₆ × 27¾ × 1½ (3.9 × 70.5 × 3.8)
NMNH 410131

At many Paiwan feasts, particularly the annual millet-planting and -harvesting celebrations, a fermented rice wine is drunk from double cups such as these. Drinking the wine becomes a ritual act. The village chief calls a man's name, and the two drink simultaneously from the same cup. To do this, they place their heads together, side by

78 (one double cup)

side, and put their arms around one another's neck.

79.
Pottery Jar, before 1962
Paiwan people; Taiwan
clay
$10^{27}/_{32} \times 12^{5}/_{8}$ (27.5 × 32)
NMNH 410078

According to Paiwan custom, wealth was reckoned in the number of pots a family possessed. A decline in a family's wealth and power was attributed to the loss of its pots. Pots with snakes in relief on the shoulder are considered heirlooms and are not presented to others or sold. It is believed that the ancestors of the Paiwan were a snake and an egg and that their spirits reside in the pots.

For ceremonial purposes, rice wine was fermented in these pots and served in a double cup. In daily use, the pots were used to store grain and seeds.

80.
KAVA CEREMONY. In Samoa, as in much of West Polynesia, the kava ceremony was synonymous with formal hospitality. At the level of chiefs it was a prelude to important discussions in the council house. Traditionally, only the aristocratic classes of chiefs and orators participated.

Upon answering an invitation to kava, a group of guests was welcomed by the host orator and the visiting group's orator responded with appropriate style and etiquette. The guests were presented with kava roots—either the large *tungase* displayed here or the smaller and slightly stronger young roots—as well as with bark cloth or mats. The guests might indicate that some of the gift kava be prepared for drinking.

The chief's virginal daughter, assisted by boys and girls of the aristocracy, usually had the honor of preparing the kava. Each guest was served as the host orator called his "drinking name," and the social ranking thereby made explicit was normally accepted with grace and dignity. Oratory at a kava ceremony required artful allusions to myth and metaphor.

a.
Kava Root (*tungase* or *'ava*), before 1962
Samoa, West Polynesia
harvested and dried kava root
38½ × 6½ × 5½ (97.8 × 16.5 × 14)
NMNH 400670

The Samoans considered the *tungase,* or large, mature kava root, suitable for presentation to a guest chief. Such a root might take four or five years to grow. To prepare the bitter root, which was mixed with water immediately before drinking, youths of the aristocratic class chewed it to a pulp. This was placed in the kava bowl, which the chief's daughter had previously brought to the appropriate side of the council house. She first removed her headdress of human hair and flowers because all persons involved in kava preparation had to be bare to the waist as a sign of respect.

b.
Kava Bowl (*tanoa'ava*), mid-19th century
Samoa, West Polynesia
wood, vegetable-fiber twine
7¾ × 23 (19.7 × 58.4)
NMNH 386698

Large kava bowls such as the one displayed here were used in council-house ceremonies. The hands of the chief's daughter were ceremonially washed before she mixed the chewed kava pulp with water in such a bowl, which, when not in use, occupied a special platform at one side of the council house.

c.
Kava Strainer (*to tan'ava*), 1924
Samoa, West Polynesia
bast fiber
5 × 24 × 12 (12.7 × 61 × 30.5)
NMNH 395991

The woman who mixed kava strained undissolved particles of the churned or pounded kava root from the beverage with a strainer stripped from the inner bark of a hibiscus tree. After drawing the strainer through the liquid kava, she wrung it and then tossed it over her right shoulder to an attendant youth. He snapped it

80 b

smartly outside the council house, thereby shaking out the undissolved particles, then tossed it back to her with stylized élan. After having brought the liquid to the requisite degree of purity and potency, the mixer sought the guests' approval by pouring it from a height that allowed all to see her feat. This gesture was timed to coincide with the rhetorical climax of the host orator. Participants clapped their hands on their thighs to express their approval of the performance.

d.
Kava Cup ('pu'ava), before 1897
Samoa, West Polynesia
coconut shell
4¼ × 6⁹⁄₁₆ (10.8 × 16)
NMNH 175209

The host orator announced the celebrant to be served kava by calling out his drinking name: "This is the cup of . . . ." If the person did not have a drinking name the orator used his aristocratic title. While carrying the kava to the drinkers, young male servers never presented the backs of their hands to the guests. They carried the cup at head height with the right hand (the left being kept behind the back), served it at chest level, and waited at a distance until the drinker was finished. The drinker first poured off a few drops to deflect mischievous spirits then murmured a prayer of thanks and drank the beverage.

81.
BEER CALABASHES. As among many other agricultural peoples in eastern Africa, beer among the Haya people is an important sign of hospitality, generosity, and conviviality. The Haya exchange quantities of beer to mark several ritual occasions, most notably those surrounding marriage.

a.
Decorated Beer Calabash with Ladle, ca. 1968–69
Haya people; Kagera region, Tanzania
calabashes, papyrus, banana leaf
calabash: 20¼ × 13⅜ (51.4 × 34)
NMNH 422176 a, b
ladle: 15¼ × 6⅛ (38.7 × 15.8)
NMNH 422177

Beer is presented from one family to another in calabashes like this one at several celebrations that mark stages in the planning and completion of a Haya marriage, from courtship to the bride's emergence from her postwedding ritual seclusion. White strands of the papyrus symbolize happiness, for in the Haya language "to be happy" and "to be white" are the same word, okw-era.

In addition to serving the everyday utilitarian functions of scooping and pouring in beer brewing, the calabash ladle assumes ceremonial status during celebrations. At these times it is used to convey beer from large storage calabashes to smaller personal ones. Etiquette dictates that men's calabashes should not be filled directly. A server of beer finds a ladle covered with a green banana leaf, which he or she removes and later uses as a "spoon plate" for the ladle.

b.
Two Beer Calabashes with Papyrus Stoppers and Straw, ca. 1972–77
Haya people; Kagera region, Tanzania
calabashes, papyrus, reed
men's: 23⅝ × 6¹¹⁄₁₆ (60 × 17)
NMNH 422171 a–c
women's: 17½ × 7½ (44.5 × 19)
NMNH 422174 a, b

Beer calabashes like these are the distinctive personal property of individual men and women. The swelling at the top of a man's calabash, which distinguishes it from a woman's, prevents its slipping from a man's hand as he walks about. (Women are not supposed to walk about sipping beer.) A woman's calabash may be carried by its owner to a celebration where beer is being served, or it may be filled with beer by the host of a celebration and given to a special guest as a private decanter. In the latter case it is closed with a papyrus stopper of the kind displayed here. Otherwise it would be fitted with a stopper and straw identical to those used for a man's calabash. The use of papyrus for this purpose is most frequent in Kiziba, the northernmost of the seven kingdoms of Hayaland.

82.
Pipe and Stem, ca. 1830–45
Ojibwa Indians; Minnesota
wood (ash?), catlinite with lead inlay
3¾ × 38¹³⁄₁₆ × 1½ (9.5 × 98.6 × 3.8)
NMNH 130786

For Native Americans tobacco was a gift from the gods, and it was returned to the gods as an offering. The Ojibwa offered both the plant and its smoke. Tobacco was smoked on many occasions—most frequently during religious rituals. It was also smoked when invoking a guardian spirit, asking for a favor, securing protection from danger, naming a child, treating the sick, or using medicines. As one Ojibwa put it, "Lighting a pipe is the same as praying, for we light our pipe and ask our helper to help us."

The symbolism of the pipe unifies diverse forces of the universe: maleness of the stem with femaleness of the bowl, the circle of the world with the straight path of human morality, brown and red of earth and sky, life and death. The pipe was handled with a series of formal gestures and motions that linked the smokers to one another and to the larger universe in a web of smoke. Smoking a ceremonial pipe (like the one displayed here) before a meeting solemnized it and set an oath on the words to be spoken, a practice that gave rise to the popular conception of "smoking the peace pipe" to end hostilities.

83.
Lidded Bowl on Stand (probably ogobanya), 1850–early 19th century
Dogon people; Mali
wood
height: 22½ (57.1)
AfA 69-31-21 a, b

The hogon, the high priest of the vegetation cult among the Dogon, uses bowls such as this to hold ritual foods, as when he petitions the gods for an abundant harvest of millet, the basis of Dogon nutrition. Other similar but less elaborate bowls are used for everyday purposes.

83

84.
Two Serving Plates (*sangdes*), before late 1960s
Tibet
copper, tin (?) lining
largest: 6⅛ × 9 (15.5 × 22.8)
NMNH 415664 a, b
Illustrated in color, p. 24

The new year is traditionally celebrated in Tibet with dance dramas, ritual offerings, and feasting. Foods are offered on home altars in plates such as these and are eaten from the same plates at New Year's feasts.

Special New Year's foods are ornamental and have symbolic significance. On the eve of the new year, for example, a traditional dumpling dish is served. Some of the dumplings contain pieces of wood, stone, wool, or the like. Others are in special shapes. An individual's fortune is foretold by what is received in one's portion. Then the dough of the dumplings is gathered together, taken outside, and hurled away from the house amid a great noise of whistling, shouting, and exploding firecrackers. This custom, like others observed in the Tibetan home, involves the concept of the new year's breaking up and casting away of the evil that may have accumulated during the old year.

85.
Incense Burner (*hyangno*), ca. 1600–1700
Korea
bronze
4²⁹⁄₃₂ × 4¼ (12.4 × 10.8)
NMNH 151618

This incense burner, probably cast in the seventeenth century, was used in Buddhist temple services and in other Buddhist ceremonies and Confucian rituals. The mythical unicorn-lion that surmounts the pierced lid is a symbol of valor, energy, and omniscient wisdom. The lion is sacred to Buddhism and is sometimes represented offering flowers to the Buddha. It also is used on the censer and flower vase that appear on the Buddhist altar on the second floor and which is discussed in 202.

85

a.
Feast Cup, ca. 1890–95
Central Pomo Indians; Léma,
northern California
willow rod, sedge root, root weft,
redbud, native twine, glass beads,
quail topknots
2¼ × 5³⁄₁₆ (5.7 × 13)
NMNH 203462; Collected 1895 by
John W. Hudson

b.
Guest's Platter, ca. 1884–89
Northern Pomo Indians; Central
Pomo or Potter Valley, northern
California
willow stem, redbud
8¾ × 24 (22.2 × 60.9)
NMNH 203257; Collected 1889 by
John W. Hudson

c.
Feast Basket, ca. 1885–90
Coast Central Pomo Indians; Bó-
keya, northern California
willow rod, sedge-root weft, sedge,
woodpecker feathers
4⅜ × 10¾ (10.6 × 27.3)
NMNH 203446; Collected 1890 by
John W. Hudson

88.
Poi Bowl, before 1909
Hawaii, East Polynesia
wood
16¹³⁄₁₆ × 7¹⁵⁄₁₆ (42.7 × 20.1)
NMNH 257978
Illustrated in color, p. 24

At nineteenth-century Hawaiian
feasts poi was served in wooden
bowls such as this one. Feasts
might be given in celebration of a
marriage or completion of an important task or as part of a religious
or state event.

Poi was usually made from kalo,
the staple tuber in the Hawaiian
diet. According to Hawaiian myth,
the god of kalo was Hāloa, born to
Wākea, personification of the sky
father. High chiefs were descendants of the kalo god's brother.
Hawaiians called their chiefs "kalo
planted in the land"—a source of
life.

Matured kalo tubers—baked or
boiled, peeled, scraped, and
pounded with a shaped-stone pound-
er on a wooden slab—are used for
poi. Water is gradually added until
the mixture reaches a smooth, but
not too soft, consistency. Then the
paste is left to ferment slightly. Poi
is eaten with one or two fingers

86.
Stoneware Jug, 1850–75
probably Pennsylvania
stoneware
11⅛ × 8³⁄₁₆ × 7¼ (28.2 × 20.6 ×
18.4)
NMAH 1979.577.4; Gift of Preston
R. Bassett
Illustrated in color, p. 24

Sometime between 1850 and 1875,
an unknown potter captured a
happy moment on this jug when he
stenciled the scene of three conviv-
ial drinkers sharing a good laugh
together. The drinkers in this scene
appear to follow the American tradition of unabashed liquor con-
sumption. Though we shall never
know their immediate cause for
celebration, we do know that from
earliest colonial days Americans
used alcohol to celebrate major
business transactions as well as
weddings, funerals, church open-
ings, deacon ordinations, and house
raisings.

87.
**POMOAN FEASTING CON-
TAINERS.** Pomoan feasts required
many kinds of containers to hold
plentiful servings of acorn soup and
of pinole, which was made from a
mixture of ground seeds. Foods
were prepared and presented in
large trays and were later divided
up into smaller containers to be
served to guests.

In addition to celebrations like
marriage and puberty rites, many
public events called for feasting.
All religious ceremonials closed
with feasts. Food trading was another such occasion. If one Pomoan
group found itself with an abundance of fish or acorns, they invited a neighboring group to trade
shell-bead money for the surplus
food. After the exchange the two
groups shared a feast served in especially beautifully made and decorated baskets.

88

dipped to the first joint, rotated once or twice, then drawn to the mouth. Business was never discussed around an open poi bowl, nor were scolding or unpleasantness tolerated. Smacking one's lips, however, was polite, for only stingy people ate in silence or behind closed doors.

89.
Sago Platter, before 1944
Aitape people; Papua New Guinea
wood
3¾ × 31¾ (9.5 × 80.6)
NMNH 387897

Aitape men celebrate bountiful harvests, which are believed to result from the blessings of spirits responsible for the growth of food crops. In ostentatious feasts they honor the spirits and serve large portions of sago, a starchy food made from the pulp of the sago palm, on flat wooden dishes like this one. The impressionistic bird form recalls similar figures on prehistoric stone bowls and other objects discovered throughout the New Guinea area. In New Guinea and many other places birds are identified with supernatural beings.

90

90.
Lidded Bowl, 1850–early 20th century
probably of Mbunda origin made for Lozi people; Zambia
wood
6½ × 13½ (16.5 × 34.2)
AfA 72-33-12 a, b

The Lozi, a people who had an elaborate culture for cooking and storing food, produced and obtained in trade a wide variety of food containers. They had an abundant and

diversified food supply and took care of it with a complex assortment of utensils and cooking and storing methods. This wooden bowl was specifically used for storing minced meats; other types of utensils also had their prescribed functions.

91.
Chalice, before 1925
Italy
silver, gold
8½ × 5¼ (21.6 × 13.1)
NMAH 179016

87 c

During the ceremony of the Mass in the Roman Catholic church, a chalice such as this Italian example is used to hold wine, which is offered, consecrated, and consumed as the blood of Christ during the ritual of Holy Communion. Before they are used in the Mass, liturgical chalices are consecrated by a bishop or abbot with holy chrism (a mixture of olive oil and balsam).

The chalice is used with the paten, a shallow plate for holding the Eucharistic host or unleavened bread, which is consecrated with the Communion wine. A veil covers both plate and cup as they are carried to the altar before Mass.

93

92.
Ladle, ca. 1820–50
Chinook Indians; Columbia River,
Oregon and Washington
wood
7 × 7¹¹⁄₁₆ × 4⅜ (17.8 × 19.3 ×
10.6)
NMNH 701

Among the Chinook of the Columbia River area of the Northwest Coast, elaborate feasting with ritual utensils was an important part of the ritual year. The Chinook feasted at the naming of a child, an ear-piercing ceremony, a child's first efforts at food gathering, a girl's puberty, marriage, the death of a chief, the succession of a new chief, and at many other celebratory occasions. The food was always abundant and servings lavish. Foods cooked in large bowls or baskets were served with carved horn or wooden ladles. The significance of the animal carved on the handle is unknown. Such decoration is a convention and also an effective device for making the handle easier to grip.

93.
Serving Tray (*zen; ozen*), 18th century
Japan
wood, lacquer, silver and gold dust or flakes
9 × 15½ × 16⅝ (22.9 × 39.4 × 42.2)
NMNH 401948 a

Before the eighteenth century only the nobility in Japan used elegant trays such as this one for dining on special occasions. During the Edo period (1615–1867), the rising merchant class appropriated the use of the trays. Since 1868 they have been used by all classes of Japanese society.

92

This is one of a pair of trays used together for serving. It is embellished with the crest of the Kyōgoku family, which had commissioned the trays for its own use. From 1658 to 1863 the Kyōgoku family ruled a region on the main island of Shikoku in Japan.

94.
Serving Spoon (*wa ke mia; wunkirmian*), ca. mid-18th century probably Dan people; Liberia and Ivory Coast
wood
2⁵⁄₁₆ × 21¹³⁄₁₆ × 7¹⁄₁₆ (5.5 × 55.2 × 17.8)
NMNH 400594

This elaborate serving spoon is an essential element of Dan celebrations. Only select women of high status own such spoons, which are carved by local master craftsmen. Women serve special foods at opulent feasts given by wealthy men who wish to increase their village and regional standing through lavish expenditures. It is considered to be a great compliment to a woman to be asked to assist the host of these celebrations. The spoon itself not only adds to the elegance of the feast but also represents the respected position of its owner.

In some Dan villages, the serving spoon is used in the traditional *wunkirle* dance. The *wunkirle* is the spirit that allows women to attain special status in her society and is thus represented by the spoon.

Another example of a Dan woman's serving spoon is displayed in the Objects Speak Gallery and is discussed in number 6.

95.
DECORATED FOOD CONTAINERS. Both of these decorated containers were for ceremonial use by Northern Plains Indians. Spoons such as this one were used only for eating, but bowls might be used for paint, medicines, and dice games and for food in both domestic and ritual contexts. With the spread of the white economy, containers obtained through trade replaced those of native manufacture and wooden bowls were gradually restricted to ceremonial use. Guests often brought their own bowls to a feast.

a.
Wooden Bowl, ca. 1875–90
Sioux Indians; Northern Plains, USA
hardwood
3 × 7¹⁄₈ (7.6 × 18.1)
NMNH 153948

b.
Horn Spoon, ca. 1876–89
Teton Sioux Indians; Northern Plains, USA
horn, sinew, tin, quill
1¹¹⁄₁₆ × 9⁷⁄₁₆ × 3¹⁄₃₂ (4.3 × 24 × 7.7)
NMNH 131337

96.
Berry Spoon, ca. 1780
Tlingit Indians; Stikine, Alaska
maple wood
1³⁄₁₆ × 16³⁄₁₆ × 1¹¹⁄₁₆ (2.1 × 41.1 × 4.2)
NMNH 224420 b

The Northwest Coast Indians believed that food was obtained only through cooperation between humans and animals. This ecological link was so strong that human and animal survival and identity were thought to be inextricably intertwined. This spoon, used to serve a meringuelike dessert of whipped berries at a feast, illustrates the close tie by showing a human and a salmon as parts of a single being.

95 b

Retelling Myth and History

Celebrations are often linked to stories, whether these be myths, epics, histories, fables, or folktales. Sometimes a narrative plot knits together the entire celebration, as in the case of pageants and parades. Pageants can become elaborate dramas, often staged outdoors, celebrating a historical event or even presenting the history of a community. At some major religious festivals—in India, for example, during the Jagannatha Car Festival at Puri, Orissa—the mythical deeds of the presiding deity and royal personages are enacted by performers.

97.
Initiatory Tablet (*lukasa*), ca. 1890–1930
Luba people; Zaire
wood
15¾ × 8¼ × 5¼ (40 × 20.9 × 13.3)
NMNH 323440

The *lukasa,* an important part of Luba initiation ceremonies, was a tablet designed to communicate or evoke ancestral myth and history. In one region its message was indicated by the arrangement of various kinds of beads on its surface. The code governing the number and placement of the beads was based on standardized principles but allowed for individual interpretation as well. In this tablet, the carved masklike heads conveyed to initiates information about their heritage and expected behavior.

98.
Puppet, ca. 1890–1930
Northwest Coast Indians; British Columbia, Canada, and Alaska
cedar, red cloth, calico cotton, red paint, grass stuffing
30½ × 13 × 4 (77.5 × 33 × 10.2)
NMNH 398057

Kwakiutl and Tsimshian secret societies used puppets to suggest to a believing audience that spirits were actually present. As part of an elaborate ritual stagecraft, puppets often appeared in acts of illusion. A box might be thrown over a fire to dim its light, whereupon a puppet would miraculously materialize from the gloom, or, at a sound from the roof, puppets might sweep down from a smokehole. In their cures, Tlingit shamans frequently used puppets to represent either a healing spirit or the illness itself.

98

99.

Esther Scroll (*megillat Ester*), early 20th century
Jerusalem
ink on parchment, olive wood
8 × 6 × 2 (20.2 × 15.2 × 5.1)
NMAH 154736

The Esther scroll is read in a carnivallike atmosphere in the Jewish synagogue on the holiday of Purim, the Feast of Lots. The story recounts how Esther and her kinsman Mordecai saved the Jews in Persia from a plot to annihilate them. The name of the villain who planned their destruction is Haman, and whenever he is mentioned in the reading children rattle special noisemakers called *gragers* (or *groggers*) to blot out the evil sound.

This Esther scroll is an example of Holy Land souvenirs from the late nineteenth and early twentieth century. Depicted on the case are the city of Jerusalem and the western wall, known as the Wailing Wall, of the Second Temple.

100.

PONGSAN MASK DANCE-DRAMA. Young Korean male dancers perform the Pongsan mask dance-drama in an open field to celebrate the spring festival of *tano* on the fifth day of the fifth lunar month. The nightlong performance may also be given when a local government has some cause for celebration and festivity. Most of the seven-act drama is devoted to scolding vice and praising virtue. Dancers wear multicolored costumes and move vigorously to forceful music. After a performance, the papier-mâché masks are burned to safeguard their purity and sanctity.

Six Pongsan Dance-Drama Masks,
before 1964
Pongsan county; Hwanghae province, Korea
papier-mâché, pigments, cotton fabric, fur, paper, wood
range: from 11½ × 8¾ × 5¾ (29.2 × 22.2 × 14.5) to 26 × 24 × 8 (66 × 60.9 × 20.3)
NMNH 404242, 404246, 404255, 404257, 404259, 404260

97

100 a

100 d

100 b

a.
Young Monk Mask (*sangjwa-t'al*)
In the opening act of the Pongsan mask dance-drama, four young monks perform a dance dedicated to the deities of the four cardinal points. Their movements are symbolic of purity and faith. This mask depicts one of the monks.

b.
Corrupt Monk Mask (*mŏkchung-t'al*)
The character personified by this mask is one of eight degenerate monks who perform a "dance of apostasy" in the second act of the dance-drama. Having renounced their own religious faith, they eventually entice an old priest into succumbing to worldly desires.

c.
Sorceress Mask (*somu-t'al*)
This mask represents a young sorceress who collaborates with the degenerate monks. At their instigation she bewitches and seduces an old priest.

d.
Monkey Mask (*wonsung'i-t'al*)
A monkey appears in the dance-drama to mock human frailty. Employed as a bill collector by a shoe salesman, the monkey selects as its first victim an old priest. The priest has bought a pair of shoes for the sorceress who seduced him. Instead of approaching the old man directly for payment, the monkey, performing a highly suggestive dance, runs after the young woman.

e.

Lion Mask (*saja-t'al*)
Buddha's traditional messenger, the lion, is capable of recognizing and punishing human shortcomings. In the fifth act of the dance-drama, the lion catches up with the eight degenerate monks and devours one of them. The others vow repentance, and the lion allows them to dance with him as a gesture of mercy.

f.

Nobleman Mask (*yangban-t'al*)
Illustrated in color, p. 25
A nobleman wears this mask in the dance-drama. It portrays a lowly village official pretending to be a high-ranking provincial functionary. In a confrontation with an arrogant, drunken commoner, the petty authority's true identity is revealed.

101.

SHADOW-PUPPET PLAYS. The Javanese people celebrate significant passages in life with nightlong shadow plays of translucent leather puppets (*wayang*). Performances confer protection and blessings on upcoming marriages, births, circumcisions, and purifications of homes. They may also celebrate the rice harvest.

Drawn from Indian epics, episodes thematically appropriate to the occasion furnish the plot for the play. The puppets represent classical characters familiar in dress and behavior to their audience. The main story concerns a feud between the five Pandawa brothers, representing good, and the ninety-nine Kurawa brothers, representing evil.

The shadows of the puppets are cast against a thin white cloth screen stretched tightly over a frame. The puppets stand by means of central sticks made of horn, which are planted in the apron of the "stage." Narrating, enacting, delivering dialogue, and singing to the accompaniment of a small percussion orchestra, the puppet master animates the puppets by moving sticks attached to their hinged arms.

Another example of a Javanese shadow puppet is displayed at the entrance of the exhibition and is discussed in number 1.

Six Shadow Puppets (*wayang*), before February 24, 1964
Java, Indonesia
leather, paint, horn
range: from 15¼ × 9½ × ¼ (38.7 × 24.1 × 0.6) to 24 × 14½ × 1 (60.9 × 36.8 × 2.5)
NMNH 402055, 402057, 402060, 402062, 402063, 402068

a.

Bima, a warrior prince, represents pure will. When his color is black, he is in a state of extreme anger and ferocity; at other times his body and limbs are gold. Bima is also known by his long red thumbnail, with which he rips enemies apart.

b.

Ardjuna is the hero of the Pandawa plays. When gold in color, his face symbolizes dignity and refinement. Usually he is shown with a black face. A white face characterizes the hero in his younger years. A skilled warrior, Ardjuna often battles ogres and wins women's hearts.

c.

As an indication of his comic role in the plays, *Semar*, a misshapen servant, wears a chili pepper in his earlobe where once he had a golden earring symbolic of his divine nature. The principal function of Semar, and his equally misshapen sons, is to serve the leading character in a story. Here he appears black, a color signifying anger.
Illustrated in color, p. 25

d.

Prajudo, one of the evil Kurawa brothers, appears here in the garb of a lesser prince.

e.

Dressed as a prince or court minister, this *Kurawa Brother* wears the diadem, hairstyle, and bracelets of royalty.

f.

Srikandi is an adventurous female warrior. Such is her courage that the hero Ardjuna entrusts his household to her when he is away. Her puppet is of a type known for its quickness and refinement of movement.

102.

TOTEMIC EMBLEMS FROM TWO TRIBAL PEOPLES OF AUSTRALIA. The symbols on these ritual emblems are abstract representations of snakes, turtles, and other design elements such as crosshatches and concentric circles. Each symbol has a broad range of meanings that are revealed in myths and in the celebration for which the emblem is used. Each symbol is "owned" by a social group. It may refer to a place or, like crosshatched lines, to relationships among groups, or to other aspects of the natural and social order. Three of the objects displayed come from a single aboriginal people, probably the Yandjinung. The fourth, a *churinga*, is a sacred object central to the religious life of the Aranda people.

a.

Totemic Emblem (*yermerlindi*), 1948
probably Yandjinung people; Milingimbi mission station, Arnhemland, Australia
wood, paper bark, human blood, bush cotton, grass, emu feathers
73½ × 8½ × 5¼ (186.7 × 21.6 × 13.3)
NMNH 387553; Collected by Frank M. Setzler

The Yandjinung people commemorate a legendary flood in their Gunabi ceremony. A narrative song describes how the Great Python rose in anger at the desecration of its well, swallowed the two female offenders and their children, caused the earth to be deluged, and flew above the flood singing Gunabi ceremonial songs. Appearing at the climax of the ceremony like the snake emerging from its watery den, the *yermerlindi* embodies the Great Python's enraged spirit. Blood used to paint the emblem represents the afterbirth and menstrual blood with which the two primordial women defiled the python's well.

b.

Totemic Emblem (*ranga*), before 1940
probably Yandjinung people; Milingimbi mission station, Arnhemland, Australia
wood, pigment, human hair, bird down
1 × 26 × 2¾ (2.5 × 66 × 6.9)
NMNH 387547; Collected by Frank M. Setzler

100 e

c.
Totemic Emblem (*ranga*), before 1948
probably Yandjinung people; Milingimbi mission station, Arnhemland, Australia
wood, pigment
½ × 23 × 2⅜ (1.2 × 58.4 × 6.1)
NMNH 387548; Collected by Frank M. Setzler

Ranga are totemic emblems used to celebrate the mythic origins of the clans during *narra* ceremonies. These observances require many *ranga*, each symbolizing a different animal or plant associated with clan origins and ancestry. Ritual procedures and sacred songs accompany every stage in the making of *ranga*. Later, clansmen dance with these emblems in public ceremonies.

d.
Totemic Emblem (*churinga*), before 1929
Aranda people; central Australia
stone
9½ × 6 (24.1 × 15.2)
NMNH 344724; Collected by A. S. Kenyon, received through exchange

The stone *churinga* of the Aranda people are engraved with totemic signs relating to ancestors or to episodes of origin myths. Aranda kin groups, each associated with a particular ancestral spirit, store these emblems in a sacred and secret place. They are used during initiation ceremonies to validate the initiate's spiritual identity. As a culmination of the initiation rites, elders lead each young man separately to the place where the *churinga* are stored. Bringing out the one that corresponds to the initiate's spiritual identity they say, "This is your body from which you have been reborn." The young man is then associated with the emblem throughout his life.

Games and Sports

Even in today's world of electronic media, sports and games are associated with celebration. At Thanksgiving and New Year's Day many of us watch important football games on television. The association is both ancient and almost universal. Ancient Greek funeral games, Aztec and Inca ceremonial ball games, and the ritual ball game of modern Cherokee Indians spring to mind. Western children play games at birthday parties, while county fairs have horse-riding events and wrestling competitions.

Games and sports, like the rituals of which they are sometimes part, combine two seemingly opposite forces—rules and "flow." The rules of a game provide a framework of action within which anything that does not properly belong to the game is screened out as irrelevant. This enables the players to enter into an altered state of consciousness called "flow," in which their action and awareness become one and their skills and the tasks confronting them are precisely matched. A well-played game (or well-performed ritual celebration) entails a high level of flow, and consequently a heightening of consciousness and a raising of spirits, both for the participants and spectators. Games of skill, strength, and chance may be used as means of divination: if one clan wins the summer hunt will be bountiful, if another wins winter hunting should be given attention.

103.
Model of Racing Canoe (*bolo ba pen*), ca. 1900
Duala people; Cameroun
wood, European oil paint
22 × 102 × 15 (55.9 × 257 × 38.1)
AfA 76-31-1

Canoe races among Duala clans were festive occasions. Elaborated and enlarged for the contests, the traditional dugout canoe became a trim, ornate craft with room for twenty or more paddlers. Success in racing was believed to depend as much on magic as on boatmanship and strength. Each canoe sported a distinctive prow ornament, the focus of the crew's trust in magic.

The German flag on this model indicates that the piece was carved during the period 1884–1919 when Cameroun was the German colony of Cameroon. Probably made for a colonial official, this canoe is one of three models extant.

104.
THE WORLD SERIES—the October Classic, as it is sometimes called—plays out before festive crowds a drama that spotlights deeply felt American values. Competitive spirit, teamwork, individual accomplishment, ethnic achievement, civic pride, personal accomplishments recorded in the annals of the game, physical and mental strength, agility, and endurance—almost all make their appearance in this annual climax to the professional baseball season.

a.
Program, World Series, Dodgers vs. Yankees, 1952
published by Harry Steven's, Inc., New York, New York
paper, ink, metal
11⅝ × 8½ × ¼ (29.5 × 21.6 × 0.6)
NMAH 310547.97

This program is a souvenir of the 1952 World Series, which pitted long-standing rivals—the Brooklyn Dodgers and the New York Yankees—against one another. The Dodgers' Joe Black won the opener, making major league baseball history in becoming the first Black pitcher to win a World Series game. The Yankees won the series in the seventh game.

b.
Autographed Baseball, Brooklyn Dodgers, 1952
Reach, Ontario, Canada, or Philadelphia, Pennsylvania
cork, yarn, leather
3 × 3 (7.5 × 7.5)
NMAH 310547.154

Some of the Brooklyn Dodger greats have autographed this ball. The names of Roy Campanella, Billy Cox, Carl Erskine, Carl Furillo, Gil Hodges, Pee Wee Reese, Jackie Robinson, and Duke Snider are included among the twenty-five signatures. The names transform this ball from an ordinary object into the valued symbol of a legendary team and a nation's pride.

105.
Pin-the-Tail-on-the-Donkey Game, ca. 1913
Washington, D.C.
textile, paint
25⅛ × 31⅛ (63.8 × 79)
NMAH 1977.763.1; Gift of Margaret K. deRuiz

Along with cake and ice cream, the pin-the-tail-on-the-donkey game is a familiar tradition at children's birthday parties in America. Children in other countries—Cuba, Brazil, Denmark, Great Britain—also play the game, though sometimes with a different animal as the object of their effort. It is especially appropriate for birthday parties because a number of children can play, their blindfolding can be supervised, and their success can be rewarded with prizes and party favors.

106.
Three Shuttlecocks (*põõhi-'prë*), before 1966
Ramkokamekra-Canela Indians; Sardinha village, Maranhão, Brazil
corn husks, twine
each: 5¼ × 3¾ (13 × 9.5)
NMNH 404923; Collected by Dr. William H. Crocker

Canela agricultural rites take a sportive turn at harvest time. The Corn Harvest Festival features a shuttlecock game that magically influences future yield. One person, the "ceremonial father," may initiate the shuttlecock throw. A crowd tries to keep the missile in play,

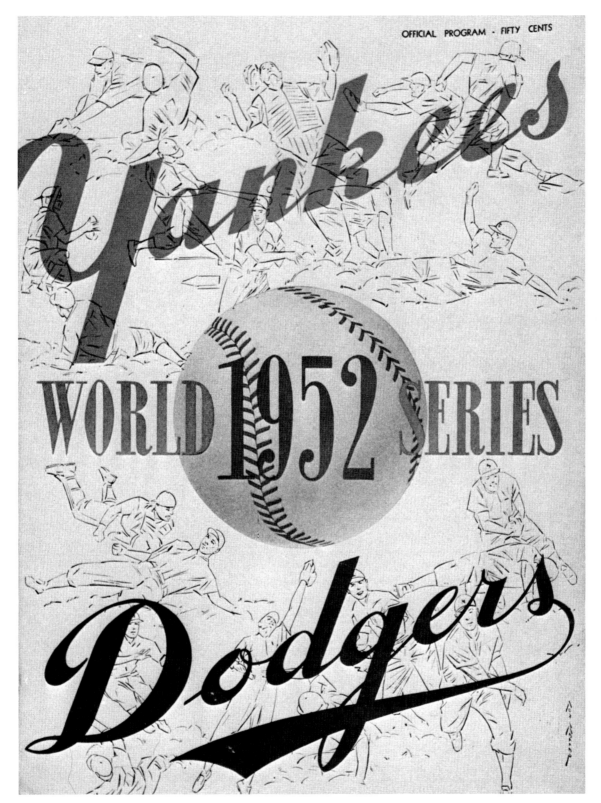

OFFICIAL PROGRAM · FIFTY CENTS

Yankees

WORLD 1952 SERIES

Dodgers

104 a

107

The centipede is vassal to one of the four Buddhist guardians. It appears frequently in Japanese festivals.

b.
Kite with Kintoki Design (Kintoki-dako), before 1963
Japan
bamboo, paper, paint
29½ × 24¾ (75 × 62.9)
NMNH 402332

Representations of Kintoki, a legendary boy warrior, are popular motifs for kites. Pink and robust, Kintoki embodies health, strength, good nature, and loyalty.

109.
NEW YEAR'S GAMES. Both of these games are played by Japanese women during the New Year holiday season. The object in both games is to match halves to make a whole. Whoever forms the largest number of complete pictures or poems wins the game.

a.
Decorated Shells (kai), ca. 1850–1900
Japan
clam shells, paper, paint, glue
each: 1 × 3 × 2½ (2.5 × 7.6 × 6.4)
NMNH 262631
Illustrated in color, p. 25

In the shell game, each of a number of bivalve shells is painted with part of a picture depicting a well-known story on one shell and the rest of the picture on the other shell. All shells are separated from their counterparts and mixed before the game is played.

b.
Poem Cards (uta-garuta), before 1896
Japan
paper, lacquer, gold and silver dust, paint, black ink
3⅜ × 4¾ × 2⅝ (8.6 × 12.1 × 6.7)
NMNH 201326

In the card game, one hundred *waka*, or thirty-one syllable poems, are written in two parts on cards. Like the shells discussed above, the cards are mixed and must be matched by the participants in the game.

batting it up with their palms. The longer the shuttlecock stays aloft, the better the current harvest of corn.

107.
Two Stilt Footrests, before 1843
Marquesas Islands, East Polynesia
wood
largest: 14 × 2¼ × 4 (35.6 × 5.7 × 10.2)
NMNH 3791, 3793; Collected by the U.S. Exploring Expedition, 1838–42

Marquesan festivals often included races and battles on stilts. Competitors tried to knock their opponents

off balance by levering their stilts out from under them. The footrests of the stilts were usually elaborately carved.

108.
In Japan, nationwide kite flying celebrates the New Year season and in May the boy's day festival. (For other objects used in this festival, see nos. 14 and 213.)

a.
Centipede Kite (mukade-dako), before 1963
Japan
bamboo, hemp strings, paper, paint
4⅞ × 36 × 10 (12.4 × 91.4 × 25.4)
NMNH 402429

110.

Gambling Sticks in Bag, ca. 1860–84

Tlingit Indians; Sitka, Alaska

hide; wood; abalone inlay; red, black, and green paint

27½ × 9 × 2½ (69.9 × 22.9 × 6.4)

NMNH 75422; Collected by John J. McLean

At feasts and potlatches, the Tlingit, Haida, and Tsimshian peoples played a stick game that invited heavy gambling. Players used sets of carved and decorated sticks, each with an individual name. The high stick of a set was called the devilfish. A set could number as many as one hundred eighty sticks, but more common were sets of fifteen to twenty. The bag shown here contains thirty-three sticks, probably two sets to provide a fresh set in case of bad luck. Players took turns shuffling the sticks and putting them under piles of shredded cedar bark. Opponents bet on the whereabouts of the devilfish. Successful guesses yielded points.

111.

CHEROKEE BALL PLAY. Ball play for the Cherokee was no mere game. Called the "friend" or "companion" of battle, it was second only to war as a manly pursuit. To play, one had to be sound of body and character and ritually pure. Only those in the best physical and spiritual shape could compete in the hotly contested games between neighboring towns.

Players took their game very seriously, training hard for two or three weeks before each contest. Many restrictions and several purification rites controlled the training period. A player could eat no salt, hot food, or rabbit (a timid animal). He had to abstain from sexual contact with women and could not even think of playing if his wife was pregnant. The day before a game he fasted.

Each team held a big dance before going to the playing field. Shamans began conjuring for victory and continued chanting after moving to the sidelines of the field. The game took place near a river so that players could purify themselves. Spectators from the competing towns gathered early and placed

108 b

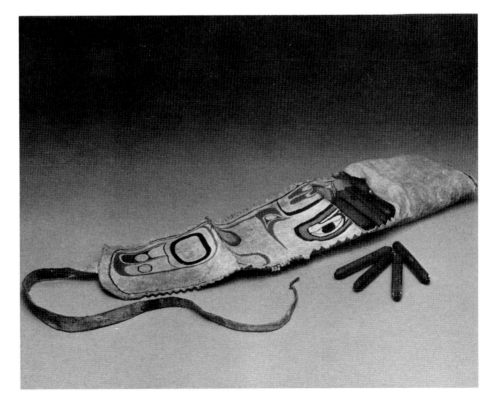

110

their bets, wagering household items like knives, trinkets, and calico. The object of the game was to put a hide ball through two uprights—poles or trees—that formed a goal. Players could handle the ball but only after scooping it up or catching it with their sticks. Definitely a contact sport, the ball game demanded aggressive play for success.

The Choctaw, a neighboring tribe, also played this game.

a.

Hide Ball, ca. 1870–80
Eastern Cherokee Indians; Yellow Hill Council House, Jackson County, North Carolina
hide, sinew, stuffing
diameter: 2 (5.1)
NMNH 63062; Collected by Dr. Edward Palmer
Illustrated in color, p. 26

In the latter part of the nineteenth century a leather-covered ball was used, where formerly it had been made of deerhair and covered with deerskin. This example appears to be one of the older balls.

b.

Ball-Play Sticks, ca. 1880–88
Eastern Cherokee Indians; Eastern Cherokee Reservation, North Carolina
wood (hickory or white oak?), rawhide string, nails
longest: 1⅝ × 29 × 3⅞ (4.1 × 73.6 × 9.8)
NMNH 383638; Probably collected by James Mooney
Illustrated in color, p. 26

The webs of traditional ball-game sticks were fabricated from Indian hemp or twisted squirrel or groundhog skin instead of from rawhide. Some groups played with a pair of sticks per man, others with a single stick.

c.

Ball-Play Trunks, ca. 1880–89
Eastern Cherokee Indians; Eastern Cherokee Reservation, North Carolina
white muslin, red cloth, bone buttons, cord, white thread
20¼ × 22½ × 1 (51.5 × 57.5 × 2.5)
NMNH 135176; Collected by James Mooney
Illustrated in color, p. 26

Before 1880 Cherokee ball players wore only loincloths, but toward the end of the nineteenth century they began to wear trunks like these, often decorated with red and blue appliqué. A complete playing costume called for a feather charm worn in the hair. This charm included an eagle's feather for keen vision, a deer's tail for speed, and a snake's rattle for intimidation of opponents. Players also rubbed their bodies with grease and charcoal and chewed sassafras bark as protective measures.

d.

George Catlin (1796–1872)
Ball-play Dance, Choctaw, 1834–35
oil on canvas
19⅝ × 27⅝ (49.8 × 70.2)
Smithsonian Institution; Gift of Mrs. Sarah Harrison
Illustrated in color, p. 26

In 1834–35 American artist George Catlin captured an intense moment of the ball-play dance. Catlin's male Choctaw players are depicted in ball-play dress as they dance and sing together to the beat of drums, rattling their sticks and raising their voices to the night sky. Chanting to the Great Spirit as they encourage their men to win, women dance in two lines between opposing groups of men. Shamans, seated where the ball-play will be started, offer smoke to the Great Spirit for wisdom to judge fairly this deadly serious sport.

112.

DISH GAME. The Iroquois were great gamblers. They played (and still play) the peach-stone, or "dish," games on celebratory occasions, including the New Year's feast of midwinter, the green-corn ceremony, and the harvest feast. During events such as these, groups competed. Individuals could vie against each other at any time for their own enjoyment. Always a betting game, the dish game could involve extensive loss of personal property, usually clothing and ornaments. Spectators responded enthusiastically and vociferously during the course of a game, which could last anywhere from a couple of hours to two or three days.

Custom held that the outcome of a game between men and women presaged the corn harvest. If the

men won, ears of corn would be long, like men. If the women won, the corn would be short. Games were also played in the presence of the sick, though more as a diversion than a cure.

a.

Gambling Bowl, ca. 1850–1900
Seneca Iroquois Indians; Tonawanda Reservation, New York
maple
3½ × 10⅛ (8.9 × 25.7)
NMNH 248723; Collected by George G. Heye

Kneeling on a blanket, two players or two competing teams face one another across a gambling bowl or dish containing peach-stone dice. The players take turns in shaking the bowl containing the dice and bringing it down with a whack on the floor.

b.

Six Peach-Stone Dice, ca. 1870
Seneca Iroquois Indians; Cattaraugus Reservation, New York
peach pits
largest diameter: ⅝ (1.6)
NMNH 248721; Collected by George G. Heye

The six peach-stone dice used in the dish game are traditionally scorched black on one side and painted white or left uncolored on the other. Points are awarded for four winning throws in the elusive combinations of six black, six white; five black with one white; and five white with one black.

113.

The Vanderbilt Cup, 1904
Tiffany and Company, New York, New York
silver
23½ × 20⅛ (59.6 × 51.1)
NMAH 310894; Gift of William K. Vanderbilt

William K. Vanderbilt, Jr. (1849–1920), began the Vanderbilt Cup Races in 1904 under the auspices of the American Automobile Association. By bringing the best foreign cars to the United States, these races helped promote the American automotive industry.

The front of the cup depicts Vanderbilt in his Mercedes and lists the winners, cars, distances, times, and dates of Cup races. The laurel

113

103

at the rim of the cup symbolizes victory.

The 1908 race was the first in which an American-made automobile (a Locomobile) won the Vanderbilt Cup. It crossed the finish line going more than 100 miles per hour, narrowly missing scores of foolhardy onlookers. Designed by A. L. Riker and driven in the winning race by George Robertson, "Old 16," as it has been affectionately called, is still in working condition today.

Celebrations for Old 16's victory over the swank European models continued day and night in a burst of American national pride. In Bridgeport, Connecticut, where Old 16 was built, a joyous homecoming several weeks later called for school holidays, parades, and banquets.

Despite severe initial opposition by farmers to the first Vanderbilt Cup races on the public highways of Long Island, the races continued in full sway (except in 1907 and 1913) until 1916. The interest in automobiles and automobile racing developed to such an intensity during these years that sleepless spectators would assemble the night before the event, celebrating with drink and merriment well before the Cup drivers began their perilous course.

114.
Soaring Bird Figure, ca. 1900–1950
Senufo people; Ivory Coast
wood
11⅜ × 25 × 27 (28.9 × 63.5 × 68.6)
AfA 78-20-1

In Senufo farming communities, bird figures like this one are awarded as trophies in hoeing contests. During each planting cycle, young men take part in the ceremonial hoeing of their chiefs' fields. Peers compete in speed and skill, working toward a marker in the form of a soaring bird. The first contestant to reach the bird marker keeps it as a memento of his victory until the next contest.

115.
DECORATED BATTLEDORES.
Japanese girls and young women play the traditional game of *hanetsuki,* or *hagoita-asobi,* during the New Year holiday season. This game resembles badminton. Highly decorated battledores or paddles, such as the ones shown here, would be impractical for actual sport; they are used instead in ceremonial gift exchanges. On January 15, the elaborately ornamented battledores are displayed in the home. Motifs for decoration include birds, flowers, and popular kabuki characters.

a.
Battledore (*hagoita*), ca. 1900–1946
Japan
wood, silk fabric, paper, paint
24⅜ × 8¾ × 1 (61.9 × 22.4 × 2.5)
NMNH 415785; Gift of Colonel and Mrs. John Soule

This battledore is decorated with the likeness of a kabuki character, the Wisteria Maiden. Her dance represents the delicacy and grace of a flower nymph.

b.
Battledore (*hagoita*), 1900–1944
Japan
wood, silk fabric, paint, feather, paper
16¾ × 5¾ × 1¼ (42.5 × 14.5 × 3.1)
NMNH 399490; Gift of James L. Honea

On this battledore, the dance costume for Dōjōji (a legendary drama of love) is readily recognizable by the priest's hat that the dancer wears and the fan she holds.

c.
Battledore (*hagoita*), ca. 1875–1946
Japan
wood, silk, brocade, paper, watercolor
24 × 9 × 2 (61 × 22.9 × 5.1)
NMNH 416909; Gift of Mrs. Kazue Johnson
Illustrated in color, p. 27

Judging from its size and elaborate ornamentation, this battledore is a ceremonial gift item for the New Year holiday display. The donor's father gave it to her when she was young.

d.
Two Battledores with Shuttlecock (*hagoita to hago*), 1900–1939
Japan
wood (probably cedar), paint, fabric, feather, silk thread, paint, soapberry nut
each battledore: 14⅜ × 4¾ × ¾ (36.5 × 11.6 × 1.9)
shuttlecock: 1 × 2⅛ × 2½ (2.5 × 5.4 × 6.4)
NMNH 398535; Gift of Mrs. Lispenard Seabury Crocker

In Japanese folk tradition the fox is messenger for the *inari* shrine, sacred to farmers. In a festival celebrating *inari,* villagers pilgrimage each year to the shrine to bring offerings of food for the fox. The figures on these two battledores allude to this annual tradition.

114

Rites of Passage

Biologically, all human beings, if they stay healthy and escape violent death, pass through the stages of birth, infancy, childhood, adolescence, early adulthood, middle age, old age, and death. Societies vary widely in the extent to which they celebrate these stages and the passages between them. For example, some develop elaborate funerary rites and ceremonies but pay little attention to birth; others emphasize marriage but have no puberty rites. In the United States we have no nationwide age or grade celebration for male or female adolescents, although we do possess localized fraternity and sorority initiations, commencement exercises, and "sweet-sixteen" parties.

Rites of passage between life's culturally defined stages themselves have three main stages. First, those going through them (the "novices") are separated from their previous stage, often by the use of symbols or symbolic actions representing death or killing, such as circumcision, scarification, or other bodily mutilation. For the novices, their old life has died. In the next stage the novices are often taken to a secluded place (a forest enclosure or a cave) and there are given instruction in sacred or secret knowledge. Often they are stripped of their former garments and either left naked or dressed in uniform garb. Their very names may be taken from them. Sometimes they are likened to the dead or to animals. They are at a threshold or "betwixt-and-between" state—neither what they were nor what they will be. They are seen as dangerous to others and as in danger themselves, usually from supernatural forces. Finally the novices are brought back into everyday society again. They are given new garments, new names, and will lead new lives at a higher level of status and responsibility. Symbols of birth and rebirth are now everywhere in evidence.

All celebrations bear traces of these three stages: separation, threshold or "limen," and reincorporation. In fact, this formula represents the progress of human life as defined by culture. To mature we all have to "die" from a previous state; to enter an unknown state full of ordeal, growth, chance, and choice; and to be reborn finally as persons in control of our lives at a more challenging level. Western societies tend not to express such passages in terms of public rituals and cultural symbols. Rather, they regard them as private, interior processes. That is one reason why non-Western objects far outnumber Western ones in this gallery.

Birth and Initiation

Entry into the human social world is a path widely and ornately hedged about by celebratory symbols. A family, clan, tribe, nation, or religious community has a potential new member whom it desires to welcome and to make its own. The biological birth itself is seldom accompanied by complex celebratory ritual. Baptism, divination for the baby's name, circumcision, and various marking and defining rites celebrate events of cultural, not biological, significance.

When it seems certain that an infant will live, its parents' kinfolk and coreligionists assemble to witness a social "birth"; that is, the marking of the infant with a social identity, a badge of membership in a group. In many societies, social birth is deferred until puberty or young adulthood. When this is the case the initiatory celebration is often long, complex, and charged with many-layered symbolism.

116.
Crib Quilt, 1841
Funkstown, Maryland
cotton top, lining, batting
50 × 43 (127 × 109.2)
NMAH T8434; Gift of Mrs. Nina Knode Heft

Ann Bender Snyder made this quilt for her godchild, Nina Knode, to celebrate the child's baptism. White, often in the West a symbol of purity and new life, is the color used for baptismal gowns and for christening blankets. The sacrament of baptism cleanses and purifies a child and is the ceremony of initiation into the Christian faith.

117.
Deep Pan, 1830
probably Exeter, New Hampshire
slipware
7 × 13½ (17.8 × 34.3)
NMAH 392412; Gift of Lura Woodside Watkins

This pan is said to have been made as a christening present for Dorothy Melissa Ann Goodrich of East Kingston, New Hampshire. It bears the initials "D m A" and the date "1830" written in slip.

118.
Christening Gown, 1891
Washington, D.C.
cotton fabric, lace
length: 42 (106.7)
NMAH 219358.1; Gift of John Fitzgerald

Catherine Holtman Lanegan wore this elaborately decorated christening dress on November 21, 1891.

In early Christian days, before the use of special white garments at baptism became common, the priest placed a white cloth on the child's head as a symbol of innocence. Mantles of bright hues, rich cloth, fine decorations, and costly furs wrapped royal and aristocratic children baptized in England through the seventeenth century. White robes with sleeves, accompanied by fancy caps, evolved as christening clothes during the eighteenth century, a tradition preserved today.

For Christians, white symbolizes purity, innocence, holiness, and glory. White emphasizes the joy of spiritual rebirth, remission of sin, and incorporation into Christ through the baptismal rite.

119.
CERTIFICATES OF BIRTH AND FAMILY MEMBERSHIP. In early America individual families (not City Hall) maintained records of births, marriages, and deaths. Such hand-decorated documents have become generally known as fraktur, though the term more specifically applies to records and writing samples of Pennsylvania-German origin.

a.
Birth Record of William Ziler, ca. 1830
USA
ink, watercolor, and gold on paper
13³⁄₁₆ × 11⅝ (34.4 × 29.5)
NMAH 329797; Gift of Mrs. E. C. Chadborne

The Zilers apparently followed the Pennsylvania-German tradition of recording each birth separately. In contrast, the Walkers listed eight births and five deaths together. A single writer appears to have entered all Walker births from 1755 to 1771, but three different hands appear to have inscribed the deaths from 1773 to 1843. Family history here recorded spans eighty-eight years.

b.
Family Record of George Walker and Elizabeth Snow, before 1974
probably Kittery Point, Maine
ink and watercolor on paper
10¾ × 8½ (27.3 × 21.6)
NMAH 312370.2

The artist of the Walker-Snow family record also appears to have painted the equally delightful Walker-Snow marriage record displayed in the "Courtship and Marriage" component of this gallery. We may speculate that the painter was a family member or a literate person familiar to the family, perhaps a local schoolteacher.

120.
Mask (*chikuza; chikunza*), 1900–1950
Luvale people; northwestern Zambia
roots, fibers, bark cloth, pigments, beeswax or resin
60 × 18 × 19 (152.6 × 45.7 × 48.2)
NMNH 399018

118

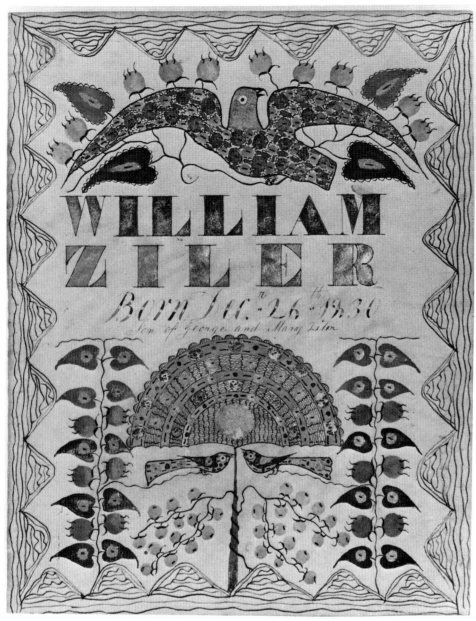

119 a

men" and the rest of the village.

The person wearing the *mbwena* mask dances alone on the sidelines of the main dance area or strolls slowly about flicking a fly whisk in each hand. He is said to represent a scavenger animal, possibly the brown hyena, which is not well known in this region.

122.
Hyena Mask (*munguli*), 1900–1950
Chokwe people; northwestern Zaire
tree branches, roots, bark cloth, fiber, pigments, resin (?)
65 × 16 (165.1 × 40.6)
AfA 75-12-1
Illustrated in color, p. 27

When newly initiated Chokwe boys return to their village after their instruction at an initiation camp, they are greeted by dancers wearing costumes like this one. The masked dancers enliven the celebration of return and familiarize the youths with the construction and special dances of the mask. The mask represents the hyena, an animal whose odd shape and behavior make it an object of fear and wonder to the Chokwe.

This mask appears only during the day and at the return of newly initiated youths, and only outstanding dancers wear it. Imitating the movements of the hyena, they crouch so that the fringe of the carapaces conceals their legs.

123.
Certificate of Completion (Ode on *Siyum*), before 1892
Rome, Italy
ink and tempera on parchment
23 × 18 (58.4 × 45.7)
NMAH 154634

This handwritten document marks the completion, or *siyum*, of the reading in Hebrew of the entire Pentateuch by a young Jewish man for the first time. Presented at a celebration of this milestone in his spiritual life, the ode includes a historical note, praise of the student's family, an extolling of the study of the sacred law, and a quote from the book of Deuteronomy.

This striking mask is worn by a senior initiated man in Luvale society. The *chikuza* spirit represented by the mask is the patron and protector of the initiation camp in which boys are secluded after their circumcision and during their transition to manhood. Walking through the village with slow, deliberate steps and stern demeanor, the masked elder gathers the young initiates and escorts them to their retreat. At the end of the initiation period he has the boys perform the ritual dances that they learned while in seclusion. They must master these dances before they can perform them publicly for the village.

121.
Mask (*mbwena*), mid-20th century
probably Luchaze people; northern Zambia
roots, fibers, bark cloth, pigment, beeswax, resin
20½ × 22 × 11¾ (52 × 55.9 × 29.9)
NMNH 399106

Like other groups in this area of Zaire, the Luchaze people have a long initiatory rite for young boys ready to pass into manhood. While in a secluded camp the initiates are guarded by persons wearing masks such as this one. When the boys have completed their training, other masks are brought out and a festive period of dance and performance is held for the "new

124.
Mask (*mbala*), 1900–1950
Yaka people; Zaire
wood, branches, raffia cloth, resin,
pigments, raffia fibers
29 × 16½ × 23½ (73.7 × 41.9 ×
59.6)
AfA 73-7-366
Illustrated in color, p. 27

The *mbala* is the most important
mask in Yaka initiation rites. After
circumcision, adolescent boys remain in a secluded camp to learn
traditional skills of manhood, especially singing and dancing. When
they return to the village as adults,
they dance in pairs wearing masks.
The best dancer performs alone and
wears a *mbala*.

The *mbala* headdress often wit-
tily depicts a surprising scene—
sometimes apparently more a
sculptural tour de force than an
ideological statement. *Mbala* imagery frequently involves subjects
not usually represented or discussed in daily life. This example
shows a woman in childbirth assisted by a midwife. The baby's
head can be seen emerging.

Villagers look forward to the performance of masked initiates. A
successful celebration in which
dancers and masks are deemed particularly fine increases the regional
prestige of a village. The group may
then tour nearby communities.
They are accompanied by their
sponsor, the man who has absorbed
all costs of their initiation and
commissioned the masks.

Another example of the *mbala*
mask is displayed in the Objects
Speak Gallery and is discussed in
number 18.

125.
Two Masks (*ndemba*), ca. 1900–
1950
Yaka people; southwestern Zaire
wood, branches, raffia cloth, resin,
pigments, raffia fiber, European
manufactured cloth
largest: 30 × 17 × 16 (76.2 × 43.2
× 40.6)
AfA 73-7-367, L66-7-2

These two *ndemba* masks are considered to be second in the hierarchy of masks in the Yaka male
initiation ceremony. Although not
as prestigious as the pointed *mbala*
mask (discussed in nos. 18 and

121

124), they are much lighter and allow their wearers more freedom of
movement.

When carving these masks, master craftsmen usually select mundane subjects—a mortar and pestle
or a hairstyle, for example—for decorating the front. The wearers of
the masks make little effort to disguise themselves and sometimes
remove the entire headdress during
a dance. These masks seem to be
valued more for their art than for
their ritual significance.

126.
String Mask and Costume (*mun-
ganji; minganji* [wearers of cos-
tume]), 1900–1950
Pende people; Zaire
raffia cord and fibers, strips of plant
epidermis
72 × 40 × 24 (183 × 101.6 ×
60.9)
AfA 72-23-29 a–h

This mask and costume were worn
by the instructors of Pende boys
going through the intensive training of an initiation camp. The *minganji*, as the masters are called, en-
force the rules of the camp. The
secret of their identity is revealed
only shortly before the newly initiated boys return to their village.
The *minganji* dance to celebrate
the return of the initiates and also
dance at other important village
events. These dancers have a special relationship with the local
chief as well as with the spirits of
the dead. Their dance may entertain the public, but it has a severe
and somewhat menacing aspect.

126

127

Family Record of Elizabeth and Solomon Newton, early 19th century probably Southboro, Massachusetts ink and watercolor on paper
20¼ × 25 × ¹⁵⁄₁₆ (51.4 × 63.8 × 2.4)
NMAH 65.855; Gift of Eleanor and Mabel Van Alstyne

Together with celebrations to mark births and deaths, Americans have kept permanent written accounts of these important life events.

Historical sources reveal that Willard Newton, listed here as the son of Elizabeth and Solomon, lived to the venerable age of ninety-two. A justice of the peace in Worcester, Massachusetts, he resided on the farm that had been the property of his ancestors for more than two hundred years.

In this patriarchal New England family, no female last names appear on the document.

128.

Girl's Initiation Costume (nâdwîn ceremony), ca. 1964
Mandalay, Burma
cardboard, cloth, wire, sequins, beads
shirt: 26½ × 22 (67.3 × 55.9)
skirt: 51½ × 33½ (130.8 × 85.1)
NMNH 408471, 408474, 408475, 408476, 408477, 408478
Shirt illustrated in color, p. 27

After their ear-piercing ceremony, which is usually held at puberty, Burmese girls are entitled to act as adult women. A girl's ear-piercing may be done as part of a boy's initiation ceremony. The master of this ceremony makes offerings to certain spirits (na') asking for their blessings. He then pierces both of the girl's earlobes with a gold pin, which may be left in the ear as an earring. The ear-piercing may also take place at home, at which time a specialist pierces the girl's ears in the same fashion but with less ceremony. A feast follows.

129.

BURMESE INITIATION CERE-MONY. Every young Burmese boy enters into the Buddhist order of monks for a short period before he becomes an adult. This initiation is a grand affair in his life. The initiation ceremony (šínpyù) begins on a day deemed auspicious by an astrologer. Dressed like a prince, the boy symbolically follows the same path as Prince Siddhartha, who left his father's palace on horseback to renounce the world and later became the Buddha. Rented for the occasion, a plywood facade, "gilded" and "bejeweled" to represent an old-style palace, is set up in front of the boy's house. From the gates of this "palace" a festive procession forms, including the "prince" on horseback, women with food offerings on their heads, clowns, a band, girls with trays of flowers, and friends and family. They proceed around the village before stopping at the east or west gate, where the boy is presented to the village's guardian spirit.

The next day, after additional ceremony, the boy enters the monastery. Head shaved and clad in yellow robes, he becomes a novice monk. Usually he remains in the monastery for three months of instruction before rejoining his village and family as a layman. Upon his return he is considered an adult and capable of all that is expected of a man.

a.

Boy's Initiation Costume (šínpyù ceremony), ca. 1964
Mandalay, Burma
cardboard, cloth, wire, sequins, beads
shirt: 13 × 17½ (33 × 44.4)
skirt: 47½ × 35½ (120.6 × 90.1)
NMNH 408462, 408463, 408465, 408467

This elaborate costume is worn during a Burmese boy's entry into the Buddhist order of monks.

b.

Two Paper Fans (ya'táun), 1964
Mandalay, Burma
paper, glue, wood
each: 15½ × 8⅛ × ½ (39.4 × 20.6 × 1.2)
NMNH 408468, 408469

A paper fan is one of the two traditional gifts given to a guest leaving a Burmese boy's šínpyù. (The other is discussed in c, below.) These fans are inscribed with the following phrase: GIFT ON THE OCCASION OF THE MERITORIOUS SINPYU

Members of a Pende secret society dance during the initiation of village boys; Zaire, 1951. Courtesy, Eliot Elisofon Archives, National Museum of African Art, Smithsonian Institution (see no. 126).

CEREMONY OF MG. SEIN LIN AND MG. SEIN MIN . . . with the date and place. The reverse side of the fan reads: WE WISH TO THANK ALL OUR FRIENDS AND RELATIVES WHO HAVE DONE US THE HONOR OF COMING TO THIS MERITORIOUS CEREMONY . . . with the names of the hosts, date, and place. The word "meritorious" is particularly significant to the Burmese, who strive to build social and religious merit (*kùδóu*) as part of a good Buddhist life. Merit is mainly earned through good behavior, including giving. Ceremonies provide opportunities to gain merit by giving food and gifts to all who attend.

c.
Face Towel in Plastic Bag
(*mye'hnaθou'pawá*), ca. 1964
Burma
cotton
4½ × 18½ × ⅛ (11.4 × 47 × 0.3)
NMNH 408470

A face towel is traditionally given, together with a paper fan, to a guest leaving a Burmese boy's *šínpyù*.

130.
FLUTE AND MASK INITIATION RITUALS. Many coastal peoples of northern New Guinea participated in ritual activities centering on flutes and masks. During a series of rituals, boys were transformed into men as rites, secrets, origin myths, songs, and identities of spirits were gradually revealed to the young initiates. The flutes and masks personified mythological water spirits that were believed to inhabit lagoons, with the flute representing the spirit's voice and the mask its

113

Costumed Burmese initiates, including a girl whose ears will be pierced, seated before offerings; Rangoon, Burma, 1964. Courtesy, William C. Sturtevant (see nos. 128, 129 a).

corporal body. The water spirits were associated with individual clans, the members of which called for their help in time of need.

During the first sequence of initiation rites, elders taught the young men secrets of water-spirit performances. At that time the youths saw the flutes for the first time. Years later, the same initiation class learned to play these instruments while living in an isolated camp far from the village. Similarly, elders displayed masks to the young men long before they revealed their meaning.

During the final phase of initiation, after an extended period of disagreeable tasks and painful scarification, the young men learned to make masks, sing sacred songs, and perform the masked dances. After initiation they returned to their villages dressed in finery provided by their sponsors. Their adornments included shell ornaments, dog-teeth armlets, and freshly woven loincloths. A weeklong festival followed, during which the new class of initiates, disguised as water spirits, performed in their own and neighboring villages.

a.
Initiation Costume
North Coast peoples; Papua New Guinea

from top:

Conical Headpiece, before 1891
vegetable fiber, red ocher
8 × 5 (20.3 × 12.7)
NMNH 153086; Exchanged with
the Royal Zoological Museum,
Florence

Mask, before 1885
wood, pigment, vegetable fiber
17 × 7½ × 4 (43.2 × 19 × 10.2)
NMNH 362551; Collected by Otto
Finsch, exchanged with the Field
Museum, Chicago

Breast Ornament, before 1943
shell, vegetable fiber, cowrie shells,
black seeds
1 × 12½ × 10½ (2.5 × 31.7 ×
26.6)
NMNH 384046; Collected by Lt.
C. T. R. Bohannan

Two Armlets, before 1943
vegetable fiber, cowrie shells, dog
teeth
largest: 2⅜ × 7½ × 3 (6 × 19 ×
7.8)
NMNH 384037, 384038; Collected
by Lt. C. T. R. Bohannan

b.
Mask, before late 19th century
wood, pigment
12½ × 6⅛ × 4½ (31.7 × 15.5 ×
11.4)
NMNH 362554; Collected by Richard Parkinson, exchanged with the
Field Museum, Chicago

131–133.
RITUAL OBJECTS. The initiation
rites of Ramkokamekra-Canela Indians in the Brazilian state of Maranhão celebrate preadolescent and
postadolescent life roles. The initiation process takes place over a period of ten or more years and has
five separate phases: each of two
rites is performed twice, and then,
much later, some males participate
in a third rite. Males who are initiated together form a lifelong age
set and participate together in
many other activities.

To the Ramkokamekra-Canela,
changes in life roles are fraught
with danger, either supernatural or

130 a (mask)

real. To negate these dangers all
members of the tribe, both male
and female, unite to protect the
vulnerable initiates. Through their
cooperation in the face of ritual
danger, the Ramkokamekra-Canela
collectively strengthen their many
subtle relationships with one another.

The Ramkokamekra-Canela use
objects and ornaments to guide
their youths and men through

these periods of transition. The
three sets of ritual objects shown
here reflect the dangers inherent in
the transitional phases of male
growth and maturity. The first set
of objects is used in the *kêêtúwayê* ceremony and helps protect
young boys against supernatural
dangers. The second set is used in
the *pepyê* ceremony and helps to
neutralize harmful pollutions fac-

ing adolescents. The third set, used in the adult men's *pepcahäc* ceremony, merely helps to deter the physical discomforts arising from competitive sport or nocturnal chill.

131.

Objects for Initiation (first phase, *kêêtúwayê*)
Ramkokamekra-Canela Indians;
Sardinha village, Maranhão, Brazil
NMNH 404843, 421734; Collected
by Dr. William H. Crocker
See colorplate, p. 28

a.

Headband with Three Vertical Macaw Feathers (*pän-yapïï*), 1964
burití palm fiber, tucum fiber, wood, macaw feathers, cotton string
2½ × 8 × 33⅞ (6.3 × 20.3 × 85.9)
Illustrated in color, p. 28

b.

Ceremonial Water Gourd (*cu'kon*), 1975
gourd, native twine
13¼ × 12½ (33.6 × 31.7)

During the *kêêtúwayê* rites, the macaw-feather headband staves off ghosts that threaten the lives and development of prepubescent boys. Water poured from the gourd by close female relatives helps boys to grow and to resist ghostly dangers. Washing serves the same purpose in postpuberty rites and also represents through ritual the close bond between unmarried boys and their close female relatives.

132.

Objects for Initiation (second phase, *pepyê*)
Ramkokamekra-Canela Indians;
Sardinha village, Maranhão, Brazil
NMNH 404733, 404864, 404865, 404861, 404844; Collected by Dr. William H. Crocker

a.

Ceremonial Lance (*krúwa-tswa*), ca. 1900–1950
wood, cotton cord, feathers, glass beads, pigment, deer hoofs
73½ × 7 × 7 (186.1 × 17.8 × 17.8)

b.

Two Initiates' Sticks (*pepyê yõõkôpo*), 1964
wood
largest: ¾ × 49¾ × 2½ (1.9 × 126.5 × 6.3)

c.

Bull-Roarer (*pĭ-'kwëc*), 1964
wood, bast fiber, *urucu* pigment
8 × 1⅜ × ¼ (20.2 × 3.5 × 0.6)

d.

Scratching Stick (*amyi-caakrêntsä*), 1964
wood
⅛ × 13 × ½ (0.2 × 33 × 1.3)

The ceremonial lance, tonged staff, and bull-roarer symbolize group unity for the pubescent boys in *pepyê*, the second set of rites. The initiates rally around the ceremonial lance, which is wielded by a group leader whenever they venture forth as a group. The whirring of the bull-roarer or the hum of the tongs on the carved staff as the initiate rubs it on his upper arm insures those in charge that each initiate remains in isolated nocturnal seclusion. During this phase of the initiation cycle, boys must guard against dangerous pollutions caused by agents such as the evil eye, moonlight, meat juices, and their own fingernails. To guard against touching themselves with their nails, they use a scratching stick.

133.

Objects for Initiation (third phase, *pepcahäc*)
Ramkokamekra-Canela Indians;
Sardinha village, Maranhão, Brazil
NMNH 404884, 404886, 405052;
Collected by Dr. William H. Crocker

a.

Gourd Face Mask (*kuc nã hatsôrtsä*), 1964
gourd, bast fiber
11 × 8¾ × 3½ (28 × 22.2 × 8.9)

b.

Necklace with Snail-Shell Whistles (*twën-kä*), 1964
snail shells, beeswax, pigment, bast twine
14⅛ × 6 × ¼ (36.2 × 15.2 × 0.6)

c.

Reed Pendant (*poopoc*), 1958
native twine, reed, native cotton
37¾ × 5 × 1½ (95.9 × 12.7 × 3.8)

d.

Mat (*catï*), 1964
burití fiber
50½ × 30½ × ½ (128.2 × 77.5 × 1.2)

The objects displayed for the adult initiation rites, *pepcahäc*, guard against no greater dangers than physical discomfort or the friendly and traditional antagonisms between certain formal male social groups. Men wear masks and play whistles similar to these when they carry out festival roles, and high ceremonial chiefs display pendants like this one to enhance their power and prestige. The mats, which ceremonial friends wear on their backs while forming a tight circle around the initiates, ward off the cold night air and eloquently symbolize the vital unity of all the celebrants.

134.

Girl's Puberty Cape, ca. 1900–1935
probably Jicarilla Apache Indians;
New Mexico
buckskin, tin, beads, paint
38 × 36 (96.5 × 91.4)
NMNH 393165
Illustrated in color, p. 28

The Apaches gave significance to a girl's entry into puberty with this special robe and the ceremonies that surrounded it. A young girl's mother or other close female relative made the robe from the finest unblemished skins. In some areas hunters took freshly killed deer away from cougars to avoid using hides marred by arrow holes. Blessings were sung over the finished dress.

A prescribed manner of dressing was strictly followed, with the garments layered in a precise order and each piece draped in a particular way. The complete outfit consisted of robe, buckskin dress, fringed cape, beads, shawl, shell earrings, shell necklace, moccasins, and magpie feathers for the hair. The girl wore this outfit for four days of ritual, dance, and feasting. On the fifth day she changed into ordinary Apache attire, and an even larger feast took place.

Although buckskin is otherwise rarely worn today by Apaches, buckskin puberty robes are still made and worn for this ceremony.

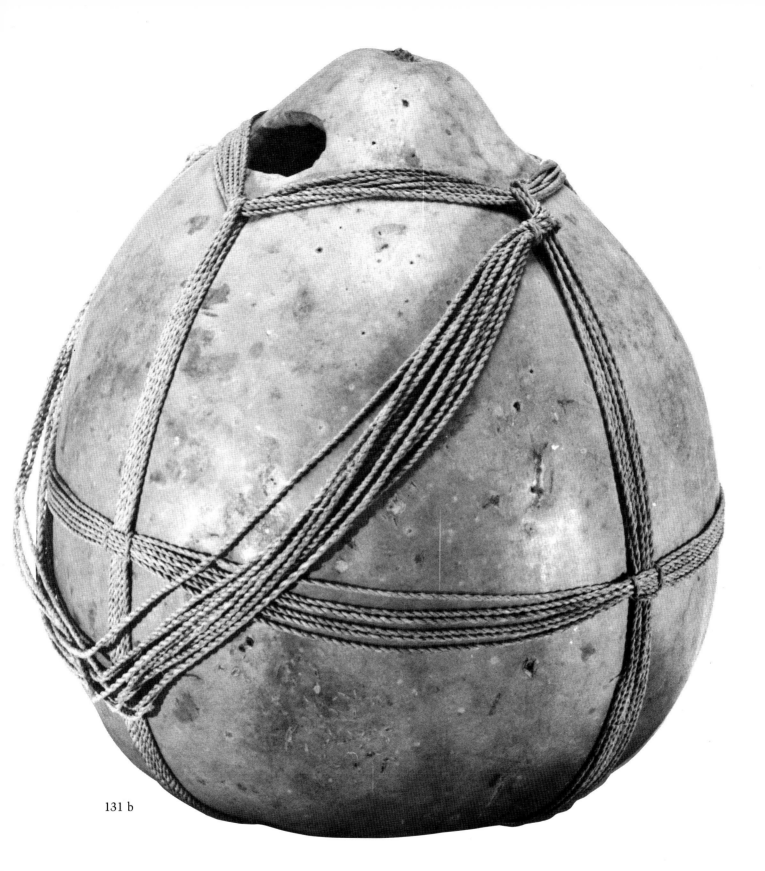

131 b

135.
THREE EFFIGY AMULETS. After the birth of a child, most Plains Indians preserved the child's umbilical cord in a beaded leather bag. The detached cord was folded, dried, and then packed, often with sweet grass, in the pouch. Lizard- and turtle-shaped pouches represent animals that are hard to kill and long lived, attributes that it was hoped would be conferred on the child.

A great deal of lore surrounded these amulets, for they were believed to contain an essential part of the child's personality. A person treated an amulet bag with respect and kept it near throughout his or her life. At death the amulet was buried with its owner.

a.
Lizard-Effigy Amulet, ca. 1900–1935
Teton Sioux Indians; South Dakota
buckskin, glass beads, unknown stuffing
8¾ × 4 × 1 (22.4 × 10.1 × 2.5)
NMNH 378164

136 b

b.
Turtle-Effigy Amulet, ca. 1900–1912
Teton Sioux Indians; North Dakota
buckskin, glass beads, unknown stuffing
5⅛ × 3½ × 1 (13 × 8.9 × 2.5)
NMNH 381374

c.
Turtle-Effigy Amulet, ca. 1880–1930
Cheyenne or Arapaho Indians; Wyoming or Oklahoma
hide, glass beads, tin jingles, yarn, hide thong
11 × 5 × 1 (27.9 × 12.6 × 2.5)
NMNH 362314

136.
MALE CIRCUMCISION. In Jewish belief, male circumcision is the sign of the sacred covenant between God and the Patriarch Abraham. The "covenant of circumcision" (*brit milah*) ceremony is performed by a specially trained circumciser (mohel), when a child is eight days old. The ritual initiates the male child into the society of those who keep the sacred covenant.

a.
Circumcision Implements and Sales Catalogue, 20th century
New York, New York
case: imitation black-grain leather, velvet, elastic
instruments: stainless (?) steel
9½ × 15⅛ × ½ (24.1 × 38.4 × 1.3)
NMAH 1979.1204.60–66

This circumcision kit was made in the workshop of Joseph and David Miller, twentieth-century New York knife makers. The kit contains a probe, forceps, scissors, clamp, and two knives, all instruments needed to perform a circumcision. These objects are used by a mohel (a specially trained circumciser) in the ritual circumcision of Jewish male infants on the eighth day of their lives.

b.
Circumcision Cup and Knife, 1863
England
cup: silver, partially gilt
knife: steel, brass, feldspar (?), semiprecious stones
cup: 3¼ × 2 (8.2 × 5.1)
knife: 5½ × ¾ × ½ (14 × 1.9 × 1.3)
NMAH 154436

137.
The prayer shawl and skull cap represent the ritual garments of a boy who becomes a bar mitzvah, or responsible man, in a celebration marking his attainment. A third traditionally necessary item, the phylacteries or tefillin, is not shown here. Occurring on the first Sabbath after the boy's thirteenth birthday, the celebration marks his attainment of responsibility for vows and sins and his right to be counted as a full member of the congregation.

a.
Skull Cap (*yarmulke*), ca. 1980
USA
rayon-satin, cotton
3½ × 7 (8.9 × 17.8)
FP R400; Gift of Mr. and Mrs. Mervin Lewis

The custom of covering the head as a sign of one's involvement in the sacred sphere of life came relatively late to the practice of Judaism. It was not until the seventeenth century that religious authorities ruled that men must cover their heads during prayer. Thereafter the custom rapidly expanded and the wearing of a head covering—in the shape of a *yarmulke*—became a religious duty for Orthodox Jewish men at all times.

b.
Prayer Shawl (*tallit*), ca. 1980
USA
rayon
72 × 17 (182.9 × 43.2)
FP R401; Gift of Mr. and Mrs. Mervin Lewis

The prayer shawl (*tallit*) is first worn by Jewish males in many communities when they are initiated into adulthood in the bar mitzvah ceremony at puberty, at about age thirteen. Thereafter one wears the shawl during morning prayers, the Sabbath rites, and when performing certain religious functions. On this example, the blessing the male recites before putting the *tallit* around his shoulders is embroidered along one edge: "Blessed art thou O Lord our god, King of the Universe, who having sanctified us with thy precepts, has commanded us to wrap ourselves in the fringed prayer shawl."

138.
Male Figure with Open Headdress
(*kwonro*), 1900–1950
Senufo people; Ivory Coast
wood
57½ × 11½ × 9 (146 × 29.2 × 22.8)
AfA 78-14-7

139

138

One of the phases of initiation into the *poro* secret society—the level at which adolescent Senufo boys become men—is called *kwonro*. A distinctive emblem of this phase is a headdress made of a high panel of wood, usually cut in an openwork pattern. This figure, which wears a similar headdress, appears to represent an idealized *kwonro* participant and may have been used during initiation for teaching.

The figure comes from the Senufo people of the Ivory Coast, who, in their traditional religion, tried to control the forces in their world through the ritual and magic techniques of the *poro* cult. *Poro* knowledge is secret and complex, and instruction in it is a long and elaborate process. To accommodate groups of different ages, the initiation and instruction cycle is divided into phases. Special dress and insignia distinguish the grades. A *kwonro* member, whose carved likeness this is, has progressed from the initial to the second stage and has several more stages to complete.

139.
Low Chair (*gba*), probably 1900–1925, possibly earlier
We people; Ivory Coast and Liberia
wood
12¾ × 14½ × 11¼ (32.3 × 36.8 × 28.6)
AfA 64-9-1

Family heads and other elders among the We- and Dan-related peoples proudly own low chairs similar to this one. They are important heirlooms and are used in many ceremonies, especially for the initiation of young women into adulthood. After designs have been painted on the initiates' faces, they carry the elders' low chairs with them during the ritual. Later, they kneel on the chairs, facing backward, to receive guests at their camp.

Courtship and Marriage

In many societies marriage entails not only the union of a man and a woman but also the alliance of two kinship groups. Its celebration is therefore often a most complicated process that involves religious, economic, political, and legal considerations and is charged with highly visible and ornate symbolism. Marriage celebrations, too, often involve competition between the bride's and groom's groups for prestige and honor, symbolized in the amount of bridewealth or dowry given, the splendor of the costumes worn, the quality and quantity of the marital feast, and the like.

Birth and death, thresholds of the unknown and invisible, evoke spare, stark, enigmatic symbols. Marriage, by contrast, is the threshold of life's most productive (and reproductive) years and evokes profuse, substantial, and relatively literal symbols. Of all types of celebrations, those centering around marriage potentially involve, both intensively and extensively, more of the basic elements of celebration.

140.
Quilt, 1850
Pawling, New York
cotton top, lining, batting; embroidery in silk and wool
103 × 103 (261.6 × 261.6)
NMAH T16323; Gift of Adelaide Pearce Green and Mira Pearce Noyes Boorman
Illustrated in color, p. 29

In the United States, quilts were sometimes made to commemorate special events. The Benoni Pearce quilt was created in the mid-nineteenth century by friends and relatives of a young man, Benoni Pearce, on the occasion of his betrothal.

This piece is called an album quilt because, like an album in which memorabilia are collected and arranged, it is composed of eighty-one individual textile greetings from Pearce's female friends and relatives. Each contributor created, crafted, and signed her own square and with it made a wish for the young man's future and a personal statement.

Some blocks speak in careful, poignant, and wistful verse:

Among the stars of sentiment
That form this bright array
This humble tribute I present
My friendship to portray
Lydia Holloway to her cousin
Benoni Pearce

I am a broken aged tree
That long has stood the wind and rain
But now has come a cruel blast
And my last hold on earth is gone
No leaf of mine shall greet the spring
No Summers sun exalt my bloom
But I must lie before the storm
And others plant them in my room.
Presented by your Aunt Anna Dodge Aged 76 This 22 Day of May 1850

Though poor the offering yet I know
That Thou wilt in a measure prize it
'Twill cause fond memory's flame to glow
In after years when Thou dost view it.
Beekmanville August 23d 1850

Album quilts were popular in America in the mid and late nineteenth century, especially in the Baltimore area. The block designs were not copied from pattern books but were shared and traded by women at county fairs and other communal gatherings. When a group of women decided to make an album quilt, each designed a block according to a predetermined size. After all the blocks were completed the women gathered in someone's home to stitch them together and quilt the colorful top to a suitable backing.

The customary recipient of a quilt at the time of betrothal was a wife-to-be. A young woman was often given a quilt by friends and relatives with whom she had quilted since girlhood. In this regard, the Benoni Pearce quilt is somewhat unusual because it was made for a young man.

141.
Ten Valentines, 1902–51
New York and New Jersey
paper, ink
largest: 7 19/32 × 12 19/32 (19.3 × 32)
NMAH 69.1; Gift of Mr. Will Barker
Illustrated in color, p. 29

The valentine that many Americans are so fond of giving to loved ones each year on February 14 has many legends surrounding its origin. The best known is that of a young Roman, Valentinus, who by sending the first "valentine" became the patron of lovers.

As the legend recounts, Valentinus helped persecuted Christians during the reign of Emperor Claudius II. Giving aid to Christians was a serious offense and Valentinus was imprisoned. Some time later he was brought before the Roman emperor, whom he tried to convert to Christianity. Impressed by the young man's sincerity, Claudius attempted to save him by encouraging him to worship the Roman gods. Failing to sway the faithful Valentinus, Claudius condemned him to death. While awaiting his execution Valentinus developed a friendship with the blind daughter of his jailer and miraculously restored the girl's sight. Unfortunately, his fate had already been sealed and he left the girl a farewell note signed "From your

Valentine." Valentinus died on the fourteenth of February and was buried in Rome. It is said that the pink blossoms of an almond tree that bloomed beside his grave became the symbol of abiding love.

Today many Americans send printed valentines like the ones shown here to express their affection for special people.

142.
Objects Used in Wedding of Constance Emily Keppler and Charles W. Millard, Jr., 1928
Elizabeth, New Jersey
NMAH 1980.0030.03, .05, .10, .13, .18

a.
Pair of Wedding Shoes
satin, lace, imitation orange blossoms
each: 5 × 9¾ × 3 (12.7 × 24.8 × 7.6)

We can see the imprint of a coin in the left shoe of Miss Keppler, who apparently followed the traditional:

Something old, something new,
Something borrowed, something
*   blue;*
And a silver sixpence in your shoe.

Aside from the shoe, we do not know how Miss Keppler may have obtained these charms for good luck and a happy union. According to custom, the "something old" should have belonged to a happily married woman; the "something new" should be the bridal attire; the "borrowed" object should be a piece of gold for wealth and fortune; and the "something blue" should be represented by a garter or some other object to show the constancy of true love.

b.
Wedding Garter, 1928
satin, elastic, lace, wax orange blossoms
1¼ × 6¾ × 7½ (3.2 × 17.1 × 19)

Miss Keppler wore this garter with her white silk stockings, apparently as part of a bride's traditional attire.

According to one source, garters worn in the eighteenth century helped to prevent "a curious hand from coming too near her [the bride's] knee."

144 e

c.
Bouquet Fragments, 1928
wax, dried flowers
1¾ × 7½ × 6¾ (4.4 × 19 × 17.1)

For her wedding in 1928 Constance Emily Keppler followed a fashion popular since the 1830s in using orange blossoms in her bridal bouquet. Orange blossoms symbolize love's innocence, purity, and endurance, as well as the promise of fertility in the fruit to come—a fitting symbol for a young woman entering married life.

d.
Wedding Book, copyright 1925
paper
12¼ × 9⅛ × ⅞ (31 × 23.1 × 2.1)

From the time of her secret engagement to that of her first home-cooked meal of soup, liver, and bacon, Constance Keppler filled *The Bride: Her Book* with treasured memories as she progressed from a bride-to-be to a new wife. The newspaper clippings, invitations, and announcements that she included in her wedding book document the festivities surrounding

American marriages. More personal are the handwritten entries—poems by noted authors, lists of wedding gifts received, names of members of the bridal party, and firsthand accounts of many gift showers, one of which, Miss Keppler wrote, she "enjoyed loads."

e.
Photograph, Wedding Portrait, 1928
10 × 8 (25.4 × 20.3)

This formal photograph of Constance Emily Keppler upon her marriage to Charles W. Millard, Jr., remains a memento of an elegant and traditional society wedding. It took place in Saint John's Episcopal Church, Elizabeth, New Jersey, on April 27, 1928. Afterward the bride's family held a reception at the Elizabeth Town and Country Club, celebrating with an orchestra, dancing, and supper for all. The *Elizabeth Daily Journal* and other local newspapers, making sure to list all the guests invited to attend this gala social event, proudly recorded the occasion with such headlines as "Many Society Folk at Miss Keppler's Wedding."

143.
Beaded Apron with Indented Fringe
(*mapoto*), 1900–1950
Ndebele people; Transvaal, South Africa
glass beads, animal skin, canvas, string, thread
14$^{11}/_{16}$ × 7¼ × ½ (37.2 × 18.4 × 1.3)
AfA 79-47-4
Illustrated in color, p. 30
See also colorplate, p. 30

Among the Ndebele, the variety of beaded apron styles indicates a girl's progression from childhood through the stages of womanhood. A young Ndebele woman makes a beaded garment like this one soon after marriage. Worn along with a black apron, the beadwork enhances her appearance and shows her new status. Older, more established women wear more elaborate beaded garments. When all of the women assemble at wedding parties and other ceremonial occasions, the diverse patterns and forms of beadwork add vigorous color to the occasion.

The geometric motifs of this apron correspond to those painted by southern Ndebele women on their homestead walls.

144.
DOWRY GIFTS. After a Newar betrothal ceremony in the vicinity of Patan, Nepal, there is a feast for the bride-to-be. During this celebration she receives dowry presents from her female relatives. Principal among them are yarn-making tools and a spinning wheel, all richly carved with religious motifs.

After her marriage ceremony the bride carries her household objects to a mountain shrine. She asks the deity of the shrine to bless her craft and leaves behind as an offering a small object, such as a bobbin or a shuttle. Once a year, in October, she anoints her household utensils with a spot of vermilion during a special ritual. The vermilion visible on the spinning wheel shown here remains from this strength-giving ritual, performed to enhance a good wife's productivity.

a.
Cotton Presser and Handle (*kekon*), possibly ca. 1880
Newar people; Patan, Nepal
wood
12 × 20½ × 8¾ (30.5 × 52 × 22.2)
NMNH 406567 a, b; Collected by Mary Slusser

This machine presses cotton into flat fiber ovals before it is spun. The inlaid carvings of frogs symbolize abundant rain and crops.

b.
Foot Piece to Cotton Presser, before November 29, 1966
Newar people; Patan, Nepal
wood
12⅜ × 2 × 1⅜ (31.4 × 5.1 × 3.5)
NMNH 406566; Collected by Mary Slusser

The lizard on this foot piece that steadies a cotton presser is another animal associated with water and its beneficence. In folk belief, lizards carry a jewel in their heads that enables them to see under water, and a hollow for such a jewel has been carved in this lizard's head. On dowry gifts, animals representing abundance symbolize the material increase and physical fertility desired by the betrothed and his kin.

c.
Carved Box (*kapi poncha*), before November 29, 1966
Newar people; Patan, Nepal
wood
4½ × 8 × 3½ (11.4 × 20.4 × 8.9)
NMNH 406564; Collected by Mary Slusser

This box stores the cotton flattened by a cotton presser before it is spun.

d.
Brass Figure, before November 29, 1966
Newar people; Patan, Nepal
brass
5 × 1½ × 1¾ (12.6 × 3.8 × 4.4)
NMNH 406558; Collected by Mary Slusser

A small statue of a Newar girl, given as a dowry gift, is placed inside the carved box before it is presented to a bride. The statuette, dressed in traditional festive apparel with large earrings, round

head ornament, and skirt cut short to reveal tattooed calves and ankles, carries a cup and jar as if offering wine to a feasting guest.

e.
Spinning Wheel (*yon* in Newari; *charkha* in Nepali), possibly 18th century but probably later
Newar people; Patan, Nepal
wood
15½ × 19 × 13 (39.4 × 48.3 × 33)
NMNH 406570; Collected by Mary Slusser

The Newari spinning wheel with its ornamental figures of gods and goddesses may be likened to a shrine with its temple carvings. Dancing goddesses like those found in temples adorn the supports that hold the wheel, and dancing milk-maids flanking the god Krishna with his flute are portrayed on panels of the arched projection opposite the wheel. Above Krishna looms the "Face of Glory" holding snakes, a motif often seen above Hindu shrines.

Each spinning wheel has a space reserved for a wooden image of its own deity at the top center of the base. Although no image is found on this piece, one can guess from the other carvings that Krishna might belong here.

f.
Handle for Spinning Wheel, before November 29, 1966
Newar people; Patan, Nepal
brass
1 × 11 × ½ (2.5 × 28 × 1.2)
NMNH 406565; Collected by Mary Slusser

Symbols on the handle and hook befit an object that celebrates a woman's contribution to the economics of marriage. The Newar associate the double water spirit on the handle, Makara, with fertility and increase and the peacock with good fortune.

g.
Hook, before November 29, 1966
Newar people; Patan, Nepal
brass
4¾ × 4¼ × 2½ (12 × 10.8 × 6.2)
NMNH 406568

147

145.
Dowry Box, before 1962
Bhubaneswar, Orissa, India
wood, treated cloth, paint
13¹⁵/₁₆ × 13⅛ × 13¹/₁₆ (35.2 ×
33.6 × 33.3)
NMNH 399418
Illustrated in color, p. 31

A box like this one holds the jewelry given to an Indian bride by her family at her wedding. More than a simple gift, the wealth is part of the dowry given to the couple by the bride's parents. The amount and contents of a dowry are negotiated between the two families. Pride dictates that the dowry be as large and as lavish as possible. Components are usually clothing (such as saris), jewelry, and cooking pots and other household goods,

which today may include a motorcycle.

The scenes on the box, done in the traditional style of the state of Orissa, are from the life of Krishna. On the top, the youthful Krishna plays his flute and dallies with young milkmaids (*gopi*). On the sides, Krishna as a child defeats three demons—his evil nurse Putana, the horse Kesin, and the whirlwind Trinivartta.

146.
Bride's Box and Cover, 1797
Germany
wood, pigment
7⁷/₁₆ × 18¹⁵/₁₆ × 11⁹/₁₆ (19 × 48 ×
29)
C-H 1962-144-6 a, b
Illustrated in color, p. 31

In 1797 a prospective groom may have presented this gaily decorated box to his intended bride. Hand-lettered on the top is his optimistic thought for their future: "Oh how my Sweetheart will laugh when we celebrate our wedding." The decoration, an idealized couple painted on the cover, is typical of brides' boxes. Young women stored lace, ribbons, and other small trousseau items in these boxes and added them to the large blanket and dowry chests that they took to their new homes after they were wed. This bride's box may have been homemade, as some boxes were, but the skillful execution of its complex designs suggests the hand of a professional artist.

149 a

147.
Chest, 1783
Lancaster County, Pennsylvania
walnut, sulfur
25 × 55 × 26½ (63.5 × 139.7 × 67.3)
NMAH 322631.14

Pennsylvania-German parents gave chests like this one to their children, both male and female, as gifts during their adolescent years or at the time of their marriages. Young women filled their chests with items they planned to take with them at marriage, although technically these articles of furniture were not considered to be "dower" chests. Rather, they were important items of storage furniture customarily given to young people and were used to store clothing, bedding, personal possessions, and money. Chests were usually placed in the bedroom for storage and for seating.

Pennsylvania-German cabinet-makers made wooden chests throughout the eighteenth century and well into the nineteenth.

148.
Four Courting Scenes from Ledger Book, ca. 1880–1906
Cheyenne Indians; Oklahoma
ledger-book pages with pencil, ink, and watercolor drawings
each: 8 × 5 (20.2 × 12.7)
NMNH-NAA 2018
Illustrated in color, p. 31

Although the Cheyenne originally required men and unmarried women to avoid each other completely, during the nineteenth century they adopted the Sioux custom called "standing in the blanket." To meet his prospective bride in the same fashion as he met the spirits, a suitor would dress in his finest clothes so as to be as sweet and pure as possible. He would then approach a consenting girl, enfold both the girl and himself in his blanket, and converse with her. A much sought-after girl might have a long line of suitors, each awaiting his turn.

The custom of drawing in ledger books grew out of the earlier Plains tradition of pictographs drawn on rocks and hides and later on cloth. Sometimes whites commissioned the drawings from imprisoned Cheyenne warriors. The most popular subject matter was war, hunting, courting, and celebrations.

149.
Carved wooden objects are important during courtship and in married life among the Bush Negro people of Surinam in northern South America. The objects are carefully designed and decorated to include forms that symbolize the personal relationship between the carver and his intended bride or his esteemed wife.

a.
Three Food Stirrers, ca. 1900–1935
Bush Negro people; Surinam
wood
largest: 13/16 × 21⅞ × 2⅜ (1.9 × 55.4 × 6)
AfA L79-7-S48, L79-7-S68, L79-7-S154

These paddles are closely involved with the personal history and experiences of married couples in Bush Negro society. They are important gifts from a man to a woman throughout the couple's courtship and marriage. The carver, usually the suitor or husband, incorporates special events or wishes into the designs on the handle. A stirrer is thus a symbolic embodiment of a couple's domestic relationship. It is also used for stirring and serving rice or stews, mainstays of Bush Negro diet.

b.
Two Combs, ca. 1900–1935
Bush Negro people; Surinam
wood
largest: 13¼ × 4¹¹/₁₆ × ½ (33.6 × 11.9 × 1.2)
AfA L79-7-S11, L79-7-S33

Bush Negro women use wooden combs of this kind to dress their hair into tufts and braids. Combs and other decoratively carved wooden objects enter into bride-wealth payments at the time of marriage.

150.
Four Love Sticks (*woguniar; okuniar*), contemporary
Truk, Caroline Islands, Micronesia
wood
largest: 35 × 1½ × ¼ (88.9 × 3.8 × 0.6)
NMNH 400954, 400957, 401641, 401645

The Trukese allow sexual experimentation among young people, provided it is kept discreet. To arrange for an evening rendezvous, a young man used to insert a "love stick" through the thatch of the hut where a young girl slept. The girl recognized the suitor by the carving on the stick and then either pushed the stick out to signal "go away," wiggled it to indicate "come back later," or drew it inside to signify "come right in."

151.
Wooden Duck (*mogan; chonan*), 19th century
Korea
wood, red and black paint
8¼ × 10⅔ × 4 (21 × 27 × 10)
Courtesy of Dr. Robert Sayers

Ducks, symbols of fidelity, play an important role in the Korean wedding ceremony. Originally live ducks were used, but specially carved wooden ducks have now taken their place. On the wedding day the groom's attendant leads a procession carrying the wooden duck to the bride's house. The bride's mother receives it and places it on a bowl of noodles. Noodles symbolize long life and were originally fed to live ducks during the ceremony. The marriage vows are exchanged before the symbolic duck.
   Wood-carvers carve a marriage duck only once in a lifetime.

152.
Ceremonial Cloth (*okorszar-kendo*), 1900–1950
Hungary
cotton with wool embroidery
65⅜ × 9½ (166 × 24.1)
NMAH T11514; Gift of Dr. Mary Davis

Throughout Hungary embroidered cloths are part of many ceremonies. This type of cloth adorned the horns of oxen that drew a cart bearing a bride's dowry from her house to the groom's. The Hungarian name of the cloth translates literally as "ox-horn kerchief." Although oxen are not used today, the cloth still adorns wreathlike loaves of wedding bread. Newlyweds decorate their homes with these embroidered panels, draping them over plates, mirrors, and pic-

150

154

Tunic and Wedding Headdress
(tunic, *gmejja*; headdress, *goufia*),
probably 1960s
Tunisia
cotton, wool, metallic wire, sequins, threads wrapped with silver
and gold
41 × 28 (104.1 × 71.1)
NMNH 420828 a, b

A traditional wedding in Tunisia
takes several days to complete. On
one day, the bridegroom sends to
the bride a collection of gifts: three
or more pieces of jewelry; a box of
perfumes; henna; silk scarves;
sugar loaves; and a "Fatima Hand,"
composed of five candles of differing lengths representing fingers. On
the same day, the marriage contract is affirmed at two separate
ceremonies. First, the fathers of the
couple agree to the terms of the
contract for the benefit of the
groom. Shortly afterward, the contract is read to the bride in her own
house and she is asked to approve
it. She signifies her acquiescence
by allowing her right hand to be
decorated with henna.

On another day, the bride is led
to her husband's house by her female friends. More ceremonies and
celebrations await her that day and
the next. Finally, after all the
guests leave, the marriage is con-
summated.

The bride wears her wedding
tunic and hat on the day the contract is read and also on the day
she moves to her husband's house.
The style of the cap is believed to
be derived from those worn by An-
dalusian Moors who immigrated to
Tunisia centuries ago.

155.
WEDDING COSTUME. In traditional China the groom sent a specially decorated sedan chair, carriage, or automobile to bring the
bride from her home. Her vehicle
came accompanied by an old-style
band of horns and drums and a
procession of men carrying lanterns, banners, and fans. All could
be hired from a carriage shop. Before entering the vehicle, the bride,
dressed in her traditional bridal finery, donned a large hat and a
mantle or veil of red, a color that
in China symbolizes joy. Then,
amid music and the noise of fire-

tures hung on the walls of a special
parlor in which family showpieces
are displayed.

153.
Wedding Dress (*bindalli*), probably
early 20th century
Turkish people; Balkan peninsula
muslin, velveteen, gold thread, paper, sequins
53⅛ × 55⅛ (135 × 140)
NMAH T11759

Elaborate customs and festivities
enhanced a Turkish wedding in the
Balkan peninsula during the time
of the Ottoman Empire. The entire
celebration could last a week. After
the terms of the marriage contract
were agreed upon, the bride sent
the bridegroom a silk packet with
shirts and handkerchiefs and a
nightshirt, shawl, and silver tobacco box. In turn he gave her a silver mirror and jewel boxes. Following this exchange the signing of the
contract took place in the men's
quarters of the house of the bride's
family. The contract was read and
agreed to by the groom three times,
with witnesses and an imam
(priest) in attendance. The imam
then went to a door or curtain behind which the bride waited and
asked for her acceptance as well.

The bride also affirmed the contract three times.

The following days were filled
with visits and exchanges between
the two families. The center of attention was the bride. Her wedding
dress and accessories were sent to
her by the groom's family. Her
friends took her in pomp to the
public bath and her future mother-
in-law blessed her and fed her
sweets. On the last day of festivities the bride dressed in her wedding gown and left her parents'
house for that of the groom. He led
her to the women's quarters, where
she was celebrated among the
women.

After evening prayers, the groom
kissed the hands of his parents and
went to the wedding chamber
where the bride awaited him with
an older matron as a companion.
The groom asked the bride her
name, which she provided. He then
asked her to remove her veil,
which she refused to do until he
gave her a present, usually a ring.
The bride then removed her veil
and kissed the bridegroom's hand.
After serving the couple a meal and
black coffee, the matron was given
a tip and discreetly retired.

155 b

The traditional Chinese bridal dress was embroidered with auspicious motifs. The butterfly is a symbol of happiness in marriage. The bat is also a symbol of happiness because in Chinese the words for "bat" and "blessings" are homonyms. Flowers have auspicious meanings as well. The peony, for example, is an emblem of love and affection and of feminine beauty and is also a sign of spring.

b.
Bride's Headdress, before 1929
China
metal, cloth, kingfisher feathers, beads, thread
14 × 8¾ (35.6 × 22.2)
NMNH 342076

In traditional China the bride wore a special headdress made of rich materials with a fringe of beads that hung over her face. This headdress was modeled after those once worn by the wives of high officers of state. The inscription on the example shown here reads, "May you prosper for five generations."

156.
Three Wedding Cups and Stand
(*saka-zuki*), before 1963
Japan
wood, lacquer, gold and silver dust
stand: 2¾ × 5³⁄₁₆ (7 × 13.2)
NMNH 401451 a–d

These three cups are used in a traditional Japanese wedding ceremony called *san-san-kudo* (literally "three times three equals nine"). All elements and movements in the ceremony are done in threes. Three cups are placed before the bride. Her attendant fills the first cup with sake by pouring three times. She drinks from it by sipping three times. Then she passes the cup to the groom, who does the same thing. The middle cup is filled and emptied in the same way, except that the groom is first to drink. The ritual for the third and largest cup, also poured and sipped in threes, is begun by the bride and is repeated by the groom. This exchange solemnizes the marriage. The decorations on the cups are auspicious symbols of married life. The crane represents long life, fidelity, and monogamy. The wave motif suggests power and resilience, like the ocean's ebb and flow.

crackers, the procession regrouped itself, now augmented by people bearing the bride's wardrobe, kitchen utensils, and a prepared feast. All of these were carried on trays or tables.

After the bride and her procession arrived at the groom's house, the marriage contract was sealed. Bride and groom bowed to the ancestral tablets of the groom's family and to the tablets of heaven and earth. The couple then drank from two cups of wine. Because the

bride was still veiled, she could only pantomime this act. After these customary rites, the bride and groom retired to an inner room where the bride's veil could be removed.

a.
Wedding Outfit, ca. 1930
Szechuan, China
silk, cotton, ribbon, lace, string, beads, paper, thread
jacket: 32½ × 27 (82.4 × 68.5)
skirt: 37 × 72 (93.9 × 182.9)
NMNH 349808 a–d
Jacket illustrated in color, p. 32

157.

Ceremonial Offering Tray (sambō), before 1888
Osaka, Japan
wood, lacquer
10⅝ × 11⅞ × 11¾ (27 × 30.2 × 29.9)
NMNH 150595

Elaborate trays such as this one are used in many Japanese ceremonies. They serve as tables on which wedding cups or offerings are placed. These tray tables usually are placed around the principal images in temples.

158.

Photograph, Marriage Certificate dated 1869
Crider Brothers, Publishers, York, Pennsylvania
13¼ × 17³⁄₁₆ (33.7 × 43.7)
NMAH CBA9004

Marriage certificates legally prove that a man and woman have been wed. Without such proof, a surviving spouse or heirs may lose certain legal rights. According to this certificate, Milton Brown and Mary Reul of Lebanon County, Pennsylvania, were wed by Lutheran minister H. Giesz on December 19, 1869.

By the mid-nineteenth century, mechanically reproduced wedding certificates became cheap and readily available due to improvements in the printing industry. These rather stiff and formal printed documents often replaced inventively hand-lettered and hand-painted records (such as the Walker-Snow family record, no. 119), which are prized today for their artistic merit.

This lithograph by A. Hoen and Company, Baltimore, Maryland, published by Crider Brothers, York, Pennsylvania, includes instructive passages from the Bible on matrimony, as did earlier hand-penned certificates. Ornately styled hearts figured prominently as symbols of love in hand-decorated certificates. Here hearts are more simply reproduced with the printing process. Individual photographs of the newly wedded couple replaced the fanciful hand drawings of bride and groom sometimes seen on earlier homemade certificates.

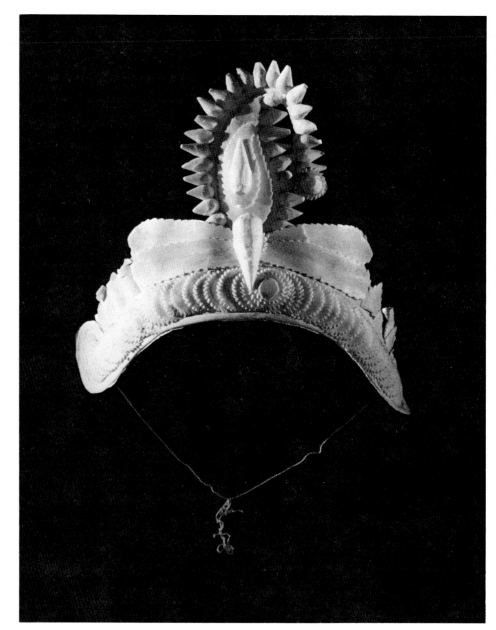

159 b

159.

BRIDE'S AND GROOM'S HEADDRESSES. When a bride in Bengal leaves her father's house and enters her husband's house, she goes as Lakshmi, goddess of wealth, and is dressed to resemble her. Her husband is also seen as a god, akin to Markando, guardian of the ancestors and husband of Sasthi, giver of babies. These godly roles reflect the new life each begins, the bride as a container of wealth and children and the groom as a guardian of that wealth.

The wedding attire of the couple helps them to embody these divine attributes. Adorning their heads are marriage coronets made with the same design and techniques, and by the same group of artisans, as the crowns that adorn deities at public festivals. The artisans are known as *malakars*, craftsmen who have made decorations for deities from ancient times. Using only one or two sharp knives, a pair of scissors, and molds, the craftsmen cut the pith of the *shola* plant into decorative flowers, garlands, wreaths for the hair, and coronets for marriage and harvest dances.

161

a.

Groom's Headdress (*shola mukut*),
before 1960
Bengal, India
pith, paper, tin foil, feathers
20 × 11 (50.8 × 27.9)
NMNH 399628
Cover

b.

Bride's Headdress (*shola mukut*),
before 1960
Bengal, India
pith, paper, bamboo, wire, string
8½ × 4 (21.6 × 10.1)
NMNH 399630

160.

Conch-Shell Horn (*shankh*), before
1879
Bengal, India
conch shell
3¾ × 4¼ × 6½ (9.5 × 10.8 ×
16.5)
NMNH 54075; Gift of the Rajah
Sourindo Mohun Tagore to President Rutherford B. Hayes

The lingering note of the conch-
shell horn augurs good fortune in
Bengali weddings. Married women
in charge of wedding rituals sound
the horn (*shankh*) during the
course of the four-day marriage ceremony. Its sonorous tone may be
accompanied by the wail of women
crying "ulu, ulu" for nuptial happiness.

Ganga ka pani sumundra ki sank,
bar kanga jag jag anand.
May Ganges water and sea-shankh
    betide,
enduring bliss to bridegroom and
    bride.
Bengali proverb

In other parts of India, conch shells
are blown at funerals, during religious festivals, and on the occasion
of bringing in the year's first harvest. Some regions assign the task
of playing the instrument to special
castes.

161.

Horn (*rana shringa; narsinga;
seeng*), before 1883
Bengal, India
brass, paint
40 × 8¼ (101.6 × 21)
NMNH 92710; Collected by the
Rajah Sourindo Mohun Tagore

Throughout India the *shringa* is
indispensable during marriages and
other festive occasions and during
funerals, when its wailing blasts
are especially pronounced. In Nepal musicians sounding these
horns lead wedding processions and
signal a bride's arrival at her husband's home. *Shringas* also sound
harvest festivals in Nepal.

162.

**Marriage Record of George Walker
and Elizabeth Snow,** ca. 1755
probably Kittery Point, Maine
ink and watercolor on paper
8½ × 11 × ⁹⁄₁₆ (21.6 × 28 × 2)
NMAH 312370.1

Family records were kept in many
different formats in eighteenth-century America. It is often difficult to
determine the archivist of the family or his or her locale by the document alone. In many instances,
families kept these records in their
heirloom Bibles.

163.

Young Girl's Wedding Party Attire:
shift (*riza*), jumper (*sukman*),
apron (*prestilka*), sash (*pojas*), un-
derbelt, overbelt, socks (*chorapi*),
shoes, 1875–1900
Bulgaria
cotton, silk, wool, metal sequins,
glass beads
49 × 35 (124.5 × 89)
NMAH 168604, 168604 a
Illustrated in color, p. 32

Until recently young maidens in
the Balkans dressed elaborately for
all village festivals. This costume
could have been worn at a wedding
or at other festive celebrations.

A girl's preparation for marriage
and adulthood included mastery of
local embroidery and weaving techniques. In addition to making her

own outfit, the bride was obliged to make up to one hundred pieces of clothing for special guests at her wedding.

Dressing the bride was a long and strictly defined process performed by female relatives. The wedding festival itself lasted for days and included elaborate feasting, dancing, and music.

164.
In Jewish tradition, a marriage contract, or *ketubah*, stipulates the legal obligations of a man to his wife. It is signed on the wedding day. The practice of writing the *ketubah* dates from the first century before the Christian era, and since the tenth century, the document has been richly illuminated.

a.
Marriage Contract (*ketubah*), 1816
Rome, Italy
ink and tempera on parchment
33½ × 21 (85.1 × 53.4)
NMAH 154633

This wedding contract was inscribed for the wedding in Rome on the twentieth of Adar 5576 (1816) between Elijah, son of Samuel Sacchi, and Mazel Tov of Castelnuevo. The margin is decorated with symbolic figures, the liturgy of the wedding ceremony, and passages from the Bible and Talmud on marriage and married life. At center top is the family crest; to the right is a boy standing on a wheel and pouring out the horn of plenty, with a motto in Aramaic, "All depends on merit and good luck"; to the left is a female figure with a tambourine and the phrase "Peace and welcome to those nigh and far." Below, to the right, appears a female figure holding two burning hearts linked by a chain and the adage "A well-mated couple is chosen by God"; to the left another female figure holds a tambourine and a flower with a quote from Isaiah 32:8. At the bottom, alluding to the bridegroom's name, is a representation of the prophet Elijah ascending to heaven in a fiery chariot with his mantle falling on Elisha.

b.
Marriage Contract (*ketubah*), 1719
Leghorn, Italy
ink and tempera (?) on parchment

37 × 23¼ (94 × 59)
NMAH 216162

This marriage contract was inscribed for the wedding in Livorno (Leghorn) on the fourth of Tammuz 5479 (1719) between David, son of Abraham Rodriguez Miranda, and Dona Esther, daughter of Moses Franco. The decoration on the contract is in the form of a Greek temple facade with the text flanked by Corinthian columns surmounted by the crests of the families brought together by the marriage. At the base of the columns are verses associated with the names of the couple:

And David behaved himself wisely in all his ways; and the Lord was with him (1 Samuel 18:14).
And Esther obtained favor in the sight of all of them that looked upon her (Esther 2:15).

165.
HAIRSTYLES AND HEADDRESSES. To the Himba people of Namibia hairstyles and headdresses make important statements. They may say, for example, that the wearer is a twin or that a child belongs to a particular clan. Adopting a new hairstyle or headdress usually marks a passage from one stage of life to another. Removing a headdress or abandoning a hairdo without replacing it signifies grief and is done during a period of mourning. When in perpetual mourning for a deceased wife, an old man may not dress his hair at all.

A boy's hairstyle changes after circumcision and also at marriage. In a special celebration after marriage, a father cuts his son's hair and then sponsors a feast for him. The son's wife receives his severed hair to lengthen her own tresses.

At his wedding, other important family rites, visits of important people, and other ceremonial occasions, a man wears a formal head covering called an *ombwiya*, similar to the one displayed here.

During a family feast celebrating the advent of her puberty, a Himba girl dons a special string headdress. Called an *ehando rokociuru*, the headdress is made of baobab-bark fiber, beads, and berries and is colored red with powdered ocher. A practical leather handle allows the owner to carry the headdress or to

hang it up when not in use.

The *ekori* is a head covering made of sheep and cow skin, iron beads, animal fat, fiber thread, wood, and red ocher. A woman receives an *ekori* in her wedding ceremony, given by her father as she is about to leave his homestead to enter that of her husband. A bride's first *ekori* may be borrowed from her mother or from another female relative. Later she fashions her own.

The soft sheepskin of the *ekori* is usually rolled up above the forehead. When she first enters the homestead of her new husband, the shy bride unrolls the sheepskin to cover her face in modesty. After several days, when she has begun to feel at home, she rolls it up again. A woman may also let the sheepskin down when mourning her husband's death.

In daily activity, a married woman of virtue wears a cap, an *erembe*, outside her house or in the company of people not from her immediate family. On ceremonial occasions at the homestead, she replaces this everyday headdress with an *ekori*.

a.
Man's Ceremonial Head Cloth
(*ombwiya*), 1955–60
Himba people; Kaokoveld, Namibia
sheepskin, red ocher, animal fat or butter, fiber thread, herbs
23 × 10 (58 × 26)
NMNH 407552; Collected by Gordon D. Gibson

A Himba man wears this head covering during his own wedding and thereafter while participating in rites of passage or receiving visits of important people to his homestead.

b.
Married Woman's Everyday Cap
(*erembe*), 1955–60
Himba people; Kaokoveld, Namibia
sheepskin, animal fat, fiber thread, herbs
6½ × 6 (17 × 15)
NMNH 407550; Collected by Gordon D. Gibson

During the routine of ordinary life, a married woman covers her head with this cap. If ever asked to remove the headgear in public, a modest woman giggles and acts coy—as if this request were an invitation to an indiscretion.

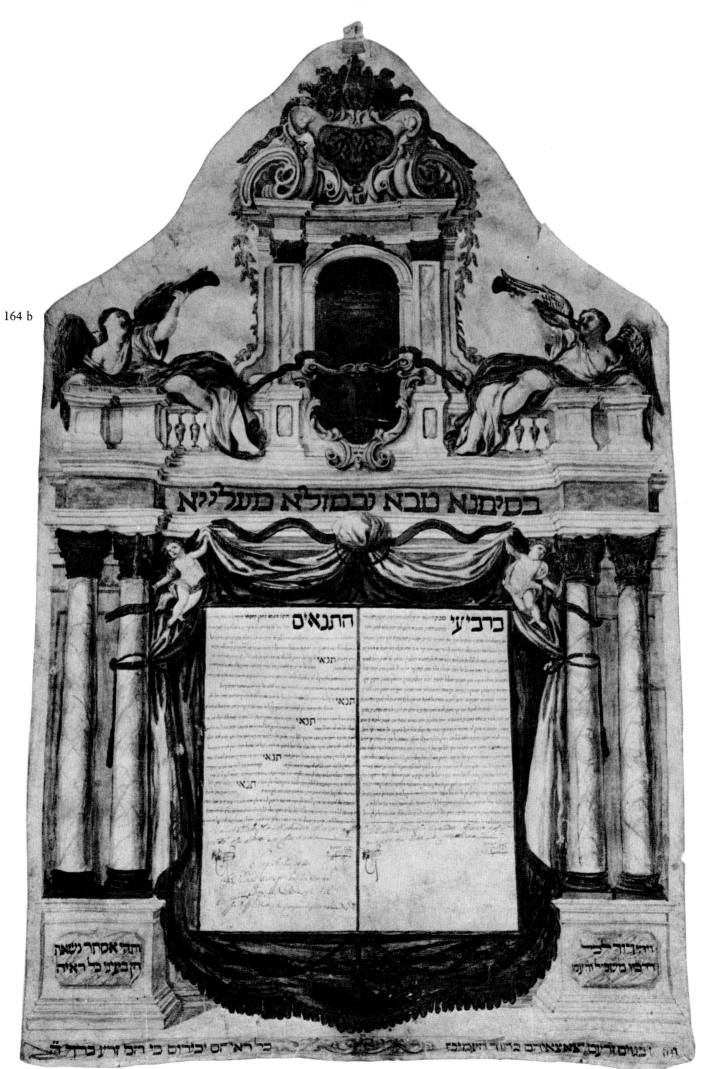

164 b

131

166.

WEDDING COSTUME. A white wedding blanket was so important a possession to a Hopi woman that some have said it was a major motivation for getting married. Without it a woman could not reach the underworld after death. Infant girls were given miniature versions of their mothers' blankets to serve as symbols of one of their goals as adults.

A complete wedding outfit consisted of a large white cotton blanket, a smaller one; a broad white cotton belt, a narrow one; high white boots; a blue and black wool dress; a white shawl with a blue border; and in some areas, a reed wrapper or cover in which some of these items were carried.

The entire wedding outfit was woven by the bride's father and her older male relatives, who worked in a ceremonial chamber over a two- to eight-week period. The bride prepared food for the weavers, and feasting and praying marked the completion of their work.

The natural white cotton fiber of the garments symbolized clouds, lightness, and breath. The long tassels of the white belt represented falling rain. The bride in her regalia was like a pure white cloud of rain, the principal focus of Hopi ritual. In later life the women wore this outfit when praying for rain, at the naming of first sons, and, finally, as a burial shroud.

a.

Wedding Blanket, ca. 1880–92
Hopi Indians; Arizona
cotton, coated with clay
62 × 47 (157.5 × 119.9)
NMNH 166790 a

b.

Wedding Sash, ca. 1890–1904
Hopi Indians; Arizona
cotton, corn husks, clay coating
49 × 8 (129.5 × 20.4)
NMNH 230105

167.

Wedding Basket, ca. 1890–1915
Navajo Indians; Arizona or New Mexico
sumac foundation and weft, natural dyes
3 × 17½ (7.6 × 44.4)
NMNH 286722

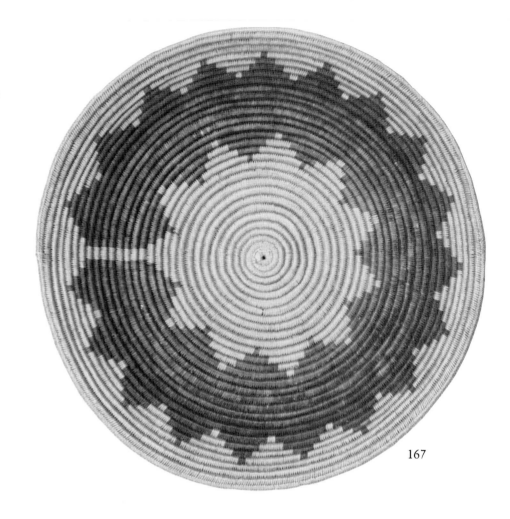

167

The basket and the cornmeal it contains play a central role in the Navajo wedding ceremony. Although ceremonial and domestic baskets look identical, only new baskets can be used for weddings. After intricate procedures involving orientation of the participants and the basket with the cardinal directions, the ritual use of whole and yellow corn pollen, and the couple's ritualized sharing of the cornmeal, the basket is passed around among the guests, who partake of its contents.

The break in the design is a "spirit doorway" and is always in line with the end of the braided rim. Like similar irregularities in Navajo blankets or Zuni pots, the break is a gesture of humility and protection, as completion and perfection are found only in the supernatural realm and in death.

During the mid-nineteenth century, before the introduction of manufactured containers, the Navajo made a variety of coiled baskets for ritual and daily use. With the later availability of manufactured containers, baskets were employed only for rituals. Eventually, because of the stringent taboos surrounding basket construction, the Navajos largely gave up making baskets and instead purchased Ute and Paiute baskets made especially for them in Navajo styles.

168.

Scroll "Love Letter," ca. 1880–87
Ojibwa Indians; Minnesota
2 × 12 × 7¼ (5.1 × 30.5 × 18.4)
NMNH 153145; Collected by Walter J. Hoffman

Courting among the Ojibwa was greatly restricted by a young girl's modesty and by society's insistence that she continually be in her mother's presence. In the evenings a suitor might play his "courting flute" outside the girl's home, but under no circumstances could she leave the lodge.

The collector of this birchbark scroll, Walter J. Hoffman, wrote in the late 1880s that this was "a letter written by an Ojibwa girl to a favored lover, requesting him to call at her lodge. Explicit directions are given to the route, and the lodge is indicated by a beckoning hand protruding from it." Since some Ojibwa did use scrolls for maps, records of migration, legends, and memory aides for songs and religious chants, this assessment is probably correct.

169.

COURTING FLUTES. Among the Plains and Woodland Indians, courting flutes were an important part of courtship rituals. A man might play his flute or sing serenades while standing outside the home of his sweetheart. He might play prearranged coded messages to her or go outside the village to play songs of loneliness and unrequited love.

a.
Courting Flute, before 1899
Sioux Indians; Northern Plains, probably North Dakota
wood, pigment, leather, lead plate, feathers
length: 32 (81.3)
NMNH 200563

b.
Courting Flute, before 1900
Kiowa Indians; Oklahoma
wood, paint, feathers, hair, glass beads, thread
length: 18½ (47)
NMNH 204546

170.

Wall Hanging *(bonad)*, ca. 1800
Småland, Sweden
paint, linen
15⅜ × 52⅜ (39.1 × 133)
C-H 1949-53-1; Gift of Richard C. Greenleaf
Illustrated in color, p. 32

During the eighteenth and nineteenth centuries in southern Sweden, peasants decorated their cottages for Christmas and other feast days with painted wall hangings. Peasant wedding processions were a favorite theme of folk painter Per Svensson (1787–1862) of Duvhult parish, Småland, Sweden, who may have painted this piece.

In this piece, which is half of a longer hanging, spirited horses drive a bride and groom, each carrying a bouquet. Four bridesmaids ride in a carriage behind the smiling couple. The wedding party is leaving the church for the bride's home, where a reception feast awaits. At the house, the bride will change her crown and elaborately embroidered dress for her "young mistress" dress and then will serve traditional fancy cakes to the guests. The letters SPAS ILD at the top right of the hanging indicate the names of the original owners, which could have been, for example, "S(ven) P(etter) A(nder) S(on)— I(nga) L(ars) D(otter) [Daughter]."

168

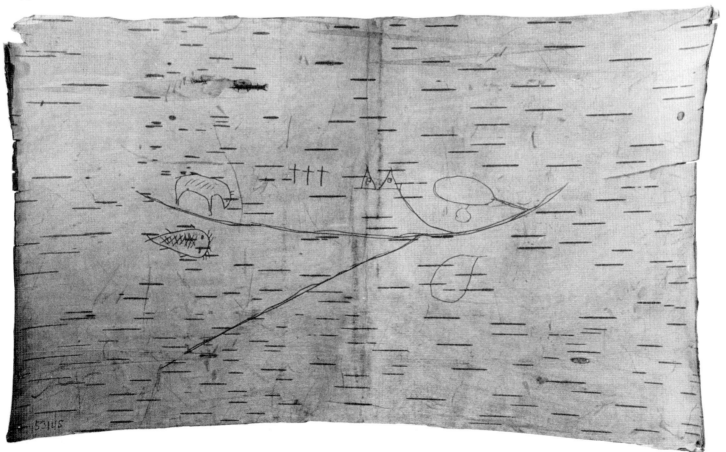

133

Death

Celebration of the dead in most societies is also celebration of the survivors. A death in these societies is a central event, an occasion for kin to revive their ties and exchange memories, a time when life seems most vivid and desirable against the backdrop of its annulment. In many preliterate societies, funerary ceremonies provide the occasion for initiation: young people are inducted into secret societies that strengthen their ties with the ancestors. Where there is belief in rebirth, death may be regarded as a necessary step toward it.

Many cultures regard life and death as opposite but complementary segments of the turning wheel of total existence. This view is reflected symbolically in many funerary celebrations; for example, the living may feed and clothe the dead so that their spirits, in turn, will protect and make fertile the living.

171.
MOURNING COSTUME. In Korea the principal male mourner wears a ritual dress to solemn celebrations of death—the funeral and subsequent memorial service.

a.
Mourner's Costume, before 1970
Kyŏnggi province, Korea (province for leggings unknown)
NMNH 414700 c, 414954–414959;
Gift of V. M. Hillyer.

From top:

Crown *(tugwan; sangju tu-gwan)*
hemp cloth, paper, glue
3¼ × 3 (7.5 × 33.5)

Cap *(hyogon; tugŏn; sangju-tugŏn)*
hemp cloth
9⅞ × 6¼ (25 × 16)

Headband *(sujil)*
rice straw
length: 16 (41)

Coat *(sangbok; chungdani)*
hemp cloth
44⅛ × 23⅝ (112 × 60)

Belt *(yojil)*
straw
length: 38.5 (97)

Leggings *(haengjŏn)*
hemp cloth
11¼ × 9½ (28.6 × 24.1)

Shoes *(chipsin)*
rice straw, paper
10 × 2¾ (25.5 × 7)

As household head and principal male heir of the deceased, the chief mourner was set apart from other mourners by his cap and crown, hemp leggings, and outer-robe, and by the square cloth tear catcher on his chest (not displayed). The other mourners also wore special ritual clothing. The headband, belt, and shoes were worn by either sex. Males wore leggings similar to those displayed here.

b.
Mourner's Hat *(p'aeraeing'i; p'yŏngnangja),* before 1883
Kyŏnggi province, Korea
split bamboo
4¾ × 15¾ (12 × 40.5)
NMNH 77064; Collected by Ens. J. B. Bernadou

After a father's funeral service, a son wears a mourner's hat similar to this one for three years, especially when he leaves his house. He also wears the hat to the memorial service held at the close of the traditional three-year mourning period.

172.
Mourning Cloth *(kuntunkuni),* 1974
Ashanti people; Ghana
white cotton cloth, colored silk threads, brown and black dyes
83¾ × 138½ (212.8 × 351.8)
AfA 74–31–12

When an Ashanti chief dies, each member of his family must wear a cloth like this one for forty days of mourning. It is during this time that the soul of the chief travels to the afterworld. The single color of the cloth's ground is regarded as obligatory. The dark designs, applied through a stamping process, are said by some to be merely stylish decoration and by others to represent ways of saying farewell to the deceased.

173.
MORTUARY COSTUME. During Bororo funeral ceremonies, which continue for nearly a month, the mourners cease all but the most essential daily chores. They ceremoniously bury the body of the deceased and water it to hasten decomposition. Months later they exhume and decorate the bones and then bury them once again. To express grief, close relatives of the dead gash their bodies and cut their hair. Songs and dances addressing supernatural spirits take place, together with rituals impersonating mythical beasts and sportive play with great wheels made of palm sticks. At the end of a funeral feast, adult males initiate young boys to manhood, being careful first to exclude women from these rites.

Bull-roarers, the sight of which is thought to be fatal to women, groan through the air at this time.

Soon after the death of a person of either sex, elders appoint a male ritual representative of the deceased. The appointed person "avenges" the dead by killing a jaguar or other carnivore, undergoing hardship and peril, both real and supernatural, on behalf of the dead. In the final phases of the funerary rites, the surrogate represents the soul of the deceased for the living when he and other Bororo men dress in ceremonial finery like the costume displayed here.

In the advent of individual death, the Bororo see energetic forces of change, fertility, and decay, called *bope*, temporarily triumphant over the permanent forces of the spirit, or *aroe*. The Bororo revenge the *bope*'s triumph by killing a meat eater and displaying its teeth in ornaments. Then, adorned with feather ornaments and body paint, they ceremonially affirm the continuity of the spirit world. Through the rites and costumes the Bororo reestablish the balance between permanence and change, mortality and immortality. They channel the forces of nature and the flow of beauty to create first a brutal, then a magnificent denial of death.

Mourning Costume, 1850–1900
Bororo Indians; Mato Grosso, Brazil

From top:

Vertical Diadem (*pariko*)
feathers, wood, fiber, native twine
26 × 31 × 2 (66 × 78.8 × 5.1)
NMNH 210805

Horizontal Diadem (*ebukejewu*)
feathers, cotton string, native twine
13⅝ × 9¼ (34.6 × 23.5)
NMNH 210806

Labret (lip ornament, *boe en-ogwa-dawo*)
shell, thread, hair, feathers, pigment
8 × 4¾ × 1¾ (21.2 × 12 × 4.4)
NMNH 210811

177

135

Two Ear Dangles (*boe e-viadawu*)
bark, feathers, rosin, native twine, down
each: 13 × 4 × 1⅛ (33 × 10.1 × 2.9)
NMNH 210808, 210809

Two Gourd Whistles (*boe e-kuie powardi*)
gourd, bamboo, feathers, cotton string, native twine, rosin
largest: 16 × 4¼ (40.6 × 10.8)
NMNH 210843, 210844
Illustrated in color, p. 33

Flute (*parira coreu*)
bamboo, feathers, down, cotton string, fiber, rosin
28¾ × 6 × 1⅛ (73 × 15.5 × 2.9)
NMNH 210849

Breast Pendant (*bakodori inogi*)
armadillo claws, native twine, cotton string, feathers, rosin, shell
16¼ × 8¹¹⁄₁₆ × 2½ (41.3 × 22 × 6.4)
NMNH 210813

Necklace (*akigu boe e-iadadawu*)
cotton string, porcupine quills
22 × 6 × 1 (55.9 × 15.5 × 2.5)
NMNH 210857

Tooth Pendant (*juko o*)
teeth, wood, leaf, cotton thread, native twine, rosin
15 × 11 × 3¼ (38.1 × 28 × 7.9)
NMNH 210816; Purchased from O. A. Derby

Tooth Pendant (*adugo o*)
teeth, wood, leaf, dye, cotton thread, native twine, rosin
10¼ × 6 × 1 (26 × 15.2 × 2.5)
NMNH 210841; Purchased from O. A. Derby

Tooth Pendant (*rie o*)
teeth, wood, leaf, dye, cotton thread, native twine, rosin
10½ × 6 × ¼ (26.7 × 15.2 × 0.6)
NMNH 210842; Purchased from O. A. Derby

Two Ornamental Feathers (*boe e-kiga*)
feathers, down, wood, quills, native twine
largest: 12¼ × 1½ × ¼ (31 × 3.8 × 0.6)
NMNH 210823, 210824

Armlets (*boe e-ido kajejewu*)
feathers, cotton string, wood
largest: 15½ × 2¾ (39.4 × 7)
NMNH T12374

At the close of the funeral rites, the ritual representative is adorned with gourd whistles, the feathered patterns of which symbolize the soul of the deceased. Feather flutes also evoke the memory of the dead, for in their sound the Bororo hear "the breath of the soul." The ornamental featherwork of the horizontal and vertical diadems, other hair decorations, ear dangles, and claw breast pendants embody the close association of the human soul with birds and the spiritual purity of the air. (The Bororo also prize feathers for their beauty and exchange them with one another as a form of currency.)

When they are ritually given a name and a soul, Bororo male youths receive a labret of shells, carved as small fish. The ritual representative includes this personal ornament in his formal dress. It shows celebrants that he is mature enough to own a soul and worthy of the trust other Bororo have placed in him to complete the funeral rites.

The Bororo are divided into many hierarchically ranked clans. The feather ornaments shown here hold heraldic meaning for Bororo clans, in much the same way that medieval flags and shields revealed family membership. When Bororo men wear feather adornments and certain other decorations, such as face and body paint, they are wearing heraldic insignias—but not necessarily for their own clan. By performing favors for members of other clans, especially in offering one another women to marry, men earn the right to wear the ornaments and body paint of the favored clan. For Bororo men to know a costume's heraldic symbols is for them to know how clans are bound to one another through mutual obligations.

174.
"View of Monument, Home and Church," ca. 1840
USA
watercolor on paper
17⅜ × 21½ × ¾ (44.1 × 54.6 × 1.8)
NMAH 65.843; Gift of Eleanor and Mabel Van Alstyne
Illustrated in color, p. 33

Young women of early–nineteenth-century New England frequently mourned the dead through their art. They created pictures like "View of Monument, Home and Church" as memorials to the deceased and mementos for living relatives and friends.

The first memorial pictures to gain widespread popularity were fashioned to honor the death of George Washington in 1799. These influenced the creation of later pieces.

Young women usually did not paint original works but rather copied from prints, from the work of their instructors, or from the work of one another. The monument, urn, weeping willow, and sorrowing relatives in black shown here were familiar and repeated symbols of death in mourning pictures. The homes and church in the background appear as symbols of continuing earthly life, a frequently expressed hopeful theme.

175.
Mourning Picture, 1896
New York, New York
hair, paint, glass, glue
13¾ × 15¾ × 1¼ (35 × 40 × 3.2)
NMAH 1980.598.1; Gift of William H. Ammarell

In 1896 Emil Moutoux created this memorial picture from human hair upon the death of his son-in-law's mother, Louisa Ammarell. Moutoux may have used hair from the head of the deceased woman or from mourners who attended her funeral. Victorians cherished mourning pictures made of human hair as deeply personal reminders of the deceased.

The intricate working of the familiar emblems of death in the picture—willow, urn, and tombstone—make it easy to see why Moutoux received an award for his craft in human hair at the Centennial Exposition of 1876 in Philadelphia.

176.
Mourning Dress, 1898–1910
USA
silk crepe, silk taffeta, sequin and
bead trim
59 × 23½ × 29 (150 × 59.7 ×
73.7)
NMAH 47101; Gift of Messrs.
Orme and R. Thornton Wilson

Sometime between 1898 and 1910
Mrs. Caroline Schermerhorn Astor
Wilson wore this elegant dress in
full mourning for the recent death
of a person close to her. The crepe
and taffeta fabric identifies the
dress as mourning attire, setting it
apart from other fashionable black
clothing commonly worn during
this period.

Among people of social standing
in nineteenth-century America, degrees of mourning were defined as
deep or full, second or half, and
light. A mourner changed colors of
clothing from black to gray or violet and eventually to other colors
as recovery from bereavement took
place. Lighter colors were also
worn for a person more distantly
connected to the mourner, such as
a national leader.

Women mourned husbands for
two years; parents, children, and fiancés for one year; and grandparents and siblings for six months.
Men did not adhere as closely as
women to mourning etiquette.

177.
Candle Labels, 1805–26
Italy
ink on parchment
largest: 5⅝ × 4⅝ (14.4 × 11.6)
NMAH 334032

The Jewish custom of burning a
memorial light (yahrzeit) originated
in Germany in the Middle Ages
and spread from there to other regions. A yahrzeit candle or lamp is
lighted on the eve of the anniversary of a death and remains burning until sunset of the next day.
The exact use of the memorial
parchments shown here is unknown, but to judge from the texts
and the evidences of burn marks,
they are closely related to the observance of the yahrzeit. A typical
text might read:

*A candle is lit for the rest of the
soul of the honorable _____
of blessed memory who departed
this world on _____. May
it please You blessed God that his/
her soul be bound in the bond of
eternity and there be good life and
peace for us and all Israel. May
this be Thy will.*

These Italian documents are inscribed to Moshe David Finzi (1819); Mrs. Roza, widow of
Shlomo Hayim (1826); and Mrs.
Yutsah, widow of Dr. Jonah Finzi
(1805).

178.
Mask with Cross Superstructure
(*kanaga*), 1900–1950
Dogon people; Mali
wood, pigments
39 × 23⅜ × 8 (99.1 × 59.4 ×
20.3)
AfA 68-36-221

Dancing to a dramatic rhythm,
kanaga maskers arrive in a long
line at *dama* funeral ceremonies.
Simulating giant birds, possibly
bustards, the dancers sweep their
masks down and around in unison.
As their masks describe great vertical circles, they all strike the
ground simultaneously with the
high stick crosses, making a spectacular climax to the dance.

179.
Mask with Protracted Upper Head
(*dannana*), 1900–1950
Dogon people; Mali
wood, porcupine quills, string, pigments
20¼ × 7 × 8 (51.4 × 17.7 × 20.3)
AfA 70-34-46

This mask is worn in a Dogon
dance that celebrates hunters, who
play a significant part in Dogon
mythology and society. The
masked dancer carries a short
sword in his left hand and a spear
in his right as he imitates movements of the hunt.

180.
Mask with Flaring Horns (*gomintogo*), 1900–1950
Dogon people; Mali
wood, pigment
22 × 7¾ × 10 (55.9 × 19.7 ×
25.4)
AfA 73-7-546

180

The mythical or extinct animal
carved by Dogon master craftsmen
corresponds to no animal known in
their region. In an agricultural
dance a performer wearing this
mask carries a baton with which
he pretends to cultivate and weed
the ground.

182 a, b

181.
Two Masks with Female Figure (*satimbe*), 1900–1950
Dogon people; Mali
wood, pigment, plant fibers, beads, rope
largest: 42½ × 8½ × 6½ (107.9 × 21.6 × 16.4)
AfA 73-7-2, 73-7-5

Wearers of these two *satimbe* masks danced in *dama* memorial rites, which were held sometime after the burial of the deceased. Because of the elaborateness and expense of the rites, several Dogon families often pooled their resources over a period of several years and offered a *dama* for their deceased relatives as a group. The funeral was given to usher the souls of the deceased out of the village and into the underworld. By honoring the departed in this manner, the family could return to normal daily life.

The female figure on the masks represents the first Dogon woman to steal mask-making fibers from the people who originally lived in the region. Afterward, the woman's husband stole the masks from her and since that time, masks have belonged to men, who perform the elaborate funerary rituals. They are aided by a woman known as the *yasingine*, "older sister of the masks," who traces her traditional role back to the daughter of the original fiber-stealing woman.

182.
DAY OF THE DEAD. In Mexico a sense of reunion surrounds November 2, All Souls' Day, when the living work together to unite in spirit with their dead family members. Before this "Day of the Dead" women prepare lavish meals, which they place on home altars decorated for the dead. The living, waiting in front of the home altar, look for a flicker of the candles, a hush—signs that the dead have arrived to eat the essence of the food. On the following days relatives share the offerings left behind. On the Day of the Dead, after the deceased have "eaten," family members go together to the cemeteries. There they clean and then decorate the graves with flowers, which are often arranged in elaborate designs. An attending Catholic priest may assist with prayers for the dead. Festive music and children's games emphasize cheer rather than gloom, but rural Indian groups may make this visit a more solemn occasion than their urban counterparts. Yellow, the pre-Conquest color of the dead, prevails in the offerings of food, candles, and flowers. The marigold, flower of the dead, predominates in floral arrangements made for this holiday.

Candy, plaster, and paper skeletons satirize death during the festivities of All Souls' Day. In Spanish slang the word for skeleton has come to mean daredevil, scapegrace, dead one, or dead duck. Bitingly satirical verses called skeletons or skulls, targeting prominent citizens, are sold on the city streets during this holiday.

Confronting death with ironic bravado while simultaneously cherishing memories of deceased relatives typify this religious celebration for many Mexicans. They mock death with toy-skeleton figurines, coffin and skull confections, skeleton puppets on a stick, and tissue-paper altar coverings with stamped designs of a skeleton's antics. Combined with these imaginative and grotesque figures are altar ornaments of animals or food offered to the dead, objects that provide comfort and a feeling of familiarity. Food and adornments together assure the spirits of the dead that they have not been forgotten in the hearts of the living, who are solaced by these tangible symbols of the presence of those they have loved.

There is a strong economic aspect to Day of the Dead celebrations. Markets bustle before this holiday as artisans, bakers, and confection makers fill their stalls with appropriate wares and foods. The lavish food offerings of All Souls' Day coincide with the height of the corn harvest. Participants celebrate lifegiving abundance as well as death, for at this time there is enough food to eat for both the living and the dead.

See colorplate, p. 34

a.
Two Candy Coffins (*tumbitas*), 1979
Mexico City, Mexico
sugar candy, icing, mixed media
largest: 4 × 2 × 5 (10.1 × 5 × 12.6)
NMNH 421286, 421287; Collected by R. M. Laughlin

183 a, b

d.
Candy Fruit Basket, 1979
Mexico City, Mexico
sugar candy, icing, pigment, wood shavings, whole clove
3 × 3½ × 3 (7.6 × 8.9 × 7.6)
NMNH 421288; Collected by R. M. Laughlin

e.
Two Toy Skeletons (*calaveras*), 1979
Mexico City, Mexico
papier-mâché, mixed media
largest: 11 × 4 × 3¼ (28 × 10.1 × 8)
NMNH 421289, 421290; Collected by R. M. Laughlin

f.
Paper Cutout, 1979
Mexico City, Mexico
tissue paper
57 × 14 (144.8 × 35.5)
NMNH 421291; Collected by R. M. Laughlin

g.
Two Ceramic Skeletons (*calaveras*), 1979
Metepec and Puebla, Mexico
earthenware, mixed media
largest: 3¾ × 4½ × 4¼ (9.5 × 11.4 × 10)
NMNH 421292, 421293; Collected by R. M. Laughlin

h.
Puppet Skeleton (*calavera*), 1979
Oaxaca, Mexico
cardboard, paint, red foil, nails, commercial string, glue, wood
15 × 3½ × ⅜ (38.1 × 8.9 × 1)
NMNH 421294; Collected by R. M. Laughlin

183.
COW FESTIVAL. There is a tradition in Patan that on the day of the cow festival a cow may push open the gates of heaven with her horns, allowing souls in wait to enter. In households where someone has recently died, families send a member out, usually a young boy, to assure that a cow stands ready at the gate. The boy parades through the town wearing the disguise displayed here—a colorful printed-paper cow's face, two bamboo "horns" decorated with paper rosettes, and a small paper poster depicting Ganesh, the elephant-headed god of good fortune. Members of the family, musicians, and other individuals dressed in differ-

b.
Candy Skull (*calavera*), 1979
Mexico City, Mexico
sugar candy, icing, mixed media
4½ × 4½ × 7 (11.4 × 11.4 × 17.8)
NMNH 421284; Collected by R. M. Laughlin

During Day of the Dead celebrations, families often place the names of deceased relatives on candy ornaments. Both the little coffins and the large candy skull head have spaces for the names of loved ones.

c.
Two Seated Candy Skeletons (*calaveras*), 1979
Mexico City, Mexico
sugar candy, synthetic fabrics, earthenware, mixed media
5½ × 5 × 5 (14 × 12.6 × 12.6)
NMNH 421285; Collected by R. M. Laughlin

The inscription behind the seated figures translates as "I love you, I love you, but you couldn't care less," emphasizing the ironic attitude toward death often expressed during All Souls' Day.

ent disguises also join the parade, while those wealthy enough may decorate a real cow to lead in the festive procession.

With much noise, gaiety, and joking, the parade moves through town. It stops at temples where special rites are performed and at certain houses where the "cows" are offered fruit, sugar cane, or other foods; money; and rice beer. Dancers may join the procession, and sometimes participants mimic plowing and planting. When participants in the celebration return home, they are worshiped at the door by other members of the household. A domestic feast follows.

This celebration honors and fulfills a family's obligations to its dead members.

a.

Poster of Cow's Face, 1965
Patan, Nepal
paper, paint
11 × 9½ (28 × 24.1)
NMNH 407238; Collected by Dr. Mary Slusser

b.

Horns for Cow Festival, 1965
Patan, Nepal
bamboo, paper, paint
24 × 5½ × 1 (61 × 14 × 2.5)
NMNH 407236; Collected by Dr. Mary Slusser

c.

Poster of Ganesh, Elephant-Headed God, 1965
Patan, Nepal
paper, paint
10 × 7½ (25.4 × 19)
NMNH 407237; Collected by Dr. Mary Slusser

184.

Quilt, 1842
Jamestown, New York
cotton top, lining, batting, thread
80 × 80 (203.2 × 203.2)
NMAH T18333; Gift of Mrs. Nancy B. Werdell

During the nineteenth century, women sometimes made quilts to mark the death of a family member. Through their art they expressed sorrow and commemorated the dead. In mourning the loss of her small grandchild, Nancy Ward Butler appliquéd an inscription resembling an epitaph on this memorial quilt.

184

185.

Figure of Woman with Child, 1875–1925
Yombe people; Zaire
wood, pigment
21½ × 11 × 10¼ (54.5 × 28 × 26)
AfA 72-41-4
Illustrated in color, p. 34

This figurine is an example of the grave decoration used by some Yombe people, who are part of a greater Kongo grouping. Only the graves of village or family leaders merited these sculptural adornments. Installed in a shed constructed directly on the grave, the wooden figures usually depicted people associated with the deceased.

The woman and child in this piece probably refer to the man's role as a husband and father. It is thought that these adornments provided the deceased with companionship or protection.

186.

Figure of Man with Child (*mintadi; ntadi*), probably 1850–1925
Kongo peoples; Zaire
soapstone, paint
11½ × 6½ × 5 (29.2 × 16.4 × 12.7)
AfA 65-1-1

Mintadi figures are special representations of leaders among certain Kongo peoples. Carved from soapstone by special craftsmen, these objects were kept in homes of village leaders to serve as guardians or as surrogates of the leaders when they were away from their villages. The figurines frequently display symbols of leadership, such as caps, bracelets, or weapons. At a leader's death the *mintadi* figures were usually placed in the cemetery.

The highlights in black paint suggest that this piece is of fairly recent manufacture.

187.
Grave Post, ca. 19th century
Crocker Island people; northern
Arnhemland, Australia
wood, pigment
50½ × 5 (125.7 × 12.7)
NMNH 416450

The fashioning of grave posts on
Crocker Island is the work of carvers of the *dua* moiety, a group to
which half the tribe belongs. The
lizard figure may represent Tjunda,
a sacred figure of the *dua* moiety.
According to myth, Tjunda was
seen by the cult hero Djunkgao and
his sister Madalait at Jelangbara,
north of Port Bradshaw.

188.
Bark Coffin, before 1950
Yirrkala people; eastern Arnhemland, Australia
wood
5 × 24 × 4 (12.7 × 60.9 × 10.2)
NMNH 387494; Collected by
Frank M. Setzler on the Joint
Smithsonian, National Geographic,
and Australian Commonwealth
Arnhemland Expedition, 1948–49

Arnhemland funerary rites include
several stages of burial and reburial. The cleaned and painted bones
of the deceased are placed inside a
hollow wooden post or bark cylinder painted with the clan emblems
of the deceased.

The clan emblems on this coffin
include a crosshatched design,
which may symbolize water, and a
turtle figure, which may refer to
the fresh-water tortoise. It is said
that during the mythic time of creation the tortoise may have been a
man named Mimala. He made four
bull-roarers (objects that make a
loud noise when whirled around at
the end of a rope) and buried them
under the public dance ground during a burial ritual. When the ritual
ended, Mimala chased the women
away, dug the bull-roarers out of
the sand, and threw them in a waterhole, where they became four
large trees. That waterhole is now
sacred and forbidden to women,
and bull-roarers are thrown into its
water each year after ritual use.

189.
Figure of Man (*kigangu; vigangu*),
1900–1950
Giryama people; Kenya
wood (usually of the *muhuhu* tree)
66 × 4¾ × 2¹¹⁄₃₂ (167.7 × 12 ×
5.9)
AfA 79-20-1

Giryama carvers made images such
as this one to represent deceased
members of a prestigious male religious cult. Surviving members
commissioned the images, which
they placed first on a deceased
member's grave and later in the
center of the village. During times
of crisis the family of the deceased
went to the image to summon its
spirit and ask it for help.

190.
Model of Grave, 1880–1912
Tlingit Indians; Alaska
wood, sinew, nails, paint
3 × 14 × 4 (7.6 × 35.6 × 10.2)
NMNH 274274
Illustrated in color, p. 34

For most Tlingits a funeral consisted of cremating the corpse and
placing its ashes in a box in a
"grave house." It was thought that
the souls of the deceased would be
more comfortable in the afterworld
near a fire.

From the position of the body
and the type of box, this Tlingit
model most likely represents the
grave of a shaman. Funerary practices for shamans were much more
involved than those for ordinary
persons. The shaman himself usually selected his grave site. There
were strictly prescribed ways for
preparing his body and for leaving
it in the grave house. Once it was
installed in the house, villagers
feared and avoided the site. Anyone
passing the grave made an offering
of tobacco to the spirit of the shaman. Tlingits believed that the
body of a shaman did not decay but
rather dried up and that the fingernails continued to grow—even
through the boards of the grave
house.

189

191.
Grave Image, ca. 1880–1920
Eskimo; Kuskokwim River, Alaska
wood, nails, paint, bone
19 × 28 × 5 (48.2 × 71.1 × 12.6)
NMNH 351076; Collected by Aleš
Hrdlička

Grave posts—this one drastically
reduced in size because it was
sawed down—marked traditional
burial sites of the Eskimo people of
the Kuskokwim River. The symbolic significance of the post, typi-
cally a human figure with out-
stretched arms, painted red face,
and inset bone eyes, is unknown.

Soon after the death of a Kuskokwim Eskimo, pallbearers removed
the flexed, skin-wrapped corpse
through a hole in the house, usually the smokehole. They placed it
in a plank coffin, which they set
either just above the ground or on
tall poles. Mourners placed images
in front of the coffin, as well as
personal possessions of the dead,
such as wooden dishes, snowshoes,
harpoons, and paddles.

Russian and Christian influence
led eventually to below-ground burial among the Kuskokwim Eskimo.

192.
**Three Objects Made of Camwood
Paste** (*mboong itool*), 1900–1950
Kuba people; Zaire
camwood paste
largest: 1¼ × 12½ × 4 (3.2 × 31.7
× 10.2)
AfA 73-7-432, 73-7-433, 73-7-434

Camwood powder is an important
element of Kuba body adornment,
social status, and tradition. At the
funeral of a Kuba family head, cam-
wood-paste objects, made by mix-
ing the powder with special oils,
are given to certain family members. Some of these objects become
heirlooms to be passed from generation to generation. Others are broken up to be used as pigment for
cosmetics or dyes. The forms of the
camwood objects vary from human
heads, animals, tools, and containers to abstract geometric forms
like these three examples, which
include an oblong, a figure eight,
and a square. To the Kuba, the
color red represents life, blood, and
energy.

193.
Portrait Skull, before 1928
possibly Iatmul people; Sepik
River, Papua New Guinea
human skull, clay, pigment, human
hair, shell
7 × 7½ × 9 (17.7 × 19 × 22.8)
NMNH 344946; Collected by Dr.
E. W. Brandes

The Iatmul honored their dead by
modeling a portrait likeness over
the skull of the deceased. A portrait skull was displayed in a lav-
ishly ornamented setting in the
men's house. During a night mortuary ceremony, men sang ancestral songs about the dead and
played ancestral flutes. Later the
skull was buried.

194.
Two Tile Plaques from Tomb
(*lauh-i-mazar*), 1971
Multan area, Punjab, Pakistan
glazed tile
11¼ × 10½ × 1 (28.6 × 26.6 ×
2.5)
NMNH 417194 a, b; Collected by
the Goddard Team

191

142

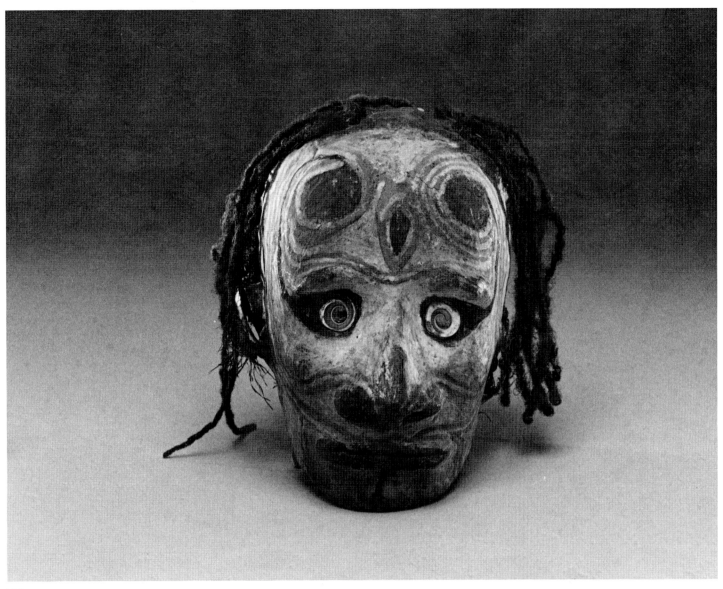

193

When Moslems in Pakistan bury a saint, they build the low structure that lies atop the grave slightly taller than the one they build for a deceased person who has not attained sainthood. The additional height accommodates two tomb plaques. One bears the name of the saint and stands at the foot of the tomb, and the other contains blessings and stands at the head. People first pay homage at the foot of the grave and then proceed around it. Proper conduct in a graveyard requires the living to wear dismal and pensive looks, to seek Allah's forgiveness, and to remember that one day they, too, will die and their remains will be brought to the tomb.

Translation of Inscriptions by Munir Rizwani
(the first and second lines are in Arabic, the remainder in Urdu)

Plaque 1
In the name of God the merciful, the compassionate
There is one God and Mohammed is his prophet
May the kindness of the Almighty shower upon your
tomb each morning and evening
May God give you a place only in the Paradise of Heaven
The name of the Saint Meeyan Ah-meed-deen whose father
was son of Shair Mohammed Chooght
Age ninety years, deceased in the month of Shawal, 1388
year of the Hijra, correspondent year 1968

Plaque 2
In the name of God the merciful, the compassionate
[indecipherable]
May you acquire peace from the evils of this world
May you exist as long as this world exists
All the good fortune we share may be attributed to you
All this was a consequence of your spending your life
ᶦin prayers

The first line is in Arabic. The third through the sixth line constitute a *roobayee*, a four-line composition in the classical Farsi language.

143

194

196

195.

Tombstone Fragment, 1918
Moore County, North Carolina
stoneware
9⅝ × 7 (24.4 × 17.8)
NMAH 68.343

This ceramic tombstone fragment
bears the inscription "MONROE.
BROWN / DIED OCT THE [bro-
ken] 1918." Hardy Brown, born
around 1815, and his son Benjamin
Brown, born in 1871, were members of a family of potters living
near the Moore County line in
North Carolina. Though we cannot
be sure that the Brown on the
tombstone fragment was related to
this family of artisans, we do know
that potters fashioned stoneware
tombstones for deceased relatives.

Ceramic tombstones were found
along much of the East Coast of
the United States, especially in the
South. They took several forms,
from slabs to the urnlike cylinder
seen here. In North Carolina the
use of ceramic tombstones has
been documented from the second
quarter of the nineteenth century
to the early twentieth century. Not
as durable as stone grave markers,
which often appeared alongside
them, ceramic tombstones rarely
remain intact today.

196.

Funeral Vase, 1865
France
porcelain
15 × 9 × 5 (38.1 × 22.9 × 12.7)
NMAH 297507.1; Gift of F. N. and
D. A. Switzer

This black vase from France stood
as a funerary decoration on one
side of Abraham Lincoln's cata-
falque in the courthouse of Chicago, Illinois, on May 1–2, 1865. It
was one of a matched pair that
held flowers. The vases were
viewed with their black sides to
the front by an estimated 125,000
mourners.

The sorrow of the people caused
the *Chicago Tribune* to exclaim,
"Thank God, He endowed Americans with hearts alive for such a
man as Abraham Lincoln. 'Behold
how they loved him!'"

Shrines and Altars

A shrine is a place of worship hallowed or honored because of its association with a superhuman, invisible power, such as a deity, ancestor, saint, or spirit. An altar is a place, often a raised platform or table, where sacrifices and offerings are made to such a power. Shrines are often complex structures with each component serving as a symbol with many meanings. The kind of stone or wood used, the orientation, the adornments, the presence of a hidden relic—all have symbolic significance. Shrines and altars are channels of communication between the invisible powers and individuals, families, communities, and polities. They range from small domestic spaces dedicated to family ancestors to elaborate constructs in large temples or churches that focus the petitions of major social units to their deities.

197.

VOODOO ALTAR. Gathered from temples, shrines, and altars in Haiti, these objects show how Voodoo believers paid homage and offered sacrifices to their gods in the early and middle parts of the twentieth century. Using these pieces, Voodoo adepts communicated with supernatural spirits as they strove to overcome the hardships of their lives—poverty, sickness, famine, and the ever-present threat of death. Voodoo has endured openly or secretly throughout the written history of Haiti. Today both peasants and city dwellers follow its complex doctrine.

The word Voodoo originates from the language of the Fon people of the Republic of Benin. It meant "god, spirit, or sacred object." Africans brought their religious beliefs with them on their forced journey to Haiti, where they were assimilated with the teachings of the Catholic clergy. When the beliefs from two different continents came into contact, the Voodoo religion emerged as a powerful force in the lives of many Haitians.

There are three kinds of deities in Voodoo: gods from African cults (called *loa*), Catholic saints, and ancestral spirits. Worshipers invoke these supernatural beings for aid in rites of passage, agricultural rituals, divinations, magic, and private and public services of thanksgiving.

Possession by African cult gods is an essential part of Voodoo. A deity, usually during a service, selects a human "horse" to mount, or possess. Upon being mounted, the worshiper falls into a trance, speaks, dances, and sometimes performs seemingly supernatural feats that reveal the character of his or her divine rider. With the aid of costumes and props, dancers in a state of possession reveal messages from the gods.

Services may be held in homes, outside in the natural world, or in a cult center, where one would find an altar like this one, which was created especially for the exhibition. A hierarchy of attendants, presided over by a head priest or priestess, cares for these independent centers of worship. Leaders act as go-betweens who cajole gods and spirits on human behalf.

Each god has a favorite emblem (or *vévé*, drawn in chalk on the floor here), tree, color, food and drink offering, set of songs and invocations, and day of the week. The pieces on the altar reveal some of these divine manifestations, while excerpts from the film *The Divine Horseman*, seen on the nearby video monitor, show some of the complex ritual salutations. As we look at the setting here, we can imagine rhythmic drums and chants, shadows, lights, and intense physical movement; smells and tastes of ritual meals; and the touch of the gods upon our spirits.

a.

Two Pairs of Iron Spits (*assen; assein*), ca. 1900–1950
Croix-des-Bouquets, Haiti
iron
largest: 20 × 8¾ × 5 (50.8 × 22.2 × 12.7)
NMNH 382557, 382558; Gift of Alfred Métraux

b.

Two Iron Crosses, ca. 1900–1950
Croix-des-Bouquets, Haiti
iron
largest: 33 × 6½ × ¼ (83.8 × 16.5 × 0.6)
NMNH 382559, 382560; Gift of Alfred Métraux

These iron spits and crosses are said to be manifestations of Damballah, the serpent god, and his female consort, Aida-Wedo. Among the most venerated of Voodoo deities, they are associated with rainfall, natural springs, and fertility.

Iron spits and standards driven into the earth in front of an altar hold food offerings or candles for the deities.

c.

Iron Gong (*ogan*), ca. 1900–1950
Croix-des-Bouquets, Haiti
iron
11⅞ × 3¼ × 2 (31.1 × 8 × 5.1)
NMNH 382563; Gift of Alfred Métraux

A percussion player strikes the iron gong (*ogan*) with a piece of metal to accompany the three Rada drums played in Voodoo dances and services. Today a hoe, chain, or piece of iron replaces the *ogan*, which is no longer made in Haiti.

d.

Gourd Bowl (*couis*), ca. 1900–1950
Croix-des-Bouquets, Haiti
iron
5½ × 11¼ × 10¾ (14 × 28.5 × 27.3)
NMNH 382571; Gift of Alfred Métraux

The chief gods of a particular center of worship each have a calabash bowl for food offerings. Though identification of this bowl is not positive, it has been suggested that "G.N.B." stands for G̲ra̲nd-B̲ois, a deity of the forest.

e.

Four Necklaces, ca. 1900–1950
Croix-des-Bouquets, Haiti
glass beads, string, snake vertebrae, ribbon, shell, metal
longest: ⅝ × 33 × 1½ (1.6 × 83.8 × 3.7)
NMNH 382208–382211; Gift of Alfred Métraux

During services, initiated members gain spiritual strength from bead necklaces like these. Each necklace contains a spirit, and a bearer of many necklaces may grow "tipsy" and reel from close association with their divine power. Initiates show their connection with a particular deity by placing a necklace on the emblem of this deity during a rite called "the descent of the necklace," which marks the last phase of their initiation.

f.

Wooden Bowl, ca. 1900–1950
Croix-des-Bouquets, Haiti
wood
3⅓ × 7¼ (8.5 × 18.4)
NMNH 382575; Gift of Alfred Métraux

The use of this bowl is not positively known, but it very likely contained food offerings for gods.

g.

Staff (*cocomacaque*), ca. 1900–1950
Croix-des-Bouquets, Haiti
wood
34⅝ × 1¼ (88 × 3.1)
NMNH 382578; Gift of Alfred Métraux

The short monkey palm, *cocomacaque*, provides Haitians with a strong weapon against sorcery and evil. The staff of the monkey palm

197 a (one pair or iron spits), b

defends Haitian travelers against magical evildoers who may threaten at crossroads or take the guise of strange animals on the road.

A person possessed by the divine Cousin Zaka, patron spirit of farmers and mountain people, seizes a *cocomacaque* as part of the impersonation. When Zaka "rides" his "mount" he appears as a peasant, wearing a blue denim outfit, carrying a knapsack, smoking a pipe, and speaking with an accent heard only in the most remote mountain villages.

h.
Bell (*clochette*), ca. 1900–1950
Jacmel, Haiti
metal, wood, string
$3\frac{5}{8} \times 2$ (9.2 × 5.1)
NMNH (no number)

The rattle usually has a small bell tied to its stem that is also used by priests and priestesses in communicating with the gods.

i.
Rattle (*asson; baksor*), ca. 1900–1950
Croix-des-Bouquets, Haiti
gourd, string, glass beads, vertebrae
8×4 (20.3 × 10.2)
NMNH 382205; Gift of Alfred Métraux

In Voodoo rites and services, the rattle enables humans to speak with the gods. Wielded by a priest or priestess, the rattle invokes deities to possess human worshipers, controls the gods when they become too violent, and dismisses them altogether when they must leave.

197 l

So essential is the rattle to the role of the priesthood that assuming this office is called literally, "taking the rattle." Training during a priest's initiation requires mastery of the eloquent language of the rattle, which is spoken through its sound and through complicated gestures made while holding it. Priests and priestesses may measure each other's ability to communicate with supernaturals through a "dialogue" of movements performed with rattles. Each manipulates the instrument in a series of gestures. One initiates movements that the other must imitate exactly. The test ends when the follower proves his or her worth, or fails. The two may then switch, with the follower taking the lead. Another example of a Voodoo rattle is displayed in the "Sound and Music" component of the Elements of Celebration Gallery and is discussed in number 45.

j.
Two Flags (drapeaux), March 1980
Jacmel, Haiti
cloth, thread, sequins, wood
red: 36 × 50 (91.4 × 127)
black: 36 × 50¼ (91.4 × 127.7)
NMNH (no number)

Flags represent the society of a Voodoo sanctuary or center of worship. The society consists of members of an initiated hierarchy that tends the sanctuary and its ritual. During services appointed members of the society use flags to salute the appearance of great deities of important human visitors. They also use flags as a barricade against worshipers possessed by unusually wild gods.

Decorations on flags identify a deity. A priest in Jacmel, Haiti, designed these emblems especially for this exhibition. The red flag bears the emblem and written name "Ogu Batagrie," master of lightning and storm; the black banner shows the emblem and name "Baron la Croix," a bawdy god of death. The priest also added his own name, "Ridoré," to the flags.

k.
Legba Staff, ca. 1900–1950
Croix-des-Bouquets, Haiti
wood, paint
51 × 14⅛ × 7½ (129.5 × 35.9 × 19.1)
NMNH 382576; Gift of Alfred Métraux

This staff symbolizes the presence of the god Legba during Voodoo worship. Though it is used as an accessory when a worshiper impersonates the god, the staff also receives copious libations during services as a semidivine object in its own right.

Legba—god of crossroads, path, and portal—must consent to open the figurative gates at any service before other deities may arrive. He is often portrayed as a crippled old man with twisted crutches, but those he possesses reel under his extraordinary power.

l.
Stones and Celts (pierres tonnerres; pierres loas), before 1950
Croix-des-Bouquets, Haiti
stone
range: from ¾ × 1½ × 1¼ (1.9 × 3.7 × 3.1) to 2⅞ × 5¼ × 4¼ (7.3 × 13.3 × 10.8)
NMNH 382204, 382564; Gift of Alfred Métraux

Certain stones, usually celts (neolithic stone tools), from Haiti's aboriginal peoples are thought to be inhabited by deities. They are believed to have been hurled from the sky by thunder gods for believers to find and place on their altars. To retain their powers, such stones must be kept in oil. These pieces, passed through generations, are often thought to contain the protective deity of a single family. Members of the family conduct elaborate sacrifices and ceremonies for the stones to retain the favor of the deity.

m.
Twin Bowl (marassa), ca. 1900–1950
Croix-des-Bouquets, Haiti
wood
5 × 12½ × 6 (12.7 × 31.8 × 15.2)
NMNH 382573; Gift of Alfred Métraux

Both West African religions and Voodoo hold in awe the supernatural power of twins. In Voodoo, twins and the child born after them form a trio of spirits who must be respected through continual offerings and yearly services. Often acting like petulant children, the spirits of twins may harass living relatives with ills and misfortunes. If favorably disposed, they may equally send remarkable cures.

This twin bowl, often placed on an altar before a picture of the Catholic martyr twins Cosmas and Damian, usually holds a small snack of candy or peanuts. During formal services in honor of twins, these bowls hold more substantial offerings.

n.
Pitcher and Stopper (criche; cruche), ca. 1900–1950
Haiti
clay, slip
11¾ × 6¼ × 6 (29.8 × 15.9 × 15.2)
NMNH 364727, 364728

Pitchers contain holy water used by priests during services. When *loa* (deities of African origin) visit humans, they come from their dry and airy spirit homeland by water. They usually contact people at springs, waterfalls, and rivers. Voodoo worshipers who wish the *loa* to attend indoor services keep the water route open for the gods' easy travel.

To entice and invite deities, a priest or priestess spills some water first at the center pole of the temple where gods descend and later at the foot of the altar. Water is offered to the cardinal directions, and a path is drawn for the gods to follow from the temple gateway to the courtyard.

During services, water is poured from the pitchers onto the earth to refresh and renew the weary *loa*.

o.
Four Candles, ca. 1900–1950
Haiti
tallow, string
largest: 12 × ¾ (30.5 × 1.9)
NMNH T7149

Candles are found wherever Voodoo worship is conducted, indoors or out, for their use is indispensable to the ritual. They are lighted to begin and intensify important ritual moments. These may include drawing the emblem (*vévé*) of a particular god, offering a sacrificial animal, or reciting prayers to attract the attention of the gods.

p.
Three Rada Drums, ca. 1900–1950
Croix-des-Bouquets, Haiti
wood, goatskin, rope, pigment
NMNH 382566, 382567, 382569;
Gift of Alfred Métraux

Seven-Pegged Rada Drum (manman; adjunto; hountor; hountogri)
37¼ × 16 (95.1 × 40.6)

Six-Pegged Rada Drum (second; grondé; moyen)
28¾ × 16¼ (73 × 41.3)

Five-Pegged Rada Drum (bula; bébé; dundun)
24 × 16 (60.9 × 40.6)

The drums of Voodoo are sacred objects imbued with great spiritual power. During services, drummers can induce and terminate trances through their exquisite rhythmic control.

The types of drums shown here originated in West Africa. Highly skilled musicians use them in the rites of the Rada cult, one of many distinct cults of the Voodoo religion. An ensemble of Rada instruments consists of three drums of differing sizes and an iron gong, also shown here.

Each phase of a drum's construction—from selecting and felling the tree to driving pegs into the wooden body—is accompanied with religious ritual. No celebrant can play a drum successfully until it is baptized and consecrated. During service, devotees respect its sanctity with reverential salutations and sacrifices.

Believers in Voodoo periodically renew the spiritual power of drums by returning them ritually to their African homeland. Worshipers put them to bed, feed them through sacrifices, mourn their departure, and then celebrate the return to Haiti of the revitalized drums.

197 p (six-pegged Rada drum)

198 a

198.

JAGANNATHA. In the Objects Speak Gallery on the first floor, the image (no. 19) of Jagannatha, Lord of the Universe, from Puri, Orissa, India, stands alone. Though he is the most important deity of the Hindu shrine at Puri, he is but one of three gods worshiped there.

In this gallery Lord Jagannatha finds a setting among objects that place him in a fuller context. He takes his position beside Balabhadra and Subhadra, his older brother and younger sister, respectively. He also appears in a picture and miniature temple sold as mementos of pilgrimages. Painted figures on these souvenirs depict some of the rich myths and symbols of the shrine and invite the faithful to reflect on the deeper religious meanings they reveal.

See colorplate, p. 35

a.

Painting of Temple of Jagannatha, ca. 1960
Puri, Orissa, India
cloth, chalk, gum, tamarind, pigment, varnish
24¾ × 19¾ (62.8 × 50.2)
NMNH 399455; Gift of the Government of India

A hereditary group of artists fabricates cloth and then paints on it pictures like this one for pilgrims to buy as souvenirs of their worship at Puri. This painting of the temple of Jagannatha, a popular artistic theme, divides vertically into three major parts, the bottom, the central portion, and the top.

The bottom depicts the main entrance to the temple, the lion gate. Outside the gate to the left stand three cars in readiness for the car festival. To the right lies the temple pond.

The central portion of the painting is the interior of the temple, enclosed by a wall decorated with patterned indentations. Several, but not all, of its gates are visible.

The main building rises in the center of the temple enclosure. Within, Balabhadra, Subhadra, and Jagannatha stand on a platform. Three priests perform their religious duty before the images of the deities. Door guardians Jaya and Vijaya flank the entrance of the building. Within, Shiva, wearing a snakelike headdress, and Brahma, identified by having four heads, worship at the Garuda pillar.

By shifting our focus to the main building and temple walls, we can discern at least two scenes from the worship of Lord Jagannatha. In one, food is being carried from the kitchen at the bottom left to be offered to the deities. In another, images of the deities are being taken to a pond at the bottom right, where they will be given a boat ride, an event associated with the final festival of the year.

At the top of the painting are three specially beloved works of art. These are actually found within the temple at Puri.

On the left is a scene from the story of King Purushottama Deva, who appealed to Jagannatha for aid in his battle with another king. A milkmaid named Manika told the king she saw two horsemen, one mounted on a black steed, the other on a white, riding toward the enemy. The king then knew through these symbolic horsemen that Jagannatha and Balabhadra were personally coming to his aid.

A scene on the right may represent the religious reformer Sankaracharya worshiping Nrisinha, the fourth incarnation of the god Vishnu.

At the very top one can decipher the ten incarnations of Vishnu, who is shown (from left) as a fish; a turtle; a boar; a *nrisinha*, or lionman; a dwarf; the owner of the ax called "Parashuim"; Rama, a hero; Krishna; Buddha, here represented as Jagannatha; and Kalki, yet to come as a person on a white horse. One can find the original sculptures of the ten incarnations of Vishnu on the walls of the dancing hall in the temple at Puri.

199

b.
Shrine, before July 1961
Puri, Orissa, India
wood, paint
17 × 8¾ × 6½ (43.2 × 22.2 × 16.5)
NMNH 398802; Gift of C. H. P. Derby
Illustrated in color, p. 35

On this wooden model of the temple, sold as a remembrance of a pilgrimage to the temple of Jagannatha in Puri, India, guardians painted on the doors watch over the deities who stare out from within the miniature shrine.

c.
Shrine Deity, Balabhadra or Balarama (Bada Thakur), before February 1962
Puri, Orissa, India
wood, treated cloth, pigment
17 × 13 × 10 (43.2 × 33 × 25.4)
NMNH 399458 a; Gift of the Government of India

d.
Shrine Deity, Subhadra (Bada Thakur), before February 1962
Puri, Orissa, India
wood, treated cloth, pigment
12½ × 5½ × 5½ (31.8 × 14 × 14)
NMNH 399458 b; Gift of the Government of India

e.
Shrine Deity, Jagannatha (Bada Thakur), before February 1962
Puri, Orissa, India
wood, treated cloth, pigment
15⅓ × 14⅓ × 10 (38.9 × 36.3 × 25.4)
NMNH 399458 c; Gift of the Government of India

These copies of Jagannatha, his older brother Balabhadra, and his younger sister Subhadra represent the deities as a worshiper might encounter them in the temple at Puri. These models were made shortly before 1963 expressly as gifts from the Indian government to the Smithsonian Institution.

The divine wooden images of the temple are surrounded by complex rites and ceremonies. About five times a century the temple figures are remade. To create the new figures, Brahmin priests and Daitapati, a special group of worshipers, locate four unblemished, four-branched trees in the forest. They

hold a ceremony that lasts several days to consecrate the trees for sacred use. At the conclusion of this ceremony worshipers touch each tree with a golden ax before carpenters cut it into logs. Specially built new four-wheeled carts transport these sacred logs, which are now covered with silk cloths, to Puri, where they enter the temple by the north gate. During the bathing festival the logs are washed along with the existing images of the temple. Later, after 108 Brahmin priests have conducted rites in special sheds to which the logs have been removed, craftsmen turn the consecrated wood into holy images. No visitors may inspect this sacred work while it is in progress.

When completed the images are brought to the temple. In the middle of the night the *brahma*, or "sacred divine" aspect, is transposed from the old images to the new. Celebrants then buy the old images along with their accouterments. The Daitapati observe mourning for ten days and on the eleventh perform rites as for the death of a near relative.

A legend explains how these images first came to be. It is said that Vishnu, the Creator himself, disguised as an old carpenter, consented to transform one of his hairs into an image of God. He agreed to do this for the king of the area if no one disturbed him while at work. The king became impatient, however, and tried to look in on him. Vishnu, angered, disappeared and left the image unfinished as Jagannatha—the form it takes today.

In the car festival for Lord Jagannatha, worshipers pull the image of the god in a huge car through streets thick with pilgrims. Faithful worshipers sometimes fall under the wheels, suffering fatal consequences. A film of this festival can be seen on the video monitor in this gallery.

199.
SHRINE TO ANCESTORS. Many Nias Island families kept small shrines of wooden figures. These wooden images contained the spirits of important deceased family members, who were ceremonially coaxed by the living to make the images their home.

Bearing gifts of clothing and ornaments, descendants would gather around the grave of a recently buried elder and adorn the burial site with their tributes. Through songs and chants they induced the "remainder of the heart"—the spirit—to rise from the grave as a small spider. A priest brought the spider to an ancestral statue and asked the spirit to live there.

The ancestor became a "blessing giver." Family members asked for blessings or favors, making offerings in return for their requests. As time passed, descendants added more ancestors to their shrine, creating a lineage of "blessing givers" who supernaturally aided the living from the spirit world.

Five Ancestor Figures, before 1906
Nias Island people; Indonesia
wood
largest: 15¾ × 3 × 3⅛ (40 × 7.6 × 7.9)
NMNH 221577, 221603, 221604, 237269, 237279; Collected by W. L. Abbott

200.
FEAST OF THE THREE KINGS.
For Puerto Ricans, Epiphany, the Coming of the Three Kings, celebrates the spirit of generosity. In the same manner that the Three Kings brought gifts to the Christ Child, so Puerto Ricans offer gifts and warmly extend hospitality to one another on January 5 and 6. Prayer, song, music, and giving in a festive yet reverent atmosphere combine to make this holiday an offering in itself to the Christ Child.

On the eve of the feast, children throughout the island set out bowls of grass and water to refresh the kings' mounts. Parents remove the bowls and replace them with eagerly anticipated gifts attributed to Melchior. In Puerto Rico it is Melchior, not Balthazar, who is the Black King of tradition. He was burned black, legend has it, by the Star of Bethlehem.

Many families participate in this rich holiday tradition by conducting a night watch. This ceremony fulfills a promise to the saints in return for the granting of a past divine favor. Activity abounds in the Puerto Rican home where the night watch takes place from dusk to dawn. Members of the household busily prepare for the event with many varied activities, which include begging in the streets for penance, preparing food, arranging for prayer leaders and musicians, and decorating the home altar.

When the night watch is held on January 5, guests of all ages arrive to recite solemn rosaries and to make merry with feasting, song, and dance. No rosary is truly successful without music. Musicians play various instruments, including rasps (guiros), examples of which can be seen in the "Sound and Music" component of the Elements of Celebration Gallery and which are discussed in number 54.

The gracious hospitality extended to all and the hearty participation of the guests keep the atmosphere both dignified yet lively. This combination imparts a special spirit to the gathering. The shout "¡Vivan los Reyes!" ("Long Live the Kings!") rings through the night at the end of each musical piece to emphasize the good will of this uniquely Puerto Rican celebration.

A gift to the saints, a bright and decorative altar similar to the one seen here provides an honorific setting for the performances of rosaries and the flow of activity during the night watch. Scenes of the Nativity and other holy images are displayed with images of the Three Kings on the altar, with candles illuminating the entire display. The central placement of the Three Kings amidst the other figures reflects the Puerto Ricans' attachment to them—second only to their love for the Virgin and Child.

The Star of Bethlehem is depicted on this altar by a rosette atop the large manger grouping.

Feast of the Three Kings Figures,
19th and 20th century
Puerto Rico
wood, gesso, paint
largest: 13 × 21 × 7 (33 × 53.3 × 17.8)

a.
Nativity (*Nacimiento*)
NMAH 278087.47; Gift of Mrs. Dorothy W. Pike

b.
Our Lady of Perpetual Help (*Virgen del Perpetuo Socorro*)
NMAH 278088.19

c.
Nativity (*Nacimiento*)
NMAH 278087.46; Gift of Mrs. Dorothy W. Pike

d.
Saint Anthony of Padua (*San Antonio de Padua*)
NMAH 278087.15; Gift of Mrs. Dorothy W. Pike

200 f

e.
Saint Isidore the Farmer (*San Ysidro Labrador*)
NMAH 278088.14; Gift of Mrs. Dorothy W. Pike

f.
The Three Kings on Horseback (*Los Tres Reyes a caballo*)
NMAH 278087.16; Gift of Mrs. Dorothy W. Pike

g.
Saint Helena (*Santa Elena*)
NMAH 278087.5; Gift of Mrs. Dorothy W. Pike

h.
Virgin of the Kings (*Virgen de los Reyes*)
NMAH 278087.10; Gift of Mrs. Dorothy W. Pike

i.
The Three Crosses and **The Bearing of the Cross** (*Las Tres Cruces y Jesús Nazareno llevando la cruz*)
NMAH 278088.24 a, b

j.
Saint Cecilia (*Santa Cecilia*)
NMAH 278085.3
Illustrated in color, p. 35

k.
Tobias and the Archangel Raphael (*Tobias y San Rafael*)
NMAH 278088.27

l.
Saint Blasius (*San Blas*)
NMAH 278088.15

Since the Spanish Conquest, Puerto Rican folk artists called *santeros* have specialized in carving, painting, and refurbishing holy statues, mostly in small sizes for home worship. Not all the makers of these expressive pieces are known. Information shows that Pedro Celestino de Arce fashioned *The Three Kings on Horseback, Saint Helena, Virgin of the Kings*, and *Saint Anthony of Padua* in the twentieth century. Born in Aguada in the nineteenth century, Celestino died in Arecibo sometime between 1940 and 1950 at the age of eighty or ninety. Flores Cabán (1870–1950), one of a family of *santeros* located in Camuy, sculpted *Our Lady of Perpetual Help* also in the twentieth century, while Domingo Rojas (died 1870) of Moca possibly created *The Three Crosses* and *The Bearing of the Cross* in the nineteenth century.

201.
Family Shinto Shrine with Figure of Daikoku (shrine, *kamidana*), before 1854
Japan
wood
13⅞ × 13⅓ × 6½ (35.2 × 33.8 × 16.5)
NMNH 4288; Collected during Commodore Matthew Perry's Expedition to Japan, 1852–54

For Shinto families the household altar is the focus of domestic religious activity. Family members approach the altar daily to pray for divine protection. On the first and fifteenth of each month, the altar receives offerings of fresh branches of the sacred *sakaki* tree and rice wine (sake). On New Year's Day the shrine is the center of an elaborate celebration.

When a family member dies, a piece of white paper is placed before the altar to protect it from the impurity of death.

Shinto deities are venerated at the altar, especially the Sun Goddess, Amaterasu; the god of fishermen and tradesmen, Ebisu; and the god of wealth, Daikoku. Daikoku, one of Japan's seven gods of good fortune, appears on this altar. A special patron to farmers, he stands on two rice bales and holds a magic hammer with which he can produce anything the heart desires. Over his shoulder he carries a large sack of treasures.

202.
BUDDHIST ALTAR. The Buddhist altar in a Japanese home is a focal point of religious ceremonials. Daily, and on special occasions, offerings of food, flowers, and incense are placed in the altar in a spirit of thanksgiving to deceased ancestors and to the Buddha. Every morning when rice is cooked, the first scoop is served out into a special brass bowl and placed on the altar. The rice remains there during a short prayer service, after which it is removed and eaten. Special treats such as red rice cooked for a wedding, the first fruits of a season, or candy may likewise be offered on the altar. A deceased family member is honored at the altar each month on the day of his or her death. Other celebrations at the altar include Obon, an annual festival honoring souls of the deceased; New Year's Day; and Ohigan, the equinoxes, a time at which special appreciation is expressed for the Buddha.

a.
Miniature Buddhist Shrine (*zushi*), before 1921
Tokyo, Japan
wood, gold, lacquer, brass
26 × 10⅜ × 9½ (67.6 × 26.3 × 24.2)
NMNH 316338; Gift of Mrs. Gertrude B. Warner in memory of Major Murray Warner

Japanese Buddhists place portable, miniature shrines on the top shelf of a tiered altar in temple sanctuaries or in homes.

In this shrine the holy figure of the Buddha Amida Nyorai, symbol of wisdom and mercy, sits in serene thought. His closed eyes and stylized hands with fingers forming a double triangle emphasize his meditative repose.

Japanese Buddhists pray before such a shrine similar to this one on such occasions as a wedding, funeral, or reunion with a family member after a long journey and during special holidays, including the day commemorating Buddha's birth, enlightenment, and death, which is celebrated in May.

b.
Censer (*kōro*), ca. 1896
Japan
alloy of copper, tin, and zinc
5 × 4½ × 3¾ (12.7 × 11.5 × 9.5)
NMNH 220057

Buddhists consider the mythical lion on the cover of this censer as the bearer of a Bodhisattva, one vowed to become a Buddha through perfection in the six virtues: generosity, morality, patience, vigor, concentration, and wisdom. Also called the Messenger of Buddha, the lion typifies the power of the Law of Buddha. Believers place the censer in the center of the lower shelf of an altar, between vase and candlestick.

c.
Votive Flower Vase (*kebyō;*
kehyō), before 1872
Tokyo, Japan
alloy of copper, tin, and zinc, and
possibly silver
4¾ × 3¾ (12.1 × 9.5)
NMNH 95417

This vase stands on the left side of
the altar. Japanese Buddhists favor
chrysanthemum flowers for decoration but also use leafy green plants.
They prefer flower arrangements
shaped like a petal, pointed at both
ends with their length twice the
height of the vase. Since vases
must remain filled, artificial metal
flowers are sometimes used when
fresh flowers are not available. The
lions on the handles of this vase
express the same symbolism—the
Law of Buddha—as lions seen in
openwork on the cover of the censer discussed in no. 85.

d.
Candlestick (*shokudai*), before 1872
Tokyo, Japan
alloy of copper, tin, and zinc
12½ × 4½ × 3¾ (31.8 × 11.5 ×
9.5)
NMNH 95416

A candlestick is always placed on
the lower right of the altar. This
example is in the form of a crane
standing on the back of a mythical
tortoise with a fringed tail. The
crane and tortoise are emblems of
longevity and frequently appear together. The crane is also the messenger of Taoist deities and is said
to bring good luck and long life.

203.
**OBJECTS FROM *THE THRONE
OF THE THIRD HEAVEN OF THE
NATIONS MILLENIUM GEN-
ERAL ASSEMBLY.*** This assem-
blage is the creation of James
Hampton, son of a Black gospel
singer and itinerant preacher from
rural South Carolina. Hampton arrived in Washington, D.C., at the
age of nineteen and lived there for
most of his adult life.

Scant details of his life do not begin to hint at the intensity of
Hampton's inner visionary experience. He believed that he was in
direct communication with God
and His angels. Beginning in the
early 1930s, Hampton devoted him-

202

self to the construction of a monument to his personal religious vision, which grew more complex
throughout his adult life.

Applying his imagination to the
transformation of discarded materials such as old cardboard, plastic,
and different types of aluminum
foil removed from store displays,
bottles, and cigarette packs, Hampton did most of his work in a
rented garage. Although his activities remained virtually undiscov-
ered until after his death, the reclusive artist left a legacy of some 180
glittering objects as a testament to

his visionary world. The permanent
installation of *The Throne* at the
National Museum of American Art
follows a platformed layout deter-
mined by Hampton himself. Paired
objects, such as the winged vase
stands and the prophet and apostle
plaques, are placed in corresponding locations, radiating from each
side of the throne. Hampton's labels indicate that the pieces on the
viewer's left refer to the New Testament, Jesus, and Grace. Those on
the right are based on the Old Testament, Moses, and Law.

204 b

are symbols for God, who is the Light of the World.

In addition to *The Throne,* Hampton also developed a cabalistic script that has yet to be deciphered. Examples of this writing can be found on the plaques exhibited here and in a notebook that may contain the key to his vision. Lacking knowledge of his cryptic language, all we can conclude is that James Hampton constructed *The Throne* as a monument to his faith in God. A Baptist by birth, Hampton never joined a specific congregation as an adult, preferring to attend services at a variety of churches. He once expressed the desire for a ministry following his retirement, and perhaps had he lived long enough he might have converted his workshop into a church. As it was, Hampton's sole form of preaching remained nonvocal to the end. Therein lies its peculiar power.

James Hampton (1909–1964)
Selection of Objects from *The Throne of the Third Heaven of the Nations Millenium General Assembly,* ca. 1950–64
Washington, D.C.
NMAA 1970.353

a.

Pair of Winged Vase Stands
wooden furniture, light bulbs, glass vases, all covered with gold and silver foils, supplemented with cardboard, kraft paper, clear plastic sheeting
each: 54 × 35 × 40 (137.2 × 88.9 × 101.6)
Illustrated in color, p. 36

b.

Prophet Plaque
wood covered with foil and kraft paper, ink on paper covered with clear plastic sheeting
14½ × 11½ × 1¼ (36.8 × 29.2 × 3.1)

c.

Apostle Plaque
painted wood, ink on paper covered with clear plastic sheeting
13 × 9 × 1¼ (33 × 22.9 × 3.1)

d.

Nations Readjustment Plan Plaque
wood covered with gold foil, ink on paper
20¾ × 27¾ × 1½ (52.7 × 72 × 3.7)

While many of the objects—throne, altar, pulpits, and offertory tables—suggest traditional church appointments, the purpose of others is obscure. Reinforcing the artist's distinction between the Old and New Testaments are the foil-decorated wooden plaques bearing on one the names of the prophets and on the other the names of the apostles. Their design and function may reflect Hampton's belief that

God had revealed to him a second set of commandments to supersede the tablets given to Moses. The plaque entitled "Nations Readjustment Plan" seems to confirm this. Hampton's purple, silver, and gold crowns, too fragile to wear, may be inspired by a citation from his favored Book of Revelations, which speaks of the crowning of brows worthy of salvation. Sometimes Hampton's choice of materials signifies particular ideas: light bulbs

204 c (Torah finials)

e.

Three Crowns
cardboard and kraft paper covered with foil, light bulb
largest: 11 × 10 × 8¾ (27.9 × 25.4 × 22.2)

204.

THE TORAH. The Torah, or Pentateuch, comprises the first five books of the Old Testament. It is the most sacred of the sacred texts of Judaism and resides in the synagogue within the Holy Ark, which is the analogue of the holiest of holy places in the ancient Jewish Tabernacle and Temple. The center of much religious ceremony and celebration, the Torah is also the object of elaborate decoration.

a.

Torah Ark Curtain (*parokhet*), late 19th century
Istanbul, Turkey
velvet, gold and silver metallic-thread embroidery
110 × 72½ (279.4 × 184.2)
NMNH 154758
Illustrated in color, p. 36

A torah is kept behind a curtain like this one in the Holy Ark of many synagogues. The border of this curtain is decorated with floral motifs, which are associated with the tree of life (Proverbs 3:18). The lamp in the center represents the eternal light that is suspended before the Holy Ark. In the four corners are inscribed the names of four angels: Raphael, Gabriel, Uriel, and Michael. At the top are the following quotations:

But the Lord is in his holy temple: let all the earth keep silent before him (Habakkuk 2:20).

I have set the Lord always before me (Psalms 16:8).

and at the sides:

Open ye the gates, that the righteous nation which keepeth the truth may enter in (Isaiah 26:2).

This gate of the Lord, into which the righteous shall enter (Psalms 118:20).

This particular ark curtain is one of the finest existing examples from the Near East. It was made in Istanbul in the late nineteenth century.

b.

Torah Mantle (*me'il*), 1878
France
velvet, metallic and polychrome silk embroidery and appliqué
34 × 17¼ (87.6 × 43.8)
NMAH 299038.1

This French-Jewish Torah mantle depicts the climactic scene from the Old Testament story of the binding of Isaac (Genesis 22:1–19). An angel stays the hand of the Patriarch Abraham, who had been ordered by God to sacrifice his only son, Isaac, as a test of faith. The symbol of the radiant eye signifying the perpetual presence of the all-seeing God is probably borrowed from Christian iconography. The letters at the top are the initial letters of the words *keter torah*— "The Crown of the Torah." The inscription at the bottom reads "Gift of Naphtali, son of Shmuel Klein and his wife Mrs. Feigele Rachel, daughter of the honored Rabbi Toutros Ville in the year [chronogram for the Jewish year corresponding to 1878]. May we be sealed in the book of life here in the sacred congregation of Rhens."

c.

Torah Finials, Shield, and Pointer
(*rimmonim; tas; yad*), ca. 1870–1900
Austria-Hungary
silver, gilt
each finial: 14 × 6½ (35.5 × 16.5)
shield: 14¾ × 11¾ (37.4 × 29.8)
pointer, length: 12⅜ (31.4)
NMAH 1978.2106.3 a, b; 315280; 315282

A Torah scroll is wound on two rods called "trees of life" (*azei hayim*). These are adorned with finials called "pomegranates" (*rimmonim*). Pomegranates are associated with the design of the robes of the high priest of the temple (Exodus 28:33). In synagogues where two or three Torahs might be used, worshipers marked a place with a shield to indicate the portion of the Torah that stood ready to be read for a particular holiday. The name of the holiday portion might be inscribed on an interchangeable panel that fit into a shield, or the names might be inscribed singly on separate shields. The blank shield displayed here was probably acquired at a workshop where it was to have been inscribed with a name. In time, the shield became highly ornamental and many examples have lost their functional purpose.

Because ancient law forbids the direct touching of the sacred text, a ceremonial pointer, or "hand" (*yad*), came into widespread use. This set of finials, shield, and pointer from Austria-Hungary is typical of nineteenth-century central-European forms.

Religious Celebrations

Whether as vast in compass as Christianity, Hinduism, Judaism, Buddhism, and Islam or as small in scope as the traditional rituals of preliterate communities, religions are based on beliefs in a divine or superhuman power or powers to be worshiped or venerated as the creators and sustainers of the world. Rituals communicate with these powers symbolically through sacrifice, prayer, invocation, dance, song, and other means. Sacred written texts in literate traditions and oral myths in preliterate traditions preserve for posterity the words and works of deities, founders, disciples, prophets, and saints. Ritual symbols are highly charged with meaning and are also believed to be powerful in themselves.

Religious ritual is sometimes said to be "mere empty formality" or "man's obsessional neurosis" (Sigmund Freud). In religious systems that are "going concerns," however, ritual is an orchestration of many cultural performances, a symphony in more than music that often includes mythical drama, choreographed dance, poetical recitations, painting, sculpture, theological oratory, hymnody, choral singing, synchronization of musical instruments, and many other forms. Indeed, such extensive ritual may be regarded as the source of many of our modern specialized art forms, for objects used in religious celebration have traditionally been crafted by the best artists in the community. Religious rituals in their premodern expression—as much festive as solemn—perhaps most fully exemplify the celebratory spirit in human culture.

205.
Funerary Figure (*mwa*), 19th or
early 20th century
Agni people; Ivory Coast
clay
15½ × 5¾ × 5 (39.4 × 14.6 ×
12.7)
AfA 69-35-16

A focal point of the elaborate Agni
funeral rites was a small clay figure
sculpted to resemble the deceased.
The family of the deceased commissioned these sculptures for any
member of the family who died,
with the exception of newborn infants. After the initial funeral ceremony the figure was kept by the
family head. Women of the family
later adorned it with cloth and
beads for a secondary funeral. After

the funeral cortege the figure was
installed in a special place in the
forest where all such figures were
taken.

The spirits of the dead were
thought to live in or near their images. Family members occasionally
brought sacrifices to the images
and women sometimes petitioned
their aid in conceiving children.

206.
Male Figure, before 1876
Easter Island, East Polynesia
wood
9⅞ × 3 × 2¾ (25.1 × 7.6 × 7)
NMNH 17537

Although the religions of Polynesian societies varied in detail, all
were built upon a similar foundation, the result of a common prehistoric heritage of migrations,
which occurred mostly between
twenty-five hundred and four
hundred years ago. A large pan-
theon of deities and ancestors were
of primary importance in the rich
mythologies of the Polynesians.
Specialized priests enforced a strict
code of ritual behavior. Gods could
be summoned to inhabit objects
such as a wooden sculpture, a sea-
shell, or a feathered image and were
given power through prayers and
offerings. Religious celebrants regularly presented offerings, chanted
incantations, sang, and danced. Although the priests alone addressed
the high gods, commoners often in-
voked the less-powerful ancestral
spirits.

Wooden figures in human form
appear to have proliferated during
the nineteenth century into several
recognizable types as a development from eighteenth-century pro-
totypes. Although these figures are
often said to represent gods, it is
more likely that they were carved
to commemorate ancestors.

The "classic" male figures
known as *moai kavakava* are char-
acterized by the emaciated appearance of the rib cage and often have
ornamental incised designs at the
top of the head. Some have a hole
for suspension and were said to
have been worn at feasts.

207.
Commemorative Head of a King
(*uhuhmwelao*), 18th century
Edo people; Benin City, Nigeria
brass (questionably bronze), iron
13¾ × 9⅛ × 8⅝ (35 × 23.2 × 22)
HM&SG 1979.230
See colorplate, p. 36

Throughout their history, the kings
of Benin in Nigeria have carefully
observed the cult of their royal
ancestors. Royal brass heads were
made in Benin City from the fourteenth century; examples such as
this one were produced in the
eighteenth century, when the style
was becoming bolder and larger in
scale than in earlier heads. The
heads represent the office—not the
person—of deceased kings and are
placed on an altar built inside the
palace compound.

Upon accession to office each
ruler constructs a special earthen
altar to the monarch who died before him. The reigning king fur-
nishes the new altar with symbolic
and magical objects such as wooden
and brass rattle staffs, diverse brass
images, and brass memorial heads,
like this one. The crowns of such
heads support carved elephant
tusks, which are symbols of power
and wealth associated with the
Benin kingship.

Until the end of the nineteenth
century a series of celebratory rites
took place at the royal ancestral altars once a year. During these rites
special priests, who traced their
origins to the founding days of the
Benin kingdom, performed sacrifices to the spirit of each deceased
king. These rites, which promoted
communication with the royal ancestral spirits, helped insure prosperity and supernatural protection
for the kingdom of Benin.

208.
Ceremonial Paddle, before 1841
Raivavae, Austral Islands, French
Polynesia
wood
47⅛ × 13 × 4 (119.7 × 33 ×
10.2)
NMNH 3714

The production of intricately
carved ceremonial paddles on Raivavae was a specialized occupation.
Combining incising and relief carving, design elements are primarily
geometric with abstract anthropo-

205

208

morphic figures at the terminals. These paddles are too frail for use in canoes. It is possible, however, that they were used in dances in view of their similarity to the dance paddles of Tonga and Easter Island. These paddles were a favorite curio of visiting whalers and many were made for sale.

209.
Sacred Straw Rope (*shimenawa*), before 1963
Hitoyoshi city, Kumamoto prefecture, Japan
rice straw, rice stalks, paper
19¾ × 6 × 1¾ (50.2 × 15.2 × 4.5)
NMNH 402734

In the Shinto tradition a sacred straw rope symbolizes purity and acts as a barrier against evil. A Shinto priest may place a sacred straw rope on a house lot while performing the purification ceremony for ground breaking. Such a rope also figures as part of the New Year decorations.

Any entryway to a sacred place—a gateway to a Shinto shrine, a dwelling, or a holy tree—may have a straw rope hung on it. When placed on the border of a farm it serves as a protective charm against crop damage and a form of prayer for a good harvest.

210.
Prayer Rug, before 1970
Konya province, Turkey
wool
57⅛ × 29¹⁵⁄₁₆ (145.1 × 76)
NMNH 411086; Bequest from Florence Deakins Becker to the National Museum of American Art, Given to NMNH

To fulfill religious duties and assure eventual entry into Paradise, a Muslim prays five times a day. When praying alone, instead of as one of a group in a mosque, he may use a prayer rug to define a solemn, undisturbed space.

A prayer rug usually has an arched shape in the center. The arch is called a mihrab and refers to the niche in the wall of a mosque that indicates the direction of Mecca. Many prayer rugs are decorated with flowers that may symbolize eternal spring or paradise.

211.
JÍVARO SOUL POWER. For Jívaro

men, staying alive meant seeking and keeping soul power. The man with a powerful soul was honest, intelligent, energetic, and industrious. Soul power was also protection against physical and magical peril, and when it disappeared a man soon met his death.

Jívaro men commonly used a hallucinogen, datura, to induce visions during which they encountered fierce or monstrous soul apparitions. After such a confrontation a seeker knew he had gained soul power when he met the specter of an ancestor. The ancestor granted the dreamer long life and successful headhunting. The struggle to take heads for Jívaro men was much more than vengeance on enemies. It was a quest for life itself, because head taking enabled warriors to renew their own soul power. Without taking heads they would die as their power gradually ebbed to nothing.

Each of the many Jívaro who died in battle was thought to own a highly dangerous avenging soul. This soul killed a head taker or one of his close relatives by becoming a lethal snake or a falling tree or by causing fatal, self-inflicted "accidents" with machetes or guns. To thwart the avenging soul, the warrior swiftly severed and shrunk his victim's head.

Several days after its arrival home with shrunken heads, a war party celebrated the first of three victory feasts. During this feast victors ritually purified themselves and the head from the pollution of killing. The second two feasts were very elaborate, with great quantities of food and manioc being consumed. Through these feasts head takers achieved great prestige, not only as brave warriors with great soul power but also as generous hosts contributing to the well being of relatives and neighbors.

Today Jívaro no longer capture or shrink enemy heads.

Jívaro warriors used their ornaments to reveal the power of their soul, state their social status and prestige, and openly attract women. The strongest souls belonged to the "powerful ones," warriors who repeatedly killed enemies, thereby earning the right to wear the most elaborate adornments.

Jívaro wore their ornaments dur-

209

b.
Headwrap (*etsemat*), ca. 1900–1934
Jívaro Indians; Ecuador
cotton thread, dye, feathers, human hair, pitch, seeds, seed pods
6 × 15¾ (15.2 × 40)
NMNH 420849; Gift of Mr. and Mrs. Donald C. Beatty, Sr.

After a youth underwent puberty rites and began to search for soul power, he began to tie up his long, loose hair with this headwrap. Later, when he captured heads, he used this same band slung over his shoulder to carry his trophy.

c.
Comb (*temashi*), ca. 1900–1934
Jívaro Indians; Ecuador
wood, cotton thread, dye
1⅞ × 2⅞ (4.7 × 7.3)
NMNH 420955; Gift of Mr. and Mrs. Donald C. Beatty, Sr.

The Jívaro attributed great strength and vitality to their hair. Hair grooming for rituals and feasts involved not only the headdress, headwrap, and head ornaments, but also the comb.

d.
Dorsal Head Ornament (*tayocunchi*), 20th century
Jívaro Indians; Ecuador or Peru
anterior beetle wings, bird bones, seeds, string, cotton
40 × 10½ (101.6 × 26.7)
NMNH T1039

ing all ceremonial visits between villages, the most important of which were the great victory feasts. Before a feast began, each male carefully groomed himself and applied body paint. He could then proudly participate in these feasts—the pinnacles of Jívaro life.

a.
Feathered Headdress, ca. 1900–1950
Jívaro Indians; Ecuador
slit reed, birdskins with feathers, twine, pitch
19 × 6½ (48.2 × 16.5)
NMNH 383650

Elaborate feather headdresses were most commonly reserved for men with soul power. Like other male adornments, however, they also showed social prestige and status.

Apart from ceremonial use, headdresses were highly prized for trade and tribute among Jívaro and their neighbors.

211 c

211 q

e.
Collar Ornament (*tayocunchi*), ca. 1900–1924
Jívaro Indians; Ecuador
bone, string, toucan feathers, glass beads
26 × 10½ × 3 (66 × 26.7 × 7.6)
NMNH 326926; Loan from J. G. Culbertson

A collar ornament most directly revealed the strength of a wearer's soul, for only "powerful ones" draped such adornments on their shoulders. The bones in the ornament, like the many bones in the dorsal head ornament, attested to the bravery of the wearer. To find these bones, Jívaro men hunted the *tayo* bird in caves where jaguars or dangerous jaguar spirits were said to live. Since only the leg bones of the birds were used, many trips had to be made to complete a single ornament.

f.
Jaguar Tooth Necklace, ca. 1900–1934
Jívaro Indians; Ecuador
jaguar teeth, glass beads, twine
11 × 1½ (27.9 × 3.7)
NMNH 420894; Gift of Mr. and Mrs. Donald C. Beatty, Sr.

A jaguar tooth necklace imparted the magical strength of these dangerous and sacred animals to its wearer. Jaguars were among the specters of the soul that Jívaro had to face with great courage when on a vision quest for soul power.

g.
Two Ear Plugs (*wachi; arus*), ca. 1900–1934
Jívaro Indians; Educador
cane
largest: ⅝ × 8¾ (1.6 × 22.2)
NMNH 420891, 420892; Gift of Mr. and Mrs. Donald C. Beatty, Sr.

h.
Beetle-Wing Ear Drops (*kuishi*), 1900–1950
Jívaro Indians; Ecuador
anterior beetle wings, cotton, cotton thread, feathers, human hair
largest: 25½ × 1½ (64.7 × 3.7)
NMNH 403361; Gift of K. P. Curtis

i.
Headband or Neck Ornament (*muha patai*), 1900–1950
Jívaro Indians; Ecuador
birdskins with feathers attached, bamboo, string, unspun cotton, thread, dye, anterior beetle wings
27 × 14½ × 3 (68.6 × 35.8 × 7.6)
NMNH 383653
Illustrated in color, p. 37

j.
Bandolier (*nupush; nu'pisle; mupush*), ca. 1900–1934
Jívaro Indians; Ecuador
insect larvae, string, feathers, anterior beetle wings, seed pods, seeds
12½ × 25½ (31.8 × 64.7)
NMNH 373868; Gift of W. A. Larner, Jr.

k.
Bandolier, ca. 1900–1932
Jívaro Indians; Ecuador
seeds, twine
4¾ × 27 (12.1 × 68.6)
NMNH 420912; Gift of Mr. and Mrs. Donald C. Beatty, Sr.

l.
Bandolier (*nupush; nu'pisle; mupush*), ca. 1900–1933
Jívaro Indians; Ecuador
insect larvae, string, seeds, feathers
35½ × 9½ × 3 (90.2 × 24.2 × 7.6)
NMNH 366076

m.
Bandolier, ca. 1900–1933
Jívaro Indians; Aguaruna, Marañón River, Ecuador and Peru
seeds, twine
5¾ × 25 (14.6 × 63.4)
NMNH 366025

Rather than symbolizing the attainment of soul power, these adornments indicated high social status. The black, many-stranded bandolier ornaments were especially reserved for high ceremonial occasions, for they required more than a year to make. Some "beads" are actually tiny insect larvae painstakingly gathered by a warrior until he had enough for his prized chest ornament. Other beads were made from seeds, and still others of glass.

n.
Belt of Human Hair (*indashi acacho*), ca. 1900–1934
Jívaro Indians; Aguaruna, Boca del Santiago, Ecuador
hair, cotton thread, feathers, string
6½ × 41¾ × 1 (16.5 × 106 × 2.5)
NMNH 373865

Belts of human hair adorned Jívaro warriors. There is discrepancy in reports about the meaning of such belts. Earlier sources state that the wearer cut the hair from a deceased enemy, wove it or glued it into a belt, then held a small feast to consecrate its power before wearing it in public on ceremonial occasions. Later sources report that the belts were made to mourn the dead person whose hair was woven into the belt.

o.
Shrunken Sloth Head (*unūshi*), 1931 or 1932
Jívaro Indians; Ecuador
sloth head, string
3¾ × 11½ × 3 (9.5 × 29.2 × 7.6)
NMNH 366007

When a boy proclaimed his reaching of manhood, he killed a tree sloth in the forest and shrunk its head. His father then sponsored one or two feasts for him. During these feasts the celebrants treated the sloth head as if it were a human trophy. It was thought possible to substitute a sloth for a human since the sloth's lethargy indicated the animal's great age— and great soul power.

If an enemy slain during a head-taking raid was related to a member of the war party, the raiders did not take the head. Instead they substituted one of a sloth, performing the same rituals and gaining the same power as for a human trophy.

p.
Lance (*shingi*), ca. 1900–1934
Jívaro Indians; Ecuador
cane, cotton string, pigment, chontawood
83 × 2 (210.8 × 5.1)
NMNH 421028; Gift of Mr. and Mrs. Donald C. Beatty, Sr.

q.
Panpipe (*kantash*), ca. 1900–1950
Jívaro Indians; Ecuador
cane, snakeskin, cotton string, pitch, pigment
½ × 11 × 7¾ (1.3 × 27.9 × 19.7)
NMNH 403362; Gift of K. P. Curtis

Both lances and panpipes helped Jívaro men to repel the avenging soul of a dead enemy. They were not, however, used together.

The Jívaro tied the freshly taken head (human or sloth) to the chontawood lance during the first purifactory feast. The magical properties of the chontawood helped to stave off the avenging soul of the head and protected the celebrants from supernatural harm.

Slayers played panpipes for a similar reason—the magic of the music protected them from being avenged by dead or living enemies.

212.
Figure with Two Bodies and Four Heads, ca. 1900–1950
Ijo people; Nigeria
wood, pigments
56⅛ × 15 × 13¾ (142.6 × 38.1 × 34.9)
AfA 78-19-1

Priests of the Ijo people commission carved images that embody the spirits of two sacred domains, water and forest. Special cults care for the images, offering feasts and music to, and petitioning blessings from, these spirits. Cult ceremonies intended to summon the spirits necessitate the cleaning, recoloring, and purifying of the image used in the ritual. Images are thought to accumulate a layer of pollution during the interval between ceremonies.

The absence of aquatic themes in this image suggests that it represents a forest figure.

212

214 c

213.
Three Warrior Dolls, ca. 1850–1900
Japan
mixed media
largest: 17 × 6 (43.2 × 15.2)
NMNH T1, T2, T3

Dolls like these are displayed on a tiered stand in the main room of a Japanese house to celebrate the boy's day festival. With its displays of warrior dolls, miniature weapons, helmets, and banners, this festival is a celebration of the healthy growth of boys, a prayer for protection from sickness and evil influences, and a means of stimulating martial values in boys through glorification of celebrated warriors.

The boy's day festival (see nos. 14 and 108) has its origin in the ancient Japanese beliefs that people could purify themselves through cleansing rituals and could acquire protection from misfortune by driving harmful spirits from their bodies. In those times the dolls were used as talismans or symbols of Kami, which are gods or incarnations of spiritual power.

The standing warrior represents the young samari as standard-bearer. Its banner translates as "God of War [and] the Great Bodhisattva [Buddha]." The gold brocade garment of the seated warrior, the purple tassels on its breast plate, and its fur-covered footwear indicate the lofty status of a high-ranking warrior. The warrior doll mounted on a galloping white horse is in full military regalia.

214.
GHOST DANCE. During the late nineteenth century, the Ghost Dance religion arose among Plains Indians who sought salvation from a harsh reservation life. The religion, a mixture of traditional Indian and Christian elements, looked back to the glorious Indian past and forward to a hoped-for return of the buffalo, resurrection of beloved ancestors, and a life free of white domination.

Although the messiah of this religion, a Paiute Indian named Wovoka or Jack Wilson, preached a code of nonviolence and kindness, the Sioux practiced a more militant version of the religion. Among the Sioux on the oppressive Pine Ridge Reservation in 1890, the infamous massacre by the army of Indians at Wounded Knee, South Dakota, took place during Ghost Dance meetings.

Central to the religion was a ritual trance induced as performers danced faster and faster in a circle, sometimes around a sacred tree. From time to time they would emerge from the trance and recount visions they had seen of the spirit world. Today some interpret the circle dance as a symbol of the unbroken hoop of relations Indians shared with nature and with one another. Many of the symbols placed on Ghost Dance costumes referred to key points of their universe—the earth, the pole star, the sun, and the tree of the world. Also depicted were eagles, magpies, crows, and turtles, creatures able to journey between these points and link them together.

The Ghost Dance religion gradually declined in the 1890s as none of its promises came true, but its influence on the shared symbols, songs, and world view of the pan-Indian movement remains to the present.

a.
Ghost Dance Shirt, ca. 1889–92
Southern Arapaho Indians; Oklahoma
deerhide, paint
34¾ × 20¼ × 1½ (88.3 × 51.4 × 3.8)
NMNH 165126; Collected by James Mooney
Illustrated in color, p. 37

When attired in their finest buckskin shirts for the Ghost Dance, Arapaho and Cheyenne participants displayed painted and beaded figures inspired by vision trances and cult lore. In keeping with the cultural revival, Ghost Dancers wore old-style clothes, often made without materials introduced by whites. The most common vision-inspired designs were eagles, crows, turtles, and stars—some visible on the shirt here.

b.
Ghost Dance Staff, ca. 1889–92
Sioux Indians; South Dakota
wood, buffalo horn, hair, hair dye, hide, felt, glass beads
57 × 7½ × 2 (144.8 × 19 × 5.1)
NMNH 165121; Gift of Victor Justice Evans

To begin most Sioux Ghost dances, the leader, while offering a prayer, waved a staff like this one over the heads of the celebrants. He then hung the staff, symbolizing the forces of growth, and other ritual objects on the sacred tree.

c.
Ghost Dance Staff, ca. 1885–97
Northern Arapaho Indians;
Wyoming
wood, hide, glass beads, cloth, sinew, bone
30 × 5 × ¾ (76.2 × 12.7 × 1.9)
NMNH 200536; Collected by Emile Granier

Though little is known about the exact use of Arapaho staffs, it is believed that such staffs were used during the Ghost Dance to stimulate hypnotic trances. Among the Arapaho, the arrow frequently symbolizes lightning.

d.
Hide Painting of the Ghost Dance, 1891
Southern Cheyenne Indians; Oklahoma
deerhide, paint
52 × 39¾ (132 × 101)
NMNH 165127; Collected by James Mooney

The author of the classic account of the Ghost Dance, James Mooney, commissioned this hide painting from Yellow Nose, a Ute captive living among the Cheyenne. Mooney reported that this painting "gives an excellent idea of the ghost dance . . . among the Cheyenne and Arapaho." The artist paid attention to such details as the paint and feathers of fully costumed dancers, a spotted shawl fallen to the ground, and the different hairstyles of the women—Cheyenne with braids, Arapaho with loosely hanging tresses. A woman holds forth a sacred crow, while men hold inanimate ritual objects: one man a shinny stick, the other a gaming wheel. The artist also shows the manner in which performers induced a hypnotic trance by waving handkerchiefs. The medicine man, a figure standing to one side, helps a man who has stretched out a blue handkerchief toward him to enter the spirit world.

215 b

215.
WHITE DEERSKIN DANCE. The Native American peoples of northwestern California—the Hupa, Yurok, and Karok—performed many ceremonies intended to renew the good things of the world and to prevent disaster and evil. Although such ceremonies fulfilled a solemn religious purpose they also provided a social occasion during which smaller, isolated communities could merge for a short time to feast, trade, gossip, and display fine possessions.

Each September the Hupa performed the White Deerskin Dance explicitly to wipe out evil brought into the world by members of society who had broken taboos. An old priest with his helper took charge of the esoteric rites. As he chanted and mimed a narrative of the world's creation, the priest addressed the spirits who dwelled in the sweat lodge, the sacred house, and the dance ground.

The regalia exhibited here figured prominently in the public performances of the White Deerskin Dance, which was performed for ten days during afternoons and evenings. In dancing with the white

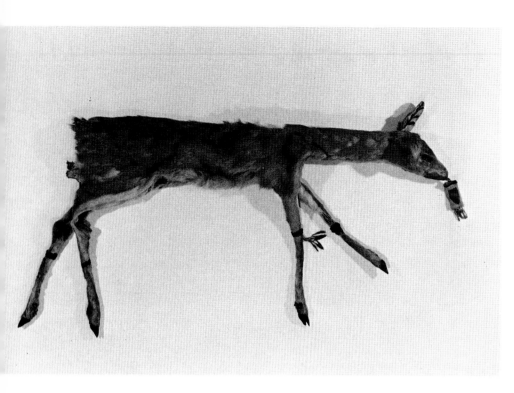

215 f

deerskins, obsidian blades, red woodpecker scalps, and other objects, both host and visiting communities vied to display their most prized valuables. Rivalry increased as the performers, lined up in two competing camps, conspicuously displayed the valued objects for all to admire as they swayed and shouted. The dances rose to a climax at the end, when each camp tried to outdo the other by showing their largest and most impressive pieces.

The Hupa privately owned and inherited their treasures. Friends and relatives combined resources to sponsor an especially lavish display of riches, which they selected from their store of valuables especially for the White Deerskin Dance.

Using some, but not all, of the regalia of the White Deerskin dances, the Hupa also celebrated other world-renewal rites, such as Jump dances, held to drive away sickness.

a.
Wolfskin Headband, ca. 1890–1930
Hupa Indians; northwestern California
wolfskin with fur, paint, buckskin
22 × 19 × 6½ (55.8 × 48.2 × 16.5)
NMNH 383442; Collected by E. G. Johnson

b.
Openweave Net Headdress, ca. 1865–75
Hupa Indians; northwestern California
native twine, jay feathers, cotton cloth
21½ × 12 × ¾ (54.5 × 30.5 × 1.9)
NMNH 21333; Collected by Stephen Powers

c.
Feathered Head Ornament, ca. 1890–1930
Hupa Indians; northwestern California
sinew, deerhide, feathers
20¼ × 2½ × 1 (51.4 × 6.4 × 2.5)
NMNH 359051; Gift of Victor Justice Evans

For the White Deerskin dances, different types of head ornaments were worn by line dancers and by lead singers. These ornaments set the dancers and singers apart from the carriers of valuable objects. During the last and most rivalrous of the White Deerskin dances, the singers alone wore elaborate feathered head ornaments of the type shown here.

d.
Dentalium-Shell Necklace, ca. 1900–1930
Hupa Indians; northwestern California
dentalium shells, glass beads, cotton threads
19 × 7 × ¾ (48.2 × 17.8 × 1.9)
NMNH 411723; Gift of Awona Harrington

During world-renewal rites, Hupa men took great pride in covering their chests with dentalium-shell necklaces. The Indians of northwestern California used long dentalium shells as a form of money, trading them in a network that extended from Vancouver Island to the Eastern Plains. So important were strings of shells that men had lines tattooed on their arms to measure the length of their wealth. Shells too short to be money became ceremonial necklaces such as this one, which was formerly owned by a Hupa named Shoemaker Robinson.

e.
Dance Apron, ca. 1880–90
Hupa Indians, northwestern California
ring-tailed cat skins, deerskin, black thread
18 × 65 (45.7 × 165.1)
NMNH 385628; Collected by Charles E. Woodruff

In the White Deerskin Dance, Hupa men wore either deerskin robes or an apron of ringed-tail catskins (probably cacomistle). Custom dictated that the lead singer in the center of the line wear a ring-tailed cat skirt, although some sources state this was only for the more important dances.

f.
White Deerskin, ca. 1880–1930
Hupa, Yurok, or Karok Indians; northwestern California
deerskin, stuffing, woodpecker scalps, abalone shell
69½ × 19 (176.5 × 48.2)
NMNH 358689; Gift of Victor Justice Evans

The Hupa valued highly rare albino and dark brown deerskins. Dancers hung such skins on poles and swung them to the movements of the dance. Ownership of these deerskins usually passed through the generations in a kind of group trusteeship, but sometimes the Hupa covertly sold them across family lines, closely guarding this secret until it was inevitably revealed at the next big dance.

g.
Obsidian Blade, ca. 1850–1908
Hupa Indians; northwestern California
obsidian
13¾ × 3¾ × 1 (35 × 9.5 × 2.5)
NMNH 248743; Collected by George G. Heye, exchanged with the Smithsonian Institution

Hupa treasured red and black obsidian blades much the same as we treasure jewels. Like jewels, the worth of the obsidian blades depended on excellent workmanship, lack of flaws, and size—the largest known reaching thirty-three inches. When not displaying the blades in dances, the Hupa stored them with great care.

216.
FANG RELIQUARIES. Spirits of important deceased family members, whose power was believed to reside in their skulls, aided Fang families to survive. Fang people preserved the skulls of their deceased leaders in sacred reliquaries. The spiritual power embodied in the skulls could be threatened, they feared, through the evil magic of antisocial elements in their own village or rival families in other villages. They attempted to counter these secret attacks by placing wooden human images like this one on the reliquaries for protection.

Ill fortune or threats to family welfare motivated rites of renewal for these guardian spirit skulls. The power of the images and that of the relics they shielded was renewed in a festive ceremony. The guardian statues danced atop a palm-leaf screen, while men of the families involved manipulated them from below to the beat of the great drums played to one side of the stage.

a.
Figure of a Crouching Man (*eyema byeri*), ca. 1900–1913
Fang people, Ntumu subgroup; Gabon and Equatorial Guinea
wood, brass, barwood pigment
23 × 5½ × 5½ (58.4 × 14 × 14)
AfA 73-7-738; Gift of Eliot Elisofon

b.
Figure of a Woman (*eyema byeri*), ca. 1850–1920
Fang people, Ntumu subgroup; Gabon and Equatorial Guinea
wood, brass, barwood pigment
height: 22 (55.8)
NMNH 323280; Gift of Mrs. Sarita Ward

Images like these once protected Fang villagers from the magic of antisocial people. The installation and the renewal of the images' powers were marked by festivities.

c.
Drum (*mbe*), ca. 1850–1900
Fang people; Gabon and Equatorial Guinea
wood, hide, rattan, pigment
45 × 12⅜ (114.3 × 31.4)
NMNH 95155; Gift of the Reverend A. Good

Fang people played drums such as this one during rites that renewed the power of sacred skulls and at the same time initiated young men into the family cult. In certain phases of this crucial family ritual, drummers were accompanied by a slit gong, xylophone, and whistles.

d.
Barrel and Lid (*nsegh byeri*), ca. 1900
Fang people; Gabon and Equatorial Guinea
bark, wood, split rattan
height: 19 (48.2)
NMNH 164870 a, b

Fang placed skulls of deceased family members, along with additional magical materials, in ordinary bark barrels, thus transforming these containers into objects with sacred qualities. Family leaders then kept barrels holding these important ancestral relics in secluded quarters.

During times of crisis families brought the barrels together in the cult place, a clearing in the forest. There, to the sound of the drums,

they showed the contents to those about to be initiated into the family cult. At the same time they performed rites to increase the power of the relics and their guardian figures.

217.
PENITENTES, NEW MEXICO. Los Hermanos Penitentes ("The Brothers of Light") trace their origins to the Third [Lay] Order of Saint Francis, established in thirteenth-century Italy. The exclusively male order was carried from Italy to Spain and was later introduced in New Mexico by Spanish Franciscans before 1700. The Mexican Revolution of 1821 ousted the clergy from the missions in New Mexico, an upheaval that threatened the survival of religious beliefs and activities among Hispanic settlers. Having lost their clergy, Hispanic groups formed their own religious society in an attempt to preserve their religious traditions. The members of this society became popularly known as Penitentes.

Performing penance is the basis of much Penitente activity today. Suffering physical discipline as they reenact the Passion of Christ, members dramatize the Passion with vivid rituals and ceremonies performed around a special prayer house equipped for Holy Week rites. Here, among other rituals, Penitentes perform the ceremony of "the darkenings," which is part of the entire Good Friday Passion. Inside the building celebrants shatter silent prayers by frenzied, continuous noisemaking produced vocally and with noisemakers such as chains, metal, and wooden blocks. The uproar imitates the agitation of the natural world at the moment of Jesus' death on the cross.

Later the Penitentes recreate the agony of Christ's Way of the Cross through the penance of self-flagellation and back-breaking processionals in which the celebrants carry heavy crosses and pull a heavy cart.

The two figures shown here represent two highly important activities in Penitente Holy Week celebrations. The statue of Christ at the Pillar is associated with the

Good Friday drama, while the figure of Death in a cart reflects the subsequent procession.

a.
Statue of Christ at the Pillar, ca. 1870–1900
Rio Arriba region, northern New Mexico
wood, gesso, water-base paint
23½ × 9¾ × 5 (59.7 × 24.8 × 12.7)
NMAH 280129.3

This statue of Christ at the Pillar, fashioned by an unknown artist, was made to stand on the altar of a Penitente prayer house. Penitentes arrange this altar to resemble as closely as possible a consecrated church altar. In the prayer house they set different holy images such as the suffering or crucified Christ, Saint John the Evangelist, and sorrowing Mary, while on the walls they hang religious lithographs. These statues reflecting the pain and sorrow of Catholics at Christ's death are prominent in the ritual dramatization of the Passion that Penitentes perform on Good Friday.

b.
Figure of Death in a Cart (Carreta con Muerto), 19th or 20th century
New Mexico
wood, gesso, paint
26¾ × 20 (68 × 50.8)
NMNH 69.94; Purchased from the May D. & F. Co., Denver, Colorado

After reenacting the Passion of Christ, Penitentes pull a cart bearing the figure of Death through the streets in several New Mexico towns during Easter Holy Week. Flanked by cross bearers and flagellants, they dramatize Christ's painful procession to Calvary. The wheels on the unusually heavy cart do not turn, which increases the strain of pulling it. The Penitentes laboriously haul the cart up hills and around corners as rough ropes cut into their bare shoulders. Good luck comes to anyone brushed by the cart during the procession.

The idea for the death cart in New Mexico probably derives from a celebration first held in Florence, Italy, in 1511. A death cart covered with black cloth and painted with skeletons and white crosses was prepared in the Hall of the Pope. Drawn by black buffaloes, it bore the figure of Death carrying a

217 a

scythe. Surrounding Death were covered tombs that opened to reveal figures of the dead whenever the procession paused. Spaniards brought to New Mexico the dramatic portrayal of triumph over Death through religion.

The death cart seen here is similar to the ones described above but is smaller and less elaborate. The figure of Death in the New Mexican cart carries a bow and arrow rather than a scythe. A bow and arrow are part of the traditional Spanish representation while northern Europeans visualize the Grim Reaper wielding a scythe.

218.
DECORATED EASTER EGGS. In pre-Christian times Ukrainians decorated eggs to symbolize the sun, life, and nature's rebirth in the spring. In A.D. 988, when Christianity arrived, eggs became part of the Ukrainian Easter ritual, which has festive rites closely related to agriculture, the memory of the dead, and the marriage season.

Russian Orthodox and Roman Catholic women decorate eggs during Easter week and give many away, usually on Easter Sunday.

Ukrainian Americans carry on these traditions, including the ritual blessing of eggs and of Easter food. Families attend a service the Saturday night before Easter, bearing their decorated eggs to the church in large baskets that also contain meat, cheese, and special breads. At that time the priest blesses the food, which the family eats the next day on Easter Sunday. Friends and relatives exchange eggs after the blessing, keeping certain eggs on display in their homes for the entire year.

a.
Painting of a Woman Decorating Eggs, made before February 6, 1931
Czechoslovakia
colored ink on paper
8 × 10 (20.3 × 25.4)
NMAH 349667

Decorating Easter eggs is itself a solemn ritual. Traditionally, women who have spent a holy day without argument or sin decorate eggs in the quiet of their homes, alone or with their immediate families. There are special times to

219 a

draw designs and to recite certain prayers and select particular designs, dyes, prayers, and symbols appropriate for each recipient.

b.
Patterns for Decorating Eggs, before June 1896
southern USSR
colored ink on paper
5 × 3¼ each (12.7 × 8.3)
NMAH 174746

c.
Two Decorated Easter Eggs (*pysanky*), 20th century
Ukraine, USSR, or Minneapolis, Minnesota
eggs, dyes, beeswax
each: 1⅞ × 2¾ × 1⅞ (4.8 × 7 × 4.8)
NMAH 379041, 379042; Gift of Mr. J. Pastushenko

d.
Decorated Easter Eggs (*kraslices*), 20th century
Czechoslovakia
eggs, dye
1⅞ × 2¾ × 1⅞ (4.8 × 7 × 4.8)
NMAH 256870
Illustrated in color, p. 37

Designs and colors of the eggs have symbolic meanings. Women choose an appropriate meaning for each person to receive an egg. For example, they present children with light, colorful eggs in floral motifs. Teenagers receive eggs decorated with white, symbolizing the blank page of their future. Married couples often receive eggs decorated with forty triangles, which represent power in all facets of their lives. Wishing the elderly passage to heaven, they give them black eggs with designs of ladders and gates symbolic of their upward journey after death.

219.
AMHARIC RELIGIOUS OBJECTS.
Churches of the Coptic faith among the Amhara of Ethiopia, like churches elsewhere, serve as local religious and social centers for townspeople and rural dwellers

in their areas. On feast days, when the laity gather in a sacred procession led by clergy—crosses held aloft, censers wafting incense, voices lifted in song—the church brings out its liturgical treasures for believers to cherish.

a.
Ornate Openwork Metal Cross, ca. 1900–1950
Amhara people; Ethiopia
brass
17¼ × 11⁹⁄₁₆ × 1½ (43.8 × 29.3 × 3.8)
AfA 72-10-2

During holy-day processions, priests of the Amharic church carry these ornate crosses, which are held aloft on long shafts. When the religious throng reaches its destination—usually a shrine or sacred pool or stream—the faithful bathe and lay the ark of the church to rest overnight. The ark is a sacred box containing scriptures or a holy slab of wood.

Priests also wield the crosses in blessing the congregation, the baptismal water, and the four corners of the church.

b.
Censer, ca. 1900–1950
Amhara people; Ethiopia
iron (probably tinned)
33½ × 7 (86.3 × 17.8)
NMNH 417053; Gift of Mrs. Betty C. Villemerette

The long association of the Horn of Africa with Christianity and incense—frankincense and myrrh—finds material expression in the censers of the Ethiopian Church. A priest or acolyte holds the censer by the handle at the juncture of the chains and swings it back and forth to waft the smoke of burning incense through the air. The censer is used within the church and, being portable, is taken outside as well, especially during holy-day processions.

c.
Two Sistrums, ca. 1900–1950
Amhara people; Ethiopia
brass, tinned iron, wood
largest: 9⅛ × 3¼ × 2⅛ (23.2 × 8.2 × 5.4)
NMNH 417048; Gift of Mrs. Betty C. Villemerette

Priests and acolytes give rhythmic accompaniment to songs and dances with sistrums like these in church services and holy-day processions. Often the metal disks are jingled to the beat of a large, single-headed drum.

220.
HANUKKAH LAMPS. The hannukah lamp is lighted on each of the eight nights of the Jewish festival of Hanukkah. The festival celebrates the military victory in 165 B.C. of Jews led by Judah the Maccabaeus over the Syrian Greeks, who had invaded and defiled the Holy Temple. After their victory the Jews cleaned and rededicated their temple. During part of these rites a miracle occurred: oil for the temple lamp, which was apparently enough to burn only for one day, lasted for eight. This is the traditional explanation for the origin of the nine-light hanukkah lamp—eight for the days of the miracle plus one that acts as "caretaker." Some scholars have seen in the celebration an older seasonal festival of the winter solstice imbued at a later date with historical significance.

The lamps themselves reflect a wide range of aesthetic styles because of the many different societies in which Jewish people live and, perhaps, because the festive quality of the celebration encourages artistic elaboration.

a.
Hanukkah Lamp (*hanukkiyah*), 19th century
Iraq
brass (glass cups missing)
10⅞ × 18 (27.6 × 45.7)
NMAH 351246

This nineteenth-century festive lamp incorporates design motifs from Middle Eastern and Islamic iconography. The overall architectural form is that of a domed building resting on four pillars. The crescent moons and stars are appar-

220 c

ently drawn from Islamic symbolism, and the hand has been a popular amulet in the Middle East for
centuries. The inscription, "Like
the seven cows of Joseph," a reference to Genesis 49:22, a verse
often used as a protection against
the Evil Eye.

b.
Hanukkah Lamp (*hanukkiyah*),
17th century
Florence, Italy
brass
8½ × 8½ (21.6 × 21.6)
NMAH 168312

The arched-gate motif in this seventeenth-century lamp is stylisti-
cally derived from the Italian Ren-
aissance, but symbolically it most
likely refers to an archway of the
Holy Temple.

c.
Lamp (*hanukkiyah*), 19th century
The Netherlands
sheet brass
10½ × 4 (26.7 × 10.2)
NMAH 377034

The hearts and roundels of this
nineteenth-century Dutch-Jewish
lamp are evidence of the vitality of
a folk culture that incorporated European motifs into a Levantine religion.

Celebrations of Increase

Many societies do not concur with the Western world view that draws watertight oppositions between humankind and nature; religion and economics; the moral order of humanity and the natural order of animals, plants, and inanimate things. In the view of these societies, humans, animals, plants, rocks, and stars are all subject to the same universe of forces, so that what influences one of these groups echoes among the others. A well-ordered ritual directed with good intent by human beings to God, the gods, or the ancestors is thus believed to bring about an abundant harvest or a plentiful supply of edible animals. Conversely, such good yields are a sign that the social body is pious and healthy. Celebrations of increase both solemnize and rejoice over the evident fact that heaven and earth, nature and society, gods and humans, the living and the dead are at least temporarily in perfect balance. Robert Browning's "God's in his heaven— / All's right with the world!" resonates with the original meaning of "economics," a word derived from the Greek *oíkos*, meaning "house" or "home." When each thing is in its home, its proper place, the economic yield is good.

221.
Christening Bottle and Bag, 1940
USA
glass, wood, crocheted bag
16¾ × 4¾ × 4⅝ (42.5 × 12.1 ×
11.8)
NASM 2780, 1973-0603

This crocheted bottle and bag were used by Mrs. H. Sayre Wheeler to christen the U.S.S. *Curtis* on April 20, 1940, in Camden, New Jersey. Celebrating the launching of a ship is a ceremonial practice at least as old as the Babylonian account of 2100 B.C. of a mariner who, like the Biblical Noah, launched his boat on the rising waters of a great flood. Although clearly religious in origin and symbolism, official ship launchings in the United States have always been civic and secular affairs.

A controversy exists as to whether wine or water is the proper medium for christening. Water and wine originally served, respectively, as a libation to supernatural powers and as a purification from evil. The choice between wine and water came to have symbolic associations with the opposition between the use of alcohol and temperance, and the medium of water was symbolically expanded by christening vessels with a mixture of water from various oceans to signify auspicious worldwide navigation.

222.
HOG BUTCHERING. Along with corn, pork was a mainstay of the American diet through the nineteenth and into the twentieth century. Farmers fattened their hogs for butchering in autumn or winter, for meat spoiled less during colder weather. Hog killing often coincided with Thanksgiving or Christmas so that holiday tables could be enriched with fresh meat.

Although paid labor was usually available, farmers often turned to neighbors and relatives to kill hogs and process pork. Throughout the Piedmont area of North Carolina, for example, a family slaughtering nine to ten hogs could expect to assemble a sturdy volunteer labor force from the community. Despite the hard work, all found time to converse, laugh, and share a noontime meal of fresh pork mixed with greens. Later in the evening, helpers received fresh pork—liver, sausage, chitterlings, or spareribs—to take home as a gesture of thanks.

At hog-butchering time neighboring farmers expected to reciprocate services. Those excluded wanted to know why. By assisting each other with hog butchering as part of the annual cycle of agricultural activities, many farmers in rural America transform a burdensome chore into an event that pleasantly bonds community ties.

The actual process of hog butchering took a whole day, beginning in the morning when several specially skilled men carried out the butchering. Once killed and drained of blood, the hog was scalded. Workers then used scrapers to remove bristles and the outer layer of skin.

Next, as shown in the painting by Illinois-born artist Jennie Cell, the carcasses were hoisted on poles and the meat divided. Nearly every part of the animal was used—even the tail was prized by children and others for playing practical jokes.

The men then either pickled or cured the cuts of meat. Farmers prided themselves in the taste of their cured pork, devising special combinations of ingredients to impart unique flavor. Meanwhile, women rendered lard, cooked entrails that could not be preserved for later use, and made sausage.

Throughout the United States beliefs about hogs affected both breeding and butchering. An example of hog lore from the Pennsylvania-German region cautioned farmers to slaughter hogs during the waxing of the moon to prevent the meat from shrinking and spoiling.

a.
Jennie Cell (born 1904)
Butchering Day, ca. 1960s
oil on fiberboard
16⅛ × 26½ (40.8 × 67.3)
NMAA 1972.55.1; Gift of Mr. and Mrs. James Mundis

This painting shows the meat being cut from the carcasses of the freshly slaughtered hogs, which have been hoisted onto poles.

b.
Hog Scraper, ca. 1902
USA
wood, metal, wire
6½ × 4 (16.5 × 10.2)
NMAH 79687Z62; Gift of William E. Salter

The scraper seen here, dating from about 1902, cleaned the hogs of P. S. Bixler and his father in Hydro, Oklahoma. Scrapers also took other forms, including blades, hoes, and bull hoofs.

c.
Sausage Stuffer, early 19th century
USA
wood, iron screw, iron hinges
10¾ × 28½ × 8¼ (27.3 × 72.4 × 20.9)
NMAH 57A23; Gift of Tel-Pak, Inc., Chicago, Illinois

One of the women's chores involved making sausage from scraps, with the hog's small intestines used for casings. Machines similar to the one shown here were used to stuff the casings.

223.
BEES. Early Americans struggled to survive on frontier homesteads, often facing scarce resources and a harsh environment. Neighbors worked together to complete large, time-consuming tasks, sharing with one another the strength of their backs and their good will. These collective efforts ("bees") on behalf of individual families combined work with fun and feasting. Often they ended with music and dancing. Bees broke the loneliness of rural life and helped to create a sense of cohesive community for scattered, isolated families. Sometimes they served as political and civic functions, and they always provided a time for people to exchange opinions.

So important were bees in the definition of community that J. G. M. Ramsey, chronicler of Tennessee in the 1850s, wrote:

. . . a failure to ask a neighbor to a raising, a chopping frolic or his family to a quilting bee was considered a high indignity . . . required to be explained or atoned for at the next muster or county court. Each settler was not only willing but desirous to contribute

222 a

his share to the general comfort and public improvement, and felt aggrieved and insulted if the opportunity to do so were withheld.

a.
Linton Park (1826–1906)
The Flax Scutching Bee, 1885
Western Pennsylvania
oil on bed ticking
31¼ × 50¼ (79.3 × 127.7)
NGA 1227; Gift of Colonel and Mrs. Edgar W. Garbisch
Illustrated in color, p. 38

In addition to being an artist, Linton Park was also a sawyer, logger, builder, raft maker, furniture maker, sign and carriage decorator, and inventor. He painted The Flax Scutching Bee in 1885, some time later than the depicted scene, which dates from the 1850s to judge from the dress of the subjects.

Considered a masterpiece of American folk art, The Flax Scutching Bee documents the particular technology of flax preparation and also captures the social atmosphere of a bee. Park usually painted from observation or, as in this case, from memory of actual events. The painting creates two distinct moods as the viewer's eye follows the action from revelry on the left to sedateness on the right.

b.
Flax Hetchel (hatchel), ca. 1850–1900
Maryville, Missouri
wood, iron nails
5½ × 18¾ × 5 (14 × 47.6 × 12.7)
NMAH 65A17; Gift of Dr. Frank Horsfall

c.
Flax Brake ("crackle"), ca. 1850–1900
USA
wood, metal
34½ × 53¼ × 5 (87.1 × 135.3 × 12.7)
NMAH 66A62; Gift of Museum of Science and Industry, Chicago, Illinois

The process of turning flax to linen took sixteen months, but the tedious procedures were well worth the effort. Since biblical times linen has been one of the most durable fabrics woven, often lasting for generations—even centuries—whereas cotton and wool disintegrates much sooner. With the advent of industrialization, the production of homespun linen virtually disappeared in the United States.

Displayed here along with *The Flax Scutching Bee* are two tools—a hetchel (or hatchel) and a brake (or "crackle"). Both date approximately from the time Park painted *The Flax Scutching Bee*—the second half of the nineteenth century. Other tools, such as scutchers (or swinglers), used with upright boards, appear only in the painting.

During the first procedure, braking, flax brakes were used to beat the woody centers out of each stalk. A brake in the lower left corner of the painting is used by a worker less formally dressed than the other men in their hats, high collars, and three-piece suits.

After braking came swingling, during which the men and women scraped away coarse plant fibers from the stalk with scutchers. A maid who lost hold of her scutcher faced kisses all around to add to the hilarity. While most of the people in the painting apply their scutchers to their task, two women on the left use theirs to punctuate their gossip.

The next task was that of carding the fibers with large nail combs or hetchels. No one is shown carding in the painting. Once the linen fibers had been patiently combed to produce the longest filaments possible, they were ready for spinning, bleaching, washing, and weaving into elegant finished cloth.

224.
Robe of Queen of Cherry Blossom Festival, before 1950
Angie, New York
satin, silver, glittering cloth, sequins, netting, pearls
120 × 120 (304.8 × 304.8)
NMAH 310738.01; Gift of the Washington Convention and Visitors Association
Illustrated in color, p. 38

Queens of the Cherry Blossom Festival wore this robe from the 1950s to the seventies. Commissioned from a New York costume designer for $750, the glittering creation was presented in the early 1950s by Mrs. Marjorie Merriweather Post to the Washington Convention and Visitors Bureau under whose auspices the festival then operated.

Today the annual Cherry Blossom Festival has evolved into the area's largest spectator event. The National Conference of State Societies (located in Washington, D.C.) sponsors its famed beauty pageant ball and ceremonies dedicated to friendship between Japan and the United States. The Downtown Junior Chamber of Commerce of the District of Columbia sponsors the parade.

More than a local celebration, the Cherry Blossom Festival also holds national significance. Many Americans make a special visit to Washington at the time of the festival to view the parade, attend the ball, and—if nature cooperates—enjoy the delicate cherry blossoms. Participants in both the parade and the beauty pageant come from across the United States. The National Conference of State Societies ensures that a princess represents every state and territory for the festival's beauty pageant, the queen of which has always been chosen by lottery. The week before the crowning, princesses and their close associates are befittingly entertained by the nation's capital with a tour of the White House, a Congressional reception, and a tea at the Japanese Embassy.

The underlying friendship between the United States and Japan encouraged the inception of the Cherry Blossom Festival. Prompted by a desire to beautify the nation's capital, the wife of President William Howard Taft, with numerous American and Japanese supporters, encouraged the mayor of Tokyo, Yukio Ozaki, to donate 3,000 cherry trees to Washington, D.C., as a gesture of goodwill. On March 27, 1912, Mrs. Taft and the wife of the Japanese ambassador planted the first two trees on the northern bank of the Tidal Basin.

In 1934 the District of Columbia Commissioners sponsored a three-day celebration in honor of the cherry trees. This event served as a forerunner to the first Cherry Blossom Festival, which took place the following year with the support of several other civic groups. The pageant performed at the coronation of the first Cherry Blossom Queen in 1949 was a mythical representation of the festival's origins. An article in the *Washington Post* issue of April 3, 1949, describes how the pageant traced the journey of the first cherry tree seedling from its Japanese birth, "attended by the High Priests, Gift Bearers, Dancing Girls, Musicians, and the Goddess of the Sun and Earth," to its ultimate welcome by "Uncle Sam." In the final act ballet dancers mimed the manner in which the seedling was "nurtured by Love," "challenged by the Elements," and "encouraged by Faith" until, at last, it "blossomed into Beauty."

Today the festival opens with the lighting of the Friendship Flame in a three-hundred-year-old lantern presented in 1954 by the Japanese ambassador Sadao Iguchi. This lantern from the Kan'euji Temple in Tokyo commemorates the one-hundredth anniversary of the first treaty between the United States and Japan, signed by Commodore Matthew Perry in 1854.

Japan has made other gifts to the city of Washington in association with the Cherry Blossom Festival. In 1957 the Mikimoto Pearl Crown, fashioned for Japan's Imperial Household and valued at $100,000, was donated for the Festival Queen to wear with her robe. In 1958 the mayor of Yokohama gave the District a stone pagoda to commemorate the 1854 Yokohama Treaty. In 1965 the Japanese government sent 3,800 more cherry trees to replace those dying of old age.

The annual Cherry Blossom Festival affects many aspects of life in Washington, D.C. Tourism and commerce thrive, while valued friendship between Japan and the United States receives dignified ceremonial recognition.

226 b

225.

Log Cabin Quilt; "Barn Raising" Pattern, ca. 1870
Lewisburg, Pennsylvania
silk top, cotton lining
68 × 68 (172.7 × 172.7)
NMAH T16909; Gift of Mrs. Edwin A. Schoen

This quilt dates from approximately 1870. Its "Barn Raising" pattern was a popular one for quilting bees, although, because the fabric is silk, this example was probably quilted by a single person. Bees were very popular before factory-made quilts became readily available at the turn of the century.

We can imagine a bee as it might have been held, since writings from colonial times to the twentieth century have vividly described this celebration of communal needlework. To make a quilt a family first chose a pattern, such as the one seen here. During spare moments they cut and pieced carefully hoarded and traded scraps (5,500 in this example) before they sent invitations to neighbors for the bee. On the day of the bee they sewed together the pieced top, lining, and back. The bee might have taken place winter or summer, indoors or out, at the home of the quilt owner or, if needed, in a larger building. The bee could have lasted more than one day if several quilts were stitched.

Women and children gathered early. The quilt, mounted on a frame, took form under the nimblest fingers. Less skillful sewers cooked to feed the party. In the evening men often came to dine. Then festivities—usually with music and dancing—were held. During the entertainment suitors could woo, while neighbors discussed politics and public affairs. At bees women often announced wedding engagements or the arrival of newcomers in town. They chatted, learned about child care and home arts, and aired concerns about community matters.

Sometimes quilts were sewn at bees to commemorate important milestones in life. Traditionally a young woman's thirteenth quilt marked her wedding engagement and was stitched with hearts and other symbols of love. A young man received a "freedom quilt" when he turned twenty-one or finished his apprenticeship. An "album quilt" such as the Benoni Pearce quilt in the "Courtship and Marriage" component of the Rites of Passage Gallery, discussed in number 140, provided a keepsake for a departing friend or community leader.

The names given to quilt patterns, such as "Barn Raising," often reflect the important preoccupations of early Americans. Some quilts, however, reflect the festive side of bees and social life, taking pattern names from square-dance calls such as "Swing in the Center" and "Hands All Around." Whatever their pattern name, quilts in their use provided much needed warmth in poorly heated homes and in their making provided a cheerful break from loneliness.

226.

STATE FAIRS. An enterprising Yankee named Elkanah Watson, equipped with two Merino sheep, is said to have mounted in 1807 the first American agricultural fair. Demonstrating methods of improved wool production, Watson went on in later years to organize larger shows in Massachusetts. His fairs included not only information on farm technology but also parades, speeches, entertainment, and prizes.

These annual events enabled early Americans (many of them illiterate) to learn new farm techniques and at the same time to enjoy a festive respite from rural isolation. By the mid-1800s agricultural associations such as the Iowa State Agricultural Society had been constituted to promote "Agriculture, Horticulture, Manufactures, Mechanics and Household Arts"—primarily through exhibition at fairs.

Today state and county fairs held in late summer and fall celebrate harvest and agricultural increase. Onlookers gather to learn from exhibits and to see the judging of livestock, produce, cooking, and handiwork. Fairs have become commercial, civic, and carnivalesque ventures as well. They draw crowds as much for beauty pageants, contests, races, stunts, food, souvenirs, games, midways, and musical shows as for education.

a.

Rochester Fair Poster, 1905
New York
lithograph
22 × 15 1/16 (55.8 × 38.3)
NMAH CBA7294; Collection of Business Americana

This saucy, eye-catching poster dating from 1905 effectively advertises an upstate New York fair at a time when printed signs did the work of today's electronic media.

Fairs have long had a tradition of celebrating feminine beauty. As Bill Riley, master of ceremony for the beauty pageant, said of the Iowa State Fair, "It's still about pumpkins, pigs, and pretty girls."

b.

Fifteen Fruit Jars, ca. 1875–1930
various manufacturers
glass, wire, zinc, cast iron, rubber, various metals
largest: 7 3/4 × 4 (19.7 × 10.2)
NMAH 76-FT-1.139, 1.406, 1.407, 1.409, 1.411, 1.412, 1.416, 1.419, 1.422, 1.429, 1.430, 1.1297, 1.1407, 1.1464, 1.1466; Gift of Mary Eloise Green
Various manufacturers include:
Ball Brothers, Muncie, Indiana
Consumers Glass Company, Toronto, Ontario, Canada
Foster Forbes Glass Company, Marion, Indiana
Hazel Atlas Glass Company, Wheeling, West Virginia
Illinois Glass Company, Alton, Illinois
Pine Glass Company, Okmulgee, Oklahoma
probably the Dominion Glass Company, Montreal, Quebec, Canada
probably the Fairmount Glass Company, Indianapolis, Indiana
Schram Glass Manufacturing Company, Saint Louis, Missouri
Sun Fruit Jar Company, New York, New York

These fruit jars, dating from the last quarter of the nineteenth century to the first three decades of the twentieth, are exhibited as if they were displayed at a state or county fair.

Home (and factory) canning in the United States began in the early decades of the nineteenth century. At this time the prize-winning, pioneering book on canning by Frenchman François Ap-

pert became available in translation as *The Art of Preserving All Substances.* Americans Robert Arthur, John Landis Mason, and Frank C. Ball, among others, invented improvements to jars and seals.

Nearly two hundred glass factories in the United States and Canada have made fruit jars in different kinds of glass and varied closures, ranging from clumsy to ingenious. Two popular methods shown here are lightning closures with wires and screw-type closures with zinc bands.

Judges of home-canned foods at fairs examine both the home-grown fruits and vegetables and the care with which they have been preserved. Experts rank jars for clean, well-sealed, uniform appearance and for color, texture, correct liquid content, flavor, and accurate labeling.

Fair prizes—whether for food or livestock—celebrate excellence in the arts and sciences of the rural economy.

227.
BROOKLYN BRIDGE OPENING.
After fourteen years of construction, the Brooklyn Bridge was completed in the spring of 1883 under the supervision of Colonel Washington A. Roebling (1837–1926), chief engineer. The reclusive Roebling had inherited the project at the death of his father, John A. Roebling. Although loyally supported by his wife and assistants, Colonel Roebling had been forced to endure occupationally related ill health, political opposition, slander, and charges of corruption in the fulfillment of the task. Roebling knew the project was a major accomplishment in civil engineering, but he desired no special opening ceremonies for this extraordinary suspension bridge. Modern technology has not moved significantly beyond the meticulous design born of Roebling's efforts and vision.

A source of inspiration even before its completion, the Brooklyn Bridge became a national symbol of progress and growth in an era that venerated industry, the wonders of science, and the triumph of man over nature. An invocation from Hart Crane's poem *The Bridge* suggests something of its impact on

228

the American imagination. Crane's imagery invokes a bridge that spans not only the entire American continent but the gap between man and God as well:

O Sleepless as the river under thee,
Vaulting the sea, the prairies'
dreaming sod,
Unto us lowliest sometime sweep,
descend
And of the curveship lend a myth
to God.

In spite of Roebling's preference, an official holiday was declared in Brooklyn to commemorate the opening of the bridge. The national significance of the event was underscored by the participation of President Chester Arthur. Together with New York's Governor Grover Cleveland, the mayors of the city's several boroughs, and numerous other dignitaries, President Arthur marched the span from Manhattan to Brooklyn, attended parades and reviews, and listened to eloquent speeches testifying to the progressive evolution of the human race. Rooftops were mobbed; the East River was crowded with boats; and streets were gaily adorned with flowers, lights, and banners. At nightfall thousands watched an elaborate display of fireworks, maintaining their vigil until the stroke of midnight, when the bridge was finally opened to public traffic.

Many years later, when astronauts first landed on the moon, an old woman told a reporter that excitement over the opening of the Brooklyn Bridge had far exceeded modern enthusiasm over that history-making voyage into space.

a.
Invitation, 1883
Tiffany and Company, New York, New York
ink on paper
6½ × 9 (16.5 × 22.9)
NMAH 1978.0803.10

Trustees of the Brooklyn Bridge issued about six thousand invitations printed by Tiffany, similar to this example, to attend speeches and ceremonies inside the Brooklyn terminal on "People's Day," May 24, 1883.

229

b.
Admission Ticket, 1883
Tiffany and Company, New York,
New York
ink on paper
2¾ × 6½ (7 × 16.5)
NMAH 1978.0803.11

Blue tickets like this one admitted
approximately seven thousand people to the festivities held on the
bridge itself the day it opened.

c.
Invitation, 1883
New York, New York
ink on paper
8 × 5 (20.3 × 12.7)
NMAH 1978.0803.12

This is one of the one thousand invitations issued by Emily Roebling,
wife of Chief Engineer Washington
Roebling, to festivities held at the
Roeblings' home after public fan-
fare terminated. This invitation
went to General M. C. Meigs.

Mrs. Roebling decked the house
with banks of flowers and drapes of
bunting. To emphasize her husband's honor, she decorated his
bust and one of his father with
flowers and laurels. The guests she
invited, among whom were the
president of the United States and
other officials, enjoyed refresh-
ments served under a grand mar-
quee in the garden while a band
played from the balcony above.

d.
Program, 1883
New York, New York
ink on paper
8 × 5⅝ (20.3 × 14.3)
NMAH 1978.0803.13

A *Programme of Exercises and Arrangements* testifies to the public
fervor and inspired speeches that
celebrated this remarkable engineering feat nearly one hundred
years ago.

228.
Figure of Woman and Child (*ere
oko*), ca. 1900–1950
Yoruba people; Nigeria
wood, pigments
25½ × 9¾ × 9¾ (64.7 × 24.8 ×
24.8)
AfA 68-13-1

Members of Yoruba religious orga-
nizations or cults place images
such as these in village shrines.

The images generally represent
priests and priestesses, mothers
with children, women carrying
bowls, and mounted warriors—
mortal people associated with the
organization or cult rather than
gods or goddesses. On designated
occasions members repaint and
adorn their images and carry them
to a special place where they feast
among them and sing their praises.
On this image, the oblong mark on
the brow of the woman is said to
be the sign of Oka, a deity who
makes farms fertile and women fe-
cund.

229.
Antelope Figure (*chi wara kung*),
ca. 1900
Bamana people; Mali
wood
44¼ × 18¼ × 3⅞ (122.4 × 46.3
× 9.8)
AfA 73-7-56

Bamana men in their twenties and
early thirties work together as a
group to clear and cultivate large
sorghum and millet fields. Their
cooperative mode of work has religious significance, for the group is
under the protection of the *chi
wara,* or "beast of work." This
spirit is represented by carved antelope figures such as this one. The
figures are attached to caps worn
by members of the working group.
Disguised from head to foot in costumes made of long black fibers,
capped men participate in a dance
that suggests the characteristic
movements of antelopes. This ceremonial dance exhorts the group of
workers to greater achievements.

230.
ABELAM HARVEST FESTIVAL.
Abelam religion is closely inter-
locked with economic life, and
only men who have passed through
an initiation can cultivate the large
yam. Beyond being a source of
nourishment, yams have great spiritual significance. They, like men,
possess a soul or spirit, and their
cultivation requires practicing special magic, observing strict taboos,
and following a selfless discipline.
In yam cultivation, rewards are not
merely economic; growing large
yams is a way to attain social recognition among one's peers.

a.
Yam Mask, ca. 1968
Abelam people; East Sepik River
province, Papua New Guinea
vegetable fiber, pigment, feathers
10¾ × 10¾ × 5 (27.3 × 27.3 ×
12.7)
NMNH 410319; Gift of Mrs. Gordon Dibble
Illustrated in color, p. 39

For the harvest festival Abelam
men decorate yams with masks,
rings, shells, and plumes. They parade the decorated yams through
the village and arrange them in
rows in the plaza at the same time
that the young initiated men dance
with their feathered headdresses.
The yams are considered to be
"like men" because they possess a
spirit that dwells both in men and
in yams. In acknowledging the spiritual identity of their yams by
treating them as men, the Abelam
encourage the growth of this staple
crop.

b.
Two Male Sculptures, before 1964
Abelam people; East Sepik River
province, Papua New Guinea
wood, pigment
largest: 71 × 14⅛ × 11½ (180.2 ×
35.8 × 29.2)
NMNH 403088, 403089

These two carved male figures are
like those that stand inside the
tamberan house, the center of Abelam social and religious life. In the
large, cleared central plaza domi-
nated by this house, Abelam villagers display their yams, exchange
pigs, and chant their clan songs. Inside the house are ritual objects endowed with supernatural power.
Carved figures such as these are associated with clan ancestors and
powers of fertility for yams.

c.
Basketry Mask (Baba-Tagwa), ca.
1964
Abelam people; East Sepik River
province, Papua New Guinea
vegetable fiber
14 × 10⅛ × 11 (35.5 × 25.7 ×
27.9)
NMNH 403086; Gift of Morton
May

A person wearing this mask, which
represents the spirit Baba-Tagwa,
appears in Abelam villages before

the planting season to impose taboos on coconuts. The same masked figure makes offerings to ancestral spirits on behalf of villagers for good crops in the year to come.

231.
CANELA MASKING FESTIVAL.
To sport a mask during the Mummers' or Masking Festival is to make merry with song, dance, and games and with antics by performers begging for food and love. A lively Canela myth tells us that the billowing masks used in the festival represent enormous foul-smelling water monsters. The monsters taught an old Canela man who visited their village the lore and behavior for the festival.

a.

Body Mask and Horns (*cu'krïtre-hô; cu'krïtre yũpär*), before 1966
Ramkokamekra-Canela Indians;
Sardinha village, Maranhão, Brazil
burití-palm fronds, twine, wood, pigment
69 × 52 × 6 (175.2 × 132.1 × 15.2)
NMNH 404909, 404910 a, b
See colorplate, p. 40

Of the eight mask designs produced, the mask shown here has no Canela name although non-Indian Brazilians call it the Espora ("spur"). The Spur gallops madly when called to perform, like the mythological Spur monster that rescued a baby of its kind from human kidnappers. Maskers spend much time begging for food, for begging is more excessive during this festival than is normally tolerated. While begging, maskers jerk or raise the vertical "face" slits and speak a humming, grunting language. Through their disguise as blameless beasts the men hide all vestiges of shame for their outrageous begging. In their humorous excesses they dramatize the society's economic model—generosity in all personal attributes, in fun and love—behavior which keeps the child "monster" alive in each Canela adult and also redistributes irregularly available food into every stomach.

230 b (one male sculpture)

b.
Food-Spearing Stick (*cu'krïtre yo 'catswer-tsa*), before 1966
Ramkokamekra-Canela Indians;
Sardinha village, Maranhão, Brazil
wood
28¾ × ½ × ½ (73 × 1.3 × 1.3)
NMNH 404914

Maskers spear their food with a pointed stick when taking what they have begged. Formerly the taboo on touching food with bare hands was very strict; today they use the stick less and less.

232.
Omer Tablet, 19th century
probably Philadelphia, Pennsylvania
ink on paper, gilded wooden frame
32 × 26½ (81.3 × 67.3)
NMAH 154404

The word omer, literally "barley," refers to the forty-nine-day interval between the Jewish festivals of Passover and Shabuoth, the Feast of Weeks. In ancient Judaism, the omer was associated with the first reaping of the grain harvest and offering at the Temple in Jerusalem. The interval of forty-nine days is counted daily in the synagogue on a seven-day week calendric device.

This omer tablet comes from a nineteenth-century American Jewish congregation, probably a Sephardic synagogue in Philadelphia. The Hebrew inscription reads: "Blessed art Thou, O Lord our God, King of the Universe, who has sanctified us with his commandments and commanded us to count the Omer"; and "May the Lord restore the worship of the Temple speedily in our days" (*Ethics of the Fathers*, 5: 23).

233.
HOPI WOMEN'S CEREMONIES.
Hopi women's ceremonies are in a sense harvest festivals, although they are not explicitly identified as such by the Hopis themselves. Taking place in the period when the main crop of corn ripens, the festivals employ a kaleidoscope of symbols referring to aspects of rain, corn, and human fertility. This season of the year, mid-September through October, is also the traditional time for Hopi weddings.

a.
Embroidered Blanket, ca. 1880–93
Hopi Indians; Arizona
cotton, wool yarn
50 × 66 × ⅜ (127 × 167.6 × 0.9)
NMNH 166790 b

Although used in Hopi women's ceremonies, the embroidered wedding blanket was not restricted to these occasions nor to use solely by women. It was also worn by men at kachina dances and other religious events.

A small white blanket was an essential element of a Hopi woman's wedding trousseau. During the first year of her marriage, a woman might embroider the blanket in designs with symbolic significance. In this example the layered triangles represent clouds, the three crosses are probably blossoms, and the winged figures are butterflies.

b.
Kachina Sash, ca. 1870–85
Hopi Indians; Oraibi (Third Mesa), Arizona
wool, red flannel, yarn
11½ × 92 × ¼ (29.2 × 233.7 × 0.6)
NMNH 128945

This sash is worn by most kachina dancers and priests and by participants in several other Hopi ceremonies. Usually it is worn like a belt with the two brocaded panels at the right side. Formerly the sashes were made of wool, but contemporary Hopi make them out of cotton.

The designs of the brocaded panels do not vary much from the Hopi village on the First Mesa to the village on the Second Mesa, but the meaning that people read into the patterns does vary. First Mesa Hopi see in a brocaded panel the mask of the Broad Face Kachina, a spirit that protects and punishes. Each panel holds two faces, one looking up, one looking down. A white zigzag at the bottom is teeth; two diamonds in the green field are eyes; white lines, both straight and hooked, are the face markings of a warrior god. For Second Mesa Hopi, the design of the brocaded panel represents summer fertility. White zigzags are lightning; green bands are fertile areas; red and white diamonds are flowers, plants, and up-

turned soil; parallel white lines on black represent falling rain; hooked white lines are paths of water in the fields or the pathways of the kachina spirits themselves. In both Hopi areas the embroidered red band between the white and brocade is called the signature line and varies with each sash weaver. The red strip of cloth sewn above the fringe is an owner's identification mark.

c.
Two Prayer Slabs, ca. 1870–80
Hopi Indians; Arizona
wood, feathers, paint, string
largest: 22 × 7 × ½ (55.8 × 17.8 × 1.3)
NMNH 41926

The *paho,* or prayer stick, is the Hopi device for catching the attention of spirits. To be effective it must be made and used with a sincere heart. Women make prayer sticks during the eight days of secret ceremonies before public dances held in connection with the Marau Society.

Women who are to be initiated into the society hold a stick in each hand and gently wave them. The feathers attached to the stick are "breath feathers" that carry the essence of prayer to the spirits. The design on the bottom represents a corncob, one of the most important Hopi food crops. The being represented is probably the fertility deity.

231 a

d.
Headdress, ca. 1860–83
Hopi Indians; Arizona
wood, feathers, hide, yarn, sinew,
cornhusk, paint
20¾ × 28 × 1 (52.7 × 71.1 × 2.5)
NMNH 69114

Like so much Hopi art, this dance headdress is a visual prayer for rain or fertility. The stepped pyramids represent rain clouds. The black rod across the forehead symbolizes a corncob, the feathers symbolize mist, and the round balls and hemispheres are corn and squash blossoms.

e.
Two Yarn Anklets, ca. 1880–85
Hopi Indians; Oraibi (Third Mesa),
Arizona
muslin cloth, yarn, buckskin strips,
hide thongs
largest: 4¼ × 11¼ × ⅔ (10.8 ×
28.5 × 1.7)
NMNH 128940
Illustrated in color, p. 40

In many Hopi and Zuni dances, anklets are frequently worn either over the moccasins or on the bare ankle of men or women. The headdress for the Buffalo Dance uses an anklet as a brow band.

Anklet decoration was traditionally worked in natural white and dyed-black porcupine quills. The anklets shown here are later examples in which yarns have been used for the designs.

f.
Kachina Doll, ca. 1900–1940
Hopi Indians; Arizona
cottonwood coated with clay,
feathers, yarn, paint, string
23 × 26 × 9 (58.4 × 67.6 × 22.9)
NMNH 418907 a
Illustrated in color, p. 41

The Hopi recognize more than 260 different kachina figures. Kachinas themselves are spirits of ancestors. They are sometimes represented by dolls, such as this one, or by masked dancers who perform at ceremonies petitioning rain and fertility. Kachina dolls are used in several ways by the Hopi. Most frequently, they are given to women, particularly girls nearing marriageable age. They are then hung on the walls from the rafters of the home. Since the early twentieth century,

Hopi men have made dolls commercially. Forms have become larger and more naturalistic than those of the older figures, which are usually smaller and without arms and legs. This figure is larger than most and was definitely made for sale.

g.
Basket Tray, ca. 1895–1930
Hopi Indians; Second Mesa, Arizona
yucca, galleta grass (?), dyes
1¼ × 11 (3.1 × 27.9)
NMNH 364629

The Hopi use basket trays such as this one for a variety of purposes, both domestic and ritual. Several of the women's dances use baskets so prominently that they are commonly called basket dances. In both Lalon and Oaqol dances performed on the last day of ceremonies, a line of women of all ages hold basket trays as they move in slow rhythm. The women then throw the baskets into the crowd as prizes for the audience. There follows a vigorous struggle for their possession.

Although coiled baskets have been made only at Second Mesa in recent years, either coiled or wicker trays may be used in all the Hopi villages. Both kinds have been widely traded among the Hopi. The design on this one is said to represent the four corners of the world, but it could also be a whirlwind design. Designs on both coiled and wicker trays often represent specific kachinas by depicting their unique attributes.

234.
Model of Dance House, ca. 1880–85
Eskimo; Nushagak, Alaska
wood, walrus ivory, nails, sinew,
gut, trade cloth, feathers, glass
beads, paint
16⅔ × 15⅓ × 15⅓ (42.4 × 38.9
× 38.9)
NMNH 76698
Illustrated in color, p. 42

Eskimo dance and music, as depicted in this walrus-ivory model, were part of winter entertainment during the ice-bound period from late December through February. The Eskimo of Nushagak celebrated hunting festivals that honored prey animals and their spirits.

This model itself was most likely made for sale to meet the rapid growth in demand for walrus-ivory carvings in the late nineteenth century. Already known for their ivory work in commercial objects such as paper cutters, salad forks, and salt spoons, the Nushagak Eskimo were the principal producers of these models. Unfortunately, little is now known about their meaning.

235.
Dance Drum, ca. 1870–85
Eskimo; Nushagak, Alaska
wood, skin membrane, string
1⅝ × 19¾ × 19¾ (4.1 × 50.2 ×
50.2)
NMNH 72505

The drum was the basic Eskimo instrument, essential for song and dance. This type—a skin stretched over a wooden hoop—was the most common. With a short heavy piece of ivory or a long slender wand, the drummer alternately struck each side of the rim, turning the drum slightly to meet each stroke. Drums came in different sizes with different tones. At times more than one drum might be used simultaneously.

236.
GAN-GUAR FESTIVAL. These figures, which together are called Gan-Guari, play an important role in the annual Gan-Guar festival, which is celebrated with great levity shortly after the spring equinox throughout India. In these rites women wish their spouses long and productive lives, thereby assuring their own welfare, while single girls wish for handsome husbands.

In their homes women set up images of Guari, wearing a full set of bridal jewelry, and her husband, Isar. The pair represents the holy couple of Shiva and Parvati, who are symbols of conjugal bliss.

During each day of the festival, women make offerings of grass, flowers, and leaves to the figures. On the final day Guari and her consort are taken, often in procession, for a ceremonial bath.

In earlier times, the Gan-Guari figures were often carried in splendid processions throughout the towns. Today this custom is less common.

233 c (one prayer slab)

a.
Female Figure (Guari), shortly before 1962
Rajasthan, India
wood, paint
38¼ × 17⅞ (97.1 × 45.4)
NMNH 399341 a
Illustrated in color, p. 42

b.
Male Figure (Isar), shortly before 1962
Rajasthan, India
wood, paint
41¾ × 16 (106 × 40.6)
NMNH 399341 b
Illustrated in color, p. 42

237.
Consolidated Fireworks Advertisement, 1892
USA
lithograph on paper
13¼ × 10¼ (33.7 × 26)
NMAH CBA9000; Collection of
Business Americana

According to this advertisement, taken from the inside front cover of the December 1892 midwinter issue of *Confectioners' Journal*, Consolidated Fireworks, Inc., planned a dazzling pyrotechnical display from the Brooklyn Bridge in commemorating the four-hundredth anniversary of the discovery of America by Christopher Columbus. As confirmation that the event took place, the *New York Times* of October 11, 1892, reported that thousands of spectators on land and water viewed brilliant Roman candles, rockets, bombs, and the glare of a fiery Niagara Falls upon a clear autumn night sky.

The discovery of combustible solid fuel in the Middle East, India, and China between A.D. 900 and 1050 led the way to the production of fireworks. In Europe the practice of using fireworks for celebrations—especially those pertaining to war victories, peace treaties, coronations, royal births, royal weddings, and religious festivals—evolved during the seventeenth, eighteenth, and nineteenth centuries.

Today fireworks figure prominently in national holidays, such as the Fourth of July and Labor Day in the United States, Bastille Day in France, and Guy Fawkes Day in England.

Celebrations of the Polity

In many preliterate (and some literate) societies it is difficult to distinguish religious from political celebrations. Chiefs may have important priestly functions and priests and shamans may play political roles, such as organizing the activities of secret societies of military associations. Many celebrations that stress political rank and reciprocity, such as the potlatch ceremony among the Northwest Coast Indians, are deeply imbued with religious ideas and values. Celebrations of succession to high rank or office are rites of passage that often involve the ritual humiliation of the candidate by priests before she or he is given increased power and authority. Here the priests represent the commonality, whose consent and witness are required to legitimize the new office holder. They also mediate between the living and the gods or ancestors, who are often identified with the spirits of deceased chiefs and priests and who stand for the moral law transmitted through rituals of installation and coronation to the new incumbent of a position of leadership.

The United States has its full share of political celebrations. One sees a fascinating point–counterpoint between our ways of celebrating political processes (such as the election of the president, which is also a celebration of the Constitution) and those of other lands. Democracy constantly celebrates individual achievements and the successes of free individuals banded together against privilege, vested interest, and autocratic rule. Monarchies, feudal systems, and despotisms celebrate permanent differences in rank and ordering both in nature and in society. They celebrate the cycle of the seasons and the repetitiveness of political and religious hierarchies. The celebratory style of the American political process responds to the ever-changing needs, interests, and aspirations of a free people.

238–241.

POTLATCH CEREMONY. The powerful and complex potlatches of Northwest Coast Indians are among the most spectacular celebratory events in North America. Involved with the maintenance and orderly transfer of power, the traditional potlatch took place at all critical junctures in the lives of a chief and his family members. These periodic and overtly self-sacrificial distributions of wealth were among the essential responsibilities of a person of rank and occurred at times requiring the change or reaffirmation of status or when the ties binding humans to each other and to the spirit world needed reemphasis. Outlawed by Canadian governmental decree for more than fifty years, the potlatch ceremony has recently been revised by all Northwest Coast tribes to mark important transitions in an individual's life and to express pride in Indian cultural identity.

The Walal was among the most important forms of Haida traditional potlatching. It celebrated the raising of a totem pole, the adoption of a child, or the construction of a new house and the consequent elevation of the owner's status to that of a household chief—a leader responsible for the welfare of several extended families. Of secondary importance was the Tsika, or mortuary potlatch, marking the death of an individual and succession of his heir. Smaller potlatches were given to welcome female puberty, to redress a public humiliation, or to ridicule an adversary.

The tribes of the Northwest Coast believed that food could be obtained only by virtue of a moral and ritual covenant between man and the spirits. The ritual display of images representing this bond, the narration of its mythic origins, the performance of related dances, and the distribution of wealth and food are essential parts of all public rituals of Northwest Coast Indians. The morally responsible person was expected to accept the burden of the past, dedicating his life and wealth to the benefit of others, in much the same way that animals sacrificed themselves for the benefit of human beings.

The philosophy of the Northwest Coast Indian emphasizes the continuing influence of the past upon the present. Ceremonial regalia almost always displays an individual or group "crest"—the image of a particular spirit whose mythic activities are partially responsible for the world in which man now lives. The identities of these totemic spirits are intertwined with those of the human beings who today reenact myths through their rituals.

In the past, a Northwest Coast chief, as representative of his extended household, became the nexus around which the various components of personal and group identity were united. From frontlet or hat downward through facial painting, jewelry, yokes and collars, robes and tunics, kilts and leggings, each piece of a chief's clothing and adornment might be decorated with distinctive crest designs. The vertical arrangement of these images thus transformed the chief into a living representation of his clan's ancestral heritage.

238.
Chief's Potlatch Costume
NMNH 20574, 380920, 88833, 88795, 89037, 89194; Collected by James G. Swan

a.
Wooden Clan Hat, ca. 1850–83
Haida Indians; Skidegate, Queen Charlotte Islands, British Columbia, Canada
cedar; copper strips and nails; red, black, and green paint; iron nails; hide strip
14 × 17½ (35.6 × 44.5)

Ceremonial headwear of the Northwest Coast Indians indicated the social and spiritual identities of the wearer. A clan hat presented the human social identity as paramount and the spiritual component as secondary; a frontlet, worn above the forehead, places human and spirit identities in balance; and a face mask presented human identity as secondary to spirit identity. The clan hat displayed here shows the chief's crest figure, Bear.

b.
Frontlet with Trailer, ca. 1850–75
Haida, or possibly Tsimshian Indians; Fort Simpson, British Columbia, Canada
wood; abalone inlay; red, black, and green paint; sea-lion whiskers; ermine skins; red and white cloth; brown felt; sinew; thread; baleen strips
51 × 13¼ × 7½ (129.5 × 33.7 × 19.1)

The frontlet shows a crest figure thought to be a raven. The crowns of frontlets were filled with eagle down, the symbol of the manifestation of spirit power in the human world. As the dancer moved and turned, the down floated out of the headpiece, filling the air with the presence of spiritual benediction.

c.
Chilkat Blanket, ca. 1890–1910
Tlingit Indians; Alaska
mountain-goat wool; cedar-bark fiber; black, yellow, and blue-green dye
55¾ × 67½ × 1½ (141.6 × 171.5 × 3.8)

The Chilkat Tlingit blanket—a ceremonial robe adopted by many other Northwest Coast tribes—expressed the idea that the chief's identity combined both human and spirit components. These blankets show, in highly stylized form, the image of a crest animal as if it were on a box and as if the four sides and lid of the box had been flattened into a single plane. A person wearing such a blanket became analogous to a treasure stored in a box. The sharing of a single soul by both crest animal and human was indicated by placing the image of the blanket's soul—a humanoid face in the center of the blanket, which represented the lid of the box—over the place in the human chest where the human soul resides. When a chief wearing a Chilkat blanket was seen from the front, he manifested his social, human self, with his imminent spirit identity shown by the image on his frontlet or crest hat. From the rear one saw only his supernatural alter ego, which had its human identity depicted as a frontlet between its ears. A chief wearing such a blanket moved and turned; he was thus continually being transformed before an onlooker's eyes.

Haida Indians pose in potlatch costumes; Klinkwan, Alaska, about 1900. Courtesy, National Anthropological Archives, Smithsonian Institution (see no. 238 d).

d.

Appliquéd Tunic, ca. 1860–83
Haida Indians; Skidegate, Queen
Charlotte Islands, British Columbia, Canada
red and blue flannel, blue satin,
white glass beads
36 × 30 (91.4 × 76.2)
Illustrated in color, p. 43

"Button blankets" and other wearable textiles made of appliquéd trade cloth present a unique synthesis of cultures. Although the materials only became available through foreign trade in the nineteenth century, their designs and use were purely native and traditional. Worn by dancers during potlatch ceremonies, appliquéd blankets, shirts, robes, and tunics always featured clan emblems. The tunic shown here has a dogfish on the front and a wolf on the back.

The preferred fabric for appliqué was Hudson's Bay Company flannel, especially red and blue. Chinese coins, brass or pearl shell buttons, and, as in this example, glass beads were all used for decoration.

e.

Speaker's Staff, ca. 1830–60
Haida Indians; Masset, Queen
Charlotte Islands, British Columbia, Canada
wood
32⅜ × 2 (82.2 × 5)

Men of position often kept speakers to make their public announcements, such as calling out recipients' names at potlatches. Professional speakers carried staffs like the one shown here, but this particular staff was used by a chief himself when distributing gifts.

In traditional Northwest Coast Indian societies, where all legitimacy came from the past, a chief stood as symbol of his house, and the carved speaker's staff he or his representative held signified his authority—analogously to the way a totem pole signified the authority of the house it stood beside. Holding such a staff indicated that the power to distribute gifts in the present derived from events that occurred in the mythic past. This particular staff, which is incomplete, shows (top to bottom) figures of Raven, Whale, Crow, Sparrowhawk, Beaver, and Mouse.

f.

Raven Rattle, ca. 1850–83
Haida Indians; Masset, Queen
Charlotte Islands, British Columbia, Canada
wood; red, black, and blue paint
6¼ × 13⅓ × 4⅜ (15.9 × 33.8 ×
11.1)

Chiefs and high-ranking members of the community used raven rattles like this to punctuate their speech and gestures in formal contexts. Most dancers of northern groups (Tlingit, Haida, Tsimshian) held their rattles upside down, with the raven's breast up, lest they come to life and fly away, as a legendary raven rattle once did.

The rattle itself is a powerful icon of spiritual transformation. Raven carries on his back a dead man toward the afterlife. The man's vital force, seen as a red bridge similar to a tongue, has been captured by Frog, a symbol of life, which is itself being captured by Kingfisher, a symbol of death. In Raven's beak is a small red object representing both the sun, which was Raven's gift to mankind, and the man's soul, which is man's reciprocal gift to the spirits. On the belly of Raven is the face of the shared soul of Raven and mankind, its beak recurved into its own mouth as symbol of the cycle of reincarnation. In its ritual use, the raven rattle reaffirmed mankind's covenant with Raven and, through its intertwined images of life, death, and rebirth, it channeled these powerful forces in a specific cycle of spiritual transformations.

239.

Copper (*tako* in Haida), ca. 1880–1920
Kwakiutl Indians; Vancouver Island and adjacent mainland, British Columbia, Canada
sheet copper, red and black paint
31½ × 26¼ × 1¾ (80 × 68.3 ×
4.5)
NMNH 360996

Copper plaques, or coppers, were one of the most treasured possessions of the Northwest Coast Indians and their exchange, sale, and sometimes destruction at potlatches was an event of the greatest significance. Through their ritual symbolism, coppers link man to the entire universe. Their shape recapitulates that of the body and

soul of a living being, symbolically associating the body of the chief, the body politic of his clan, and the bodies and souls of all of the animals that the clan has captured. The color of the copper symbolizes the red of salmon flesh on which mankind subsists and the fire by which man both cooks his food as the myths require and burns his wealth and his corpses so that they become food for the spirit beings.

Throughout the Northwest Coast, shield-shaped coppers were prestige items. For the Kwakiutl they carried special significance, appearing at every potlatch and required for every marriage. To prove his wealth, the owner of a copper sometimes broke it into pieces and threw them into the sea or a fire. A rival might destroy an equal or greater copper in a struggle for prestige. As long as its **T** ridges remained intact, a copper could be remade, and individual coppers had long histories of ownership and competitive use, proudly recited each time they were brought out. As tokens of wealth, coppers came to be valued in precise equivalents of vast numbers of Hudson's Bay Company blankets.

Northern groups, the Haida included, differed from the Kwakiutl in their treatment of coppers. They used them during status-affirming potlatches—for pole raising or house building—whereas the Kwakiutl used them during status-rivalry feasts. Among the Haida, coppers were valued at four or five or even ten slaves each.

240.

BOWLS AND BOXES. For the Northwest Coast Indians, all treasures—the food eaten, the clothing worn, the ceremonies performed, the bodies occupied—were considered to be gifts from the spirits. The display, storage, and distribution of any treasure therefore required a reaffirmation of the link between human and treasure-bestowing spirit. This reaffirmation was achieved in part by decorating the containers in which treasures were stored and distributed with crest images, which represented the close connection between everyday life and the lives of the spirits. Featured in the distribution of food and treasure, these containers symbolically embody the underlying philosophy of the potlatch ceremony.

a.
Horn Ladle, ca. 1850–80
Tlingit Indians; Alaska
mountain-sheep horn
24 × 13 × 6⅞ (61 × 33 × 17.5)
NMNH 45989

Ladles made of mountain-sheep horn were fabricated by first steaming and bending the horn on a mold and then carving the desired design. Ravens and birds of prey—symbols of death and reincarnation—are frequently depicted. The figure with the recurved beak represents the shared soul of man and spirit, intermediate between bird and human.

b.
Storage Chest, ca. 1860–83
Haida Indians; Skedans, Queen Charlotte Islands, British Columbia, Canada
cedar; black, blue, and red paint
23 × 50½ × 21¼ (58.4 × 128.2 × 54)
NMNH 89034
Illustrated in color, p. 43

Large chests such as this one were used to store family valuables, which might include masks, coppers, costumes, and ceremonial paraphernalia. Chests also served as ceremonial furniture and sometimes even as coffins. Because the corners of this particular chest are skillfully dovetailed in the Chinese manner, which was not a native joining technique, it may be speculated that a Chinese carpenter did the initial construction work.

The complex way in which shared identities and transformations are depicted in Northwest Coast Indian art is well illustrated in the decoration for this Haida chest. The spirit of Cirrus Clouds appears on one face and the spirit of Eagle on the other. The shared human soul of the two spirits is shown both in its spirit form, located beneath the mouths of the spirit beings, and in its human form, represented in profile to either side of the faces of the two spirit beings. On the sides of the chest, the bear crest of a clan is represented in two forms as well,

239

first as animal and then human.

Symbolic oppositions, which are expressed in and overcome through ritual, are clearly represented on this Haida box. Cirrus Clouds and Eagle are opposites in that Cirrus Clouds are the prevalent clouds of the Northwest Coast summer, while Eagle—who flies in cumulus clouds—is the lord of the winter sky. But Eagle and Cirrus Clouds together stand in opposition to Bear and to humans, both of whom are land creatures. Bear and humans are opposed in that the former is most active in the summer, while the latter performs rituals more frequently in the winter. All these oppositions, these separate identities, are combined to form a single coherent entity with all differences reconciled in a box for storing powerful sacred objects.

c.

Crow Feast Dish, ca. 1850–83
Haida Indians; Skidegate, Queen Charlotte Islands, British Columbia, Canada
wood
4⅛ × 10 × 6 (10.5 × 25.4 × 15.3)
NMNH 89136

Wooden bowls were used to serve seal oil and candlefish oil, two highly prestigious foods. This bowl shows two aspects of the human-spirit transformation: Crow with his human soul emerging from his mouth and the shared human-bird soul with its characteristic recurved beak in Crow's tail.

d.

House Screens, ca. 1850–1900
Tlingit Indians; Wrangell, Alaska
wood, fiber lashing, red and black paint, non-Indian frames
each: 91 × 88 × 3½ (231.1 × 223.5 × 8.9)
NMNH 233498 a, c; Collected by John R. Swanton

The Northwest Coast Indians believed that people, like other treasures, should be stored in boxes and that these boxes should be decorated with images that depict the close association between humans and spirits. House fronts were decorated with images of the spirit ancestor of the group within. House screens served as room partitions to separate families living in

a single building, creating smaller containers of social and spiritual identity within the larger box of the house, which was itself a partitioned-off space in the larger box of the universe.

241.

Totem Pole Model, ca. 1850–83
Haida Indians; Lasheek village, Queen Charlotte Islands, British Columbia, Canada
wood
50¾ × 5½ × 10⅝ (128.9 × 14 × 26.9)
NMNH 89094; Collected by James G. Swan

From the early nineteenth century, some Haida craftsmen specialized in producing items for sale to visiting merchants, sailors, tourists, and anthropologists. This miniature totem pole follows traditional design patterns. The figures on it represent legendary characters of clan history and celebrate a specific lineage and its heritage. At the top, three guardians watch over their kinsman's life. The other figures are Sparrowhawk, the mother of Crow, wearing a lip plug; Crow, who has just revealed his human identity; and Halibut.

242.

CARGO SYSTEM. The Spanish language describes the responsibility a public-office holder bears as a burden or *cargo.* Today, certain Latin American communities have evolved a system of rotating offices that requires villagers, by choice or by draft, to share the burdens of local political or religious duties. English speakers have come to call this the "cargo system" and its participants "cargo holders." In various forms, the cargo system appears from the Southwest United States to Andean South America. The objects shown here are from the Mexican state of Chiapas and from Guatemala. Usually both men and women may hold office, but only select offices are filled by women. Men must be married to qualify (unless a close female relative can assist him), whereas marriage rules may or may not apply to female cargo holders.

Today, as in the past, cargo holders gain prestige through personal sacrifice of time and wealth. Performing duties in office raises their

status in the village, but at the same time it drains their resources and savings, in part because of their hospitable support of many helpers who aid to complete myriad cargo tasks.

In many communities with cargo systems, offices are ranked. A cargo holder must serve at one level before proceeding to the next, and religious and political levels often alternate.

Religious cargo holders celebrate village saints' days with special festivities surrounding the village patron saint. Political cargo holders usually maintain village order, preside at native law courts, collect taxes, and mediate between native and nonnative governments.

Religion and politics often mix. For example, some religious fiestas reenact historic events of great political significance. During these (and other religious fiestas) native actors may mock cultural differences between Indians and non-Indian Latins. As a group, non-Indians usually wield more power than native peoples. Through irony a religious fiesta can emphasize a native perception of social, political, and economic injustice.

Both political and religious office holders pray and sacrifice to gods for village welfare, repeatedly requesting divine blessings. All cargo ritual, whether for political or religious participants, requires great attention to complex detail involving prayers, purification, banquets, ritual drinking, singing, dancing, and sacrifice to the deities. At times a cargo holder's failure to perform, whether in politics or religion, is said to cause divine punishment such as crop failures, epidemics, and political strife.

During cargo-sponsored fiestas, villagers not burdened by cargo chores throng to churches, markets, and law courts to attend to religious, economic, and civil matters. For entertainment they eat, drink, chat, watch fireworks and masquerades, and sometimes dance and sing. As they say in the village of Chamula, Chiapas, during fiestas people and gods alike take a moment "to rest their hearts."

240 c

a.
Model of House, probably 20th century
probably Maya Cakchiquel Indians;
Lake Atitlán region, Guatemala
mixed media
11½ × 17¾ × 16 (29.2 × 45.1 × 40.6)
NMNH T7272
Illustrated in color, p. 43

This extraordinarily detailed model, which seems to have no ceremonial use, offers a glimpse of a cargo-sponsored religious festival. The figures of two cargo holders and their wives face one another in a yard before a house as they dance to airs performed by ritual musicians. It seems that other celebrants have drunk considerable amounts of home-distilled liquor and are resting, being dragged away, or beginning to fight. Many Indian groups have traditionally encouraged cargo holders to free their souls with liquor so that open and

eloquent speech may be made to the gods. The Indians also know, however, that drunkenness can lead to violence, as the house model shows. In some communities, such as Chamula in Chiapas state, leaders have begun to discourage the use of alcohol, advocating soft drinks instead. Inside the house a sacred picture, perhaps of the holy person being celebrated, decorates the wall. Out of deference to this image, all of the rowdy behavior takes place in the further yard. The flag in the model represents a saint important to the community. During certain saint's-day celebrations, a cargo holder (usually with the title of "standard-bearer") honors his saint by furling his sacred banner, praying, and offering sacrifices.

b.
Cargo Holder's Hat (*pixalal*), 1930–70
Tzotzil-speaking Maya Indians; San Andrés Larrainzar village, Chiapas, Mexico
straw, synthetic ribbons, cotton thread, wool, synthetic thread tassle
5½ × 14 × 14 (14 × 35.5 × 35.5)
NMNH 419537

c.
Cargo Holder's Sandals (*chak xonobil*), 1930–70
Tzotzil-speaking Maya Indians; San Juan Chamula, Chiapas, Mexico
cowhide, nails
each: 4⅞ × 11 × 4⅓ (12.4 × 27.9 × 10.9)
NMNH 419540

Cargo holders usually emphasize their important position in the community on ceremonial occasions by wearing attire specific to each office. Although the shape of the hat shows strong Spanish influence, its ribbons and the design of the high-backed sandals may well reflect pre-Conquest Mayan ancestry. Mayan stelae show high-ranking men in ceremonial attitudes with similar high-backed footwear. Ribbons on the hat may well have replaced the feathers cascading from noble Mayan heads, which are especially visible in scenes of Mayan ceremonies.

d.
Diatonic Harp (*7arpa*), ca. 1870–1900
Tzotzil-speaking Maya Indians;
Chamula village, Chiapas, Mexico
wood, metal, glue
45 × 24½ × 15¾ (114.3 × 62.2 × 40)
NMNH 93517

e.
Violin (*ravol*), ca. 1875–1900
Tzotzil-speaking Maya Indians;
Chamula village, Chiapas, Mexico
wood, twisted gut, glue
22⅓ × 7½ × 1½ (56.6 × 19.1 × 3.7)
NMNH 93552

f.
Flute (*7ama*), ca. 1875–1900
Tzotzil-speaking Maya Indians;
Chamula village, Chiapas, Mexico
clay, pigment, glaze
9¼ × ¾ × ¾ (23.5 × 1.9 × 1.9)
NMNH 93554

These musical instruments from the Mayan community of Chamula were made to accompany religious cargo holders as they performed rituals, songs, and dances. All date from about the third quarter of the nineteenth century, although Chamula artisans fashion nearly similar instruments for the same purpose today. Ranked junior and senior musicians play such instruments for religious fiestas and ceremonies but never for secular entertainment. Music intensifies the sacred atmosphere and is said to please gods and humans alike.

While the harp is still used in both Chamula and Zinacantan, today the violin is used almost solely in Zinacantan. Chamulas reserve the shrill tones of the kind of clay flute shown here, accompanied by the sound of trumpet and drum, to mark the change of a religious office.

g.
Bull-Shaped Candleholder with Candle (*vakax lum xchi7uk nichim*), 1980
Tzotzil-speaking Maya Indians;
Chamula village, Chiapas, Mexico
bull: clay, slip
candle: wax, string
12 × 12¾ × 4⅛ (30.5 × 32.4 × 10.5)
FP R101,102

Indians of Mexico's Chiapas highlands offer candles as a sacrifice to the gods whenever they pray. Some Indians believe that the candles provide divine food, while others say that they only provide light and beauty. Worshipers may place candles directly on the ground, hold them in their hands, place them on a board, or set them in a holder such as the one shown here.

Bull-shaped candleholders sit on home altars and play a role in both private and cargo rituals. Cargo holders may own several dozen such candleholders, lighting their offerings whenever they recite important prayers of praise or petition for divine vigilance.

Bulls and deer are said to be pack animals for the earth gods, but the Chamula have yet to explain why these two particular animals and no others are fashioned into candleholders. It is possible that as divine beasts of burden they may be thought specially suited to carry a present from humans to the earth gods. Candles placed in these holders need not, however, necessarily be offered to the earth gods alone but can be offered to any god a worshiper chooses.

Such clay candleholders gain prominence away from the home altar when cargo holders called stewards, or "flowers," change office in Chamula. The wives of outgoing stewards and flowers then transport these flower-decorated candleholders, with much accompanying ritual, to the altar of the incoming stewards. Chamulas offer white candles like the one shown here as especially fine gifts to the gods of the upperworld, while reserving tawny candles of tallow for the earth deities.

h.
Incense burner (*yav 7ak' al*), 1980
Tzotzil-speaking Maya Indians;
Chamula village, Chiapas, Mexico
clay, slip
14½ × 10 × 10 (36.8 × 25.4 × 25.4)
FP R100

For centuries Maya Indians have offered the smoke of copal-pine incense to their gods as life-giving food. This incense burner was made to hold smoldering copal pine resin or copal chips. Today, whenever worshipers honor or ask a favor of the gods, whether in cargo ceremonies or in private home rituals, they almost always sacrifice costly copal incense.

In the village of Chamula, it is believed that a cargo holder seriously offends the deities and evokes their wrath upon himself and the community if he deprives them of their daily sustenance of incense. During cargo celebrations, special female helpers guard the incense burners. They keep the resin lit and raise the vessels aloft before all that is sacred at key points in the ritual.

The meaning of the three sets of three prongs on the incense burners is not known, but in northern and central Mexico birds of a very similar shape decorate the rims of similar vessels. In all of the native religions of Mexico, birds have traditionally served as messengers from humans to the gods in the upperworld.

243.
CHAMULA CARNIVAL. For Tzotzil-speaking Maya Indians of Chamula in the state of Chiapas, Mexico, the traditional run through fire on Shrove Tuesday (Mardi Gras) marks the climax of their pre-Lenten carnival—the most important festival of the year. Carnival, like many fiestas sponsored by cargo holders in Latin America (discussed in no. 242) commemorates the history of its celebrants, in particular the Caste War or Cuzcat Rebellion of 1868. In this case, Chamula recall centuries scarred by wars, oppression, and uprisings. At the same time they mock Ladinos and other Mexicans, who have often been their political adversaries.

Symbols of military power pulse through the celebration: a warrior dance; military titles for cargo holders; sacred flags and lance tips (as carried by the Passion in red, here); and rituals of shouting, running (like the run through fire), and blasting of trumpets. In a dramatic carnival event, a town crier continually refers to military action, while a carnival mock battle fought with dried horse dung reenacts the 1910 Mexican-Guatemalan border war.

Carnival also celebrates the life of Christ, who in Chamula belief "played" as a child before he was crucified. Residents of Chamula allude to this playing by calling carnival "The Festival of the Games."

Sacred silver lance heads made from old Mexican coins and "clothed" in bright ribbons, as recreated here at the tip of this flag pole, represent Christ, Mary, and other sacred persons. A cargo holder called Passion carries the lances, helping them run, dance, and walk to celebrate the fiesta. So sacred are the flags and lances that the Passion may not touch the pole with his bare hands but wraps it in the red bandanna displayed here to keep it pure.

During carnival, cargo holders strive to make the most lavish offerings affordable to the lance heads and other gods. They also provide banquets for one another and for crowds of eager onlookers. If cargo holders withhold offerings or show disrespect for the deities, they, and perhaps the whole community, can expect supernatural punishment. The gods indicate their displeasure by sending rain during the festival, which causes the local government to take action. Angered at their failure to please the gods, Chamula's political cargo holders seek out and put the guilty religious cargo holder or holders in jail.

Bearing flags aloft, the runners—religious cargo holders, their "Monkey" helpers, and other ritual assistants—purify themselves by running a fiery gauntlet made of burning thatch from abandoned houses. A fall into the fire reveals guilt of a serious wrongdoing and impending punishment by the gods. Today fire-running takes

242 d

place on the last day of major public festivity during the Chamula carnival. Like Catholics throughout the world, the Chamula reckon the date of carnival by the Catholic calendar. In pre-Conquest times, however, the ancient Maya, when celebrating a New Year troubled by bad omens, also strode upon burning coals for purification.

For the Chamula, fire also bears close associations with the sun, a deity worshiped as Christ and God the Father. The Sun, Christ, and God the Father bestowed life and food upon the Chamula—especially corn, the Mayan staple. Around

carnival time Maya farmers traditionally burn corn fields just before planting. It is possible that the run through fire enacts the path of the sun with its life-giving rays across the heavens. The run then becomes a fertility rite as well as a purification.

a.
Passion's Costume
Tzotzil-speaking Maya Indians; Chamula village, Chiapas, Mexico (except the Blue Turban from San Andrés Larrainzar village and Red Scarf from an unknown Mexican village)

FP R200–211
Illustrated in color, p. 44

From top:

Hat (*pixalal yu7un*), 1979
palm fibers, dyes, thread, commercial ribbon
5¼ × 15⅞ × 15⅞ (13.3 × 40.3 × 40.3)

Blue Turban (*yaxal pok'yu7un*), 1980
thread, dyed cotton cloth
14½ × 64 (36.8 × 162.6)

Necklace (*natz'il yu7un*), 1979
ribbon, thread, beads, metal
33 × 16 × 2 (83.8 × 40.6 × 5.1)

White Shirt (*sakil k'u7ul*), 1979
commercial cotton cloth, thread, buttons
22¼ × 28½ (56.4 × 72.4)
Not illustrated

Red Velvet Jacket (*tzajal k'u yu7un*), 1979
synthetic cloth, thread, metal, gilt
52 × 23 (132 × 58.5)

Belt (*xchuk'*), 1980
synthetic and wool yarn
2¾ × 160 (7 × 406.4)

White Trousers (*sakil vexal*), 1979
commercial cotton cloth, thread
27½ × 19 (69.9 × 48.2)

Red Velvet Trousers (*tzajal vexal yu7un*), 1979
velvet, thread, embroidery thread, metal, gilt, cotton cloth
27½ × 19 (69.9 × 48.2)

Heeled Sandals (*chak xonobil*), ca. 1970–80
leather
each: 4 × 4⅝ × 11 (10.2 × 11.8 × 27.9)
Not illustrated

Flowered Flag (*nichimal banderex*), ca. 1970–80
cotton cloth, thread
30½ × 64½ (77.5 × 165.1)
Not illustrated

Ribbons for the Tip of the Flag (*lixtonal sjol jtotik*), ca. 1970–80
ribbons, thread
average: 13 × 15 (33 × 38.1)
Not illustrated

198

Red Scarf (*tzahal pok'*), 1980
red-dyed cotton cloth, thread
22½ × 22½ (57.1 × 57.1)
Not illustrated

The red-suited figure shown here represents the most prestigious cargo holder of Chamula—an outgoing Passion. His suit is derived from the attire of a seventeenth-century Spanish gentleman. Red, a color associated with heat, indicates that the outgoing Passion, by having held office, has intensified the symbolic heat of his own body.

Each year three incoming and three outgoing Passions celebrate carnival in complex ritual groupings that echo military organization. Numerous other cargo holders and their assistants accompany them. Although carnival lasts for five days in the plaza, preparations before and clean-up afterward can extend the expense and duties for the cargo holders over a six- to eight-week period.

b.
Monkey's Costume
Tzotzil-speaking Maya Indians; Chamula village, Chiapas, Mexico (except for the Red Scarves from an unknown Mexican village and Jacket from San Cristóbal village)
FP R300–313

From top:

Hat (*batz'*), 1970
monkey skin and fur, ribbons, thread, wooden sticks
17 × 10½ (43.2 × 26.7)

Turban (*pok'*), 1977
dyed cotton cloth, thread
32 × 34½ (81.3 × 87.5)

Red Scarf (*tzahal pok'*), 1980
dyed cotton cloth, thread
22½ × 22 (57.1 × 55.8)

White Scarf (*pok'*), ca. 1980
cotton, thread
39 × 37½ (99 × 95.1)

Scarf (*panyo*), ca. 1970–80
dyed synthetic cloth, thread
27⅜ × 29⅛ (69.5 × 74)

White Shirt (*manta k'u7ul*), 1980
cotton cloth, thread, buttons
25⅝ × 20 (65.1 × 50.8)

Jacket (*sk'u7* or *leva*), 1975
cotton cloth, thread, button
40¾ × 19¼ (103.5 × 48.8)

Red Scarf (*tzahal*), 1980
dyed cotton cloth, thread
22½ × 23 (57.1 × 58.4)

Belt (*xchuk*), ca. 1978
wool and synthetic yarn, thread
2¼ × 120 (5.7 × 304.8)

White Trousers (*sakil vexal*), ca. 1975
white cotton cloth, lining, thread, metal zipper, clasp
38½ × 17 (97.8 × 43.2)

Leather Trousers (*nukulal vexal*), 1970
deerskin, thread
25½ × 17 (64.7 × 43.2)

Drinking Horn (*xulub vakax*), ca. 1970–80
cow horn, deerskin, brass tacks, wood, string
3¼ × 20 (8.2 × 50.8)

Tin Funnel (*burne*), ca. 1970
tin
2⅞ × 3¼ × 3¼ (7.3 × 8.2 × 8.2)

Bull-Penis Rod (*yat vakash*), 1979
bull penis, metal rod, cotton cloth, ribbon, thread
length: 23 (58.4)
Not illustrated

Shoes (*batz'i varachil*), ca. 1980
rubber, leather, metal
each: 4⅜ × 3¾ × 10⅝ (11.1 × 9.5 × 26.9)
Not illustrated

The most active and important helpers for the Passion are his "Monkeys." Dressed in a costume that imitates the uniform of a French grenadier of the 1860s (dating from the French intervention in Mexico), the Monkey keeps order, distributes food and drink, leads song and dance, and supervises other significant events, such as the horse-dung war. Monkeys also run with Passions, usually bearing smaller, less highly sacred flags with no silver tips.

Monkeys serving Passions and other cargo holders often act like soldiers to keep the crowds in line. This military connection is emphasized in the name for their jacket. It is called *leva*, meaning "draft" in Spanish. Monkeys carry a rod made from the penis of a bull (usually one sacrificed by an outgoing Passion for his banquet) stretched over a wire rod. When the Passion runs, anyone carelessly in the path receives a disciplinary blow from the Monkey's weapon.

Some Chamula men and boys dress like Monkeys during carnival to dance, sing, play musical instruments, and beg for food in the village square. Chamula sometimes liken these "free" Monkeys to lustful devils. Even such free Monkeys must keep order and obey the cargo holder's Monkeys. If free Monkeys step out of line, then they too must duck the well-aimed rod.

Monkeys, as do many carnival-ritual participants, combine religious and political themes. Acting as soldiers they keep order and help cargo holders worship the gods while also engaging in rousing, militarylike ritual with strong political overtones.

243 b

244.
Beaded Cloth Mask, ca. 1900–1950
Bamiléké peoples; Cameroun
banana fiber, raffia, or jute cloth;
thread; glass beads; metal bells
50 × 23½ × 9 (127 × 59.7 × 22.9)
AfA 79-13-39

In the political hierarchy of traditional Bamiléké kingdoms, several men's associations were ranked just below the king's council. These groups enjoyed the king's favor and served him in the administration as well as in the protection of the realm. Membership in the prestigious societies was either bought or earned by merit.

The associations used wealth from initiation fees to purchase glass trade beads. The beads were used in fabricating masks, of which this stylized elephant's head is an example. Such masks usually belonged to groups with martial functions that gave their king invaluable support in wartime.

Members performed masked dances on solemn ceremonial occasions. At state funerals and during their own biennial meetings, the associations danced before the highest dignitaries of the kingdom.

245.
Uncle Tom's Cabin, 1894
Strasbourg, Virginia
earthenware
16 × 15 × 15 (40.6 × 38.1 × 38.1)
NMAH 1978.107.3 a–c

In 1894, Levi Bergerly and Theodore Fleet of Eberly Pottery, Strasbourg, Virginia, made this earthenware sculpture to commemorate the thirtieth anniversary of the Battle of Fisher's Hill. The title seems to have no relation to that used by Harriet Beecher Stowe for her famous novel.

Incised on the roof of the piece are the words FROM / FISHER S HILL / BATTLE FIELDS / SEPT 1864, perhaps a reference to its having been made from clay taken from the battle site. A well and the potter's mark have been broken off the front of the piece.

The Battle of Fisher's Hill took place during the Civil War near Strasbourg. Led by General Philip H. Sheridan, who pitted his forces against Confederate troops under

244

General Jubal A. Early, the Union army prevailed. For many years afterward former Confederate soldiers who had fought in the battle held reunions at Fisher's Hill every August. These became notable events in the social life of the Shenandoah Valley, and one such reunion may well have been the occasion for the creation of this earthenware group.

246.
"Emancipation House," 1964
Texas
mixed media
19½ × 23½ × 18½ (49.5 × 59.2 × 47)
NMAA 1976.60
Illustrated in color, p. 44

George W. White, Jr. (1903–70), created this work to commemorate the emancipation of American slaves. In Texas, Emancipation Day on June 19 commemorates the freeing of the slaves in 1865 and is celebrated in a holiday called "Juneteenth."

White's reverence for President Abraham Lincoln as The Great Emancipator strongly emerges in this piece. He places on the cabin both the date of Lincoln's birth, 1809, and a reproduction of Thomas Nast's depiction of Lincoln's first inauguration, clipped from the February 1960 issue of *National Geographic.* Inside the cabin, a picture of Lincoln—who changed the future for all generations of Black children—looms over a small child on a bed. At one time, when the piece had a slightly different composition and its electrical wiring functioned, the interior was lit.

For 124 years in some parts of Texas, Juneteenth was not a legal holiday. Many Blacks, however, took off from work, celebrated with baseball games and pit barbecues, and participated in civic events. The unofficial status of the holiday led some Blacks to lose their jobs or face derision when attending these culturally meaningful festivities. In 1979 Juneteenth became an official state holiday in Texas, and today the right of Blacks to celebrate an event so crucial to their history is acknowledged by all Texans.

247.
Plaque, 1975
Santa Barbara, California
varnished maple
36 × 36 × 5 (91.4 × 91.4 × 12.7)
NMAH 320049.1; Gift of Anita Dwyer

Carved by Joseph Perrotta to commemorate the nation's bicentennial, this plaque depicts symbols of our history. The covered wagon represents westward expansion; the city street, industrialization; the light bulb, invention; and the moon landing, further exploration and technological advancement.

248.
Appliquéd Scene, ca. 1900–1933
Fon people; Republic of Benin
appliquéd cotton cloth
68⅜ × 38¾ × ⅞ (173.6 × 98.4 × 2.2)
AfA L79-7-T6

Among the Fon, ownership and display of appliquéd cloth were royal prerogatives. The fabric adorned the walls inside the king's palace and made up the umbrellas, tents, and banners used in his processions out of doors. Scenes depicted in appliqué often dealt with the power and conquests of the kings of Dahomey.

The lion in this piece represents King Glélé, who ruled from 1858 to 1889. Guns and knives do not deter him as he overpowers his enemy.

249.
Uncle Sam Costume, 1936
USA
cotton, wool, brass
hat: 12 × 9 (30.5 × 22.9)
pants: 16 × 38½ (40.6 × 97.8)
coat: 19 × 38 (48.2 × 96.5)
NMAH 227739.1936.C5, 6; Ralph E. Becker Collection

The Uncle Sam Club of Buffalo, New York, used this costume at the Republican National Convention in 1936.

The figure of Uncle Sam originated during the War of 1812 with Samuel Wilson (1766–1854), a meatpacker from Troy, New York. Working under a government contract, Wilson stamped inspected and approved meat for the United States army with the initials U.S.

Wilson, an outgoing man who liked to spin yarns, was called "Uncle Sam" by relatives and friends. American soldiers who grew to like the loquacious visitor to their camps called themselves "Uncle Sam's soldiers" and declared that Uncle Sam issued their provisions.

During the nineteenth century, the popular symbol of Uncle Sam took many graphic forms, even rotund and beardless ones. It was Thomas Nast, the famous political cartoonist of the mid-nineteenth century, who popularized a gaunt and goateed figure and so the symbol has remained.

Uncle Sam has come to personify the United States as an individual, a man who expresses various emotions (anger, dismay, pride, and the like) about national and international affairs.

250.
Schley Loving Cup, ca. 1902
USA
silver
21 × 12 (53.3 × 30.5)
NMAH 39572; Gift of Mrs. R. S. Wortley (nee Virginia Schley)

During the Spanish-American War of 1898, many Americans admired Admiral Winfield Scott Schley (1839–1911) for his exploits during the Battle of Santiago. The bluff, hearty, and popular naval officer saw his first action in the American Civil War, after his graduation from the United States Naval Academy. He received his commission as a lieutenant in 1862 and won acclaim for his courage during the Civil War. In 1884 he made a heroic rescue of the survivors of Adolphus Greely's ill-fated Arctic expedition, after two other attempts had failed.

After the Spanish-American War, Americans celebrated Schley's naval exploits and feted him with banquets and parties and with gifts such as this silver loving cup from the citizens of Dallas, Texas, presented on October 20, 1902.

Though he was publicly acclaimed, a bitter controversy raged in the Navy over Schley's conduct during the 1898 combat. Schley himself called a naval court of inquiry at the end of 1901 to clear his name, but the court reached a judgment that in general was adverse to him.

Despite his censure, Schley's nationwide popularity continued. This cup, presented after the verdict, gives evidence in engraved script to the "affectionate regard and grateful appreciation of the city of Dallas, Texas for his illustrious achievements in the service of his country."

251.
Silver Ewer, 1861
Tiffany and Co., New York, New York
silver gilt
14½ × 8 × 7 (36.8 × 20.3 × 17.8)
NMAH 282163.01; Courtesy of Dr. Sidney Peerless

This ewer, a presentation piece to Abraham Lincoln upon his first inauguration, bears the words:
For the President of the United States—Abraham Lincoln—From his Washington friends—March 4, 1861.

The design on the ewer reflects support of Lincoln's stand to preserve the Union. The engraved inscription encircles thirty-three stars, which in turn encircle the great seal of the United States. These stars, symbolizing the thirty-three states that form one nation, clearly deny the existence of a Confederacy formed from seven states that had seceded earlier.

Taking office has traditionally been a time of political celebration for presidents, but tension and fear were in the air when Lincoln became commander-in-chief. Though in his inaugural address he entreated the South to remain peaceful, four more states seceded almost immediately upon his taking office. On April 12 the Civil War began.

245

252.
Torah and Cover, 1914
USA
silk, parchment
15 × 8 (38.1 × 20.3)
NMAH 31842; Gift of Israel Fine
Illustrated in color, p. 44

This scroll honors the one-hundredth anniversary of the composition of *The Star-Spangled Banner.* It bears a hymn in Hebrew written by Israel Fine and translated into English by Dr. Tobias Salzman.

253.
Commemorative Blanket, ca. 1836–39
Mexico or Peru
wool yarn
74 × 62 (188 × 157.5)
NMNH 367923; Gift of Clara de N. Abercrombie
Illustrated in color, p. 45

Textiles commemorate festive and triumphal occasions in Latin America, where they were used to decorate balconies and windows. This blanket was collected in Mexico during the Mexican-American War of 1846 and extols a president named Herrera. It has, therefore, been suggested that José Joaquín Herrera, twice acting president (1844–45) and then president (1848–51) of Mexico, is the subject of the weaving. It is more likely, however, that the hero whom it celebrates is a Peruvian, Don Ramón Herrera.

The woven symbols derive from South Peruvian coins minted between 1837 and 1839. The boat and the tower reflect the mixture of cultures in Peru. Spanish civilization came to the New World in ships and conquered the Inca, represented here by symbols of Inca culture taken from Cuzco's coat of arms. The smoking volcano, representing Peru's landscape, is a motif in Arequipa's coat of arms. The horn of plenty with coins rolling out has been part of Peru's general coat of arms since 1825 and is an obvious symbol of wealth. The flags, the garland of laurel, the crossed muskets, and the drum and cannon are military images appropriate to the status of Ramón Herrera as a triumphant general.

The weaver used abbreviations to fit a lengthy statement around the

249

border of the blanket. The expanded Spanish text reads: "SOY PARA EL ABRIGO DE LA YLUSTRE PERSONA EXC[ELENTE] S[IMÓN] D[ON] RAM[ÓN] HERR[ER]A CAP[ITÁN] J[ENE]RAL Y PRESIDENTE D[E]L ESTADO SUDPER[UANO]." It translates: "I am for the protection of the illus-trious person his excellency Don Ramón Herrera, Captain General and President of the State of South Peru."

The fate of this weaving may speak of defeat as much as it does of triumph. Political upheaval caused the once-favored President Ramón Herrera to flee Peru in 1839 and live the rest of his life in exile. It is possible that he stopped on his way to Europe to visit his relatives, the Mexican Herreras, and made them a gift of the blanket.

254.

ARAPAHO MEN'S SOCIETIES.
Throughout the Plains, warriors met periodically in ceremonial associations known as societies, lodges, or dances. The activities of the societies varied from nation to nation, but most provided military services during war, discipline on the hunt, and police duties in camp. Among the Arapaho, neither these responsibilities nor religion were the members' main purpose. The meetings of the societies were entirely social in nature, and the members' internal ranks, or degrees, mirrored their external standing in the community.

Although membership was not compulsory, almost every Arapaho male over the age of twelve belonged to one of the Arapaho's eight societies. Membership was progressive, or age-graded; an individual could join a particular society only after having been a member of a group below it. A man thus progressed with his peers from youth to old age. No formal initiation into these societies was required. Members, singly or in groups, merely had to be instructed about the ways and customs of the lodge by an elder member called the "grandfather." The grandfather also gave new members a proper set of regalia to be used in public dancing, singing, feasting, and gift giving.

The societies gave identity, meaning, and coherence to the shared experiences of a group of peers. They distributed power and responsibility among men and provided for the orderly succession of power, thereby lessening the destructive aspects of competition. The societies also preserved Arapaho ideals and helped maintain social order, by providing a means whereby men could direct their energies communally to the benefit of society and to the harmony of the cosmic order.

250

a.
Two Ceremonial Clubs (age-grade 17–20), ca. 1880–1903
Southern Arapaho Indians; Oklahoma
wood; hide strip; cornhusk; red stroud cloth; lime; buffalo or horsehair; sinew; red, green, and black paint; feathers
largest: 45¾ × 4⅓ × 2⅔ (116.2 × 10.9 × 6.7)
NMNH 165768, 233095

Like other badges of office, paraphernalia of a member of an age-graded society expressed the expansion of his identity from a personal to a more public level. The only regalia of the Tomahawk age group, which was composed of young men between the ages of seventeen and twenty, was a ceremonial club resembling a war club. Since youths of this age were just entering the ranks of warriors and would not have accumulated war honors, the simplicity of their regalia emphasizes their as-yet-unrealized military potential. The buffalo head at the end of one club links its possessor to the strength and protection of the buffalo; the sharpened point, enabling the club to be stuck into the ground, brings the power of the buffalo to the place where the owner is; the cornhusks symbolize both the bounty of the earth and the harvest of slain enemies; and the red and black paint symbolizes the powers of creation and destruction.

b.
Men's Society Regalia (fourth age-grade, 20–30), ca. 1880–90
NMNH 165821, 165821c, 200788, 200906

From top:

Feathered Head Ornament
Northern Arapaho Indians; Wyoming
rawhide, quills, eagle feathers, lime
12 × 3⅞ × ⅛ (30.5 × 9.8 × 0.3)

Armband
Northern Arapaho Indians; Wyoming
rawhide, quills, brass bell, buffalo hair
6¾ × 3½ (17.1 × 8.9)

Hide Kilt
Southern Arapaho Indians; Oklahoma
buffalo hide, red stroud cloth, tin jingles, crow feathers, red and green paint, quills
15 × 30 × ⅓ (38.1 × 76.2 × 0.8)
Illustrated in color, p. 45

Two Fur Legbands
Southern Arapaho Indians; Oklahoma
fur, quills
2½ × 22 × 1 (6.3 × 55.8 × 2.5)

The Plains Indians believed that power and knowledge came from the alignment of the individual with the order and beauty of the cosmos. This set of regalia—complete except for a lance—for the fourth age group (twenty to thirty years) of an Arapaho society emphasizes the relationships between its possessor and natural and spiritual forces. The crosses symbolize

the morning star, father of mankind, who makes life good; the red stroud-cloth border represents the color of the evening star; the four vertical green lines stand for completeness, the four days of the lodge's meeting, and the straight paths of the moral life; and the notches on the lower edge represent clouds. Here, as in other regalia, the feathers indicate the expansion of human action outside its normal earthly range and the giddy speed of supernatural power.

c.
Hide Sash (sixth age-grade, about 50), ca. 1880–97
Northern Arapaho Indians; Wyoming
hide, eagle feathers, quills, blue and white beads, red stroud cloth, root
8 × 80¾ (20.3 × 205)
NMNH 200538
Illustrated in color, p. 45

A member of the sixth age group, or lodge, wore a long sash like this one, with his left arm and shoulder thrust through the slit. The four circles represented the four generations of the world. The gray eagle feather at the end, from an old bird, reflected the age—about fifty—of the warrior who wore the sash.

d.
Dewclaw Rattle Stick (sixth age-grade, about 50), ca. 1860–90
Southern Arapaho Indians; Oklahoma
wooden stick, rawhide, quill, dewclaws, red stroud cloth, feathers, porcupine tail
25 × 5 × 1½ (63.5 × 12.7 × 3.7)
NMNH 165760

The four crosses on the rattle's handle represented the morning star. All eagle-bone whistles for this lodge were strung on hide split into seven strands, each strand wound in seven places with cornhusks. This pattern referred to the seven men most senior in rank, who directed the entire Arapaho ceremonial organization.

e.
Eagle Bone Whistle (sixth age-grade, about 50), ca. 1880–91
Northern Arapaho Indians; Wyoming
eagle wing bone, quills, blue glass beads, buckskin
19¾ × 8½ × ¾ (50 × 21.6 × 1.9)
NMNH 153056

Eagles were important symbols of the way in which spiritual power could soar majestically and omnisciently above the earth, and eagle feathers were an essential part of nearly every Plains Indian costume. The beating of eagle wings was envisioned as a great rain-bringing wind, sweeping clean the world and producing a state of purity. This power was evoked with ceremonial eagle-wing brushes and eagle-wingbone whistles. Blowing such a whistle and sweeping the world clean with his motions, a dancer symbolically became an eagle restoring purity and order to the world.

255.
GURO DYE CULT. Among the Guro, members of the *dye* cult are masked as they dance and sing at feasts or funerals. On these occasions, an ensemble of *dye* maskers emerges from the forest to entertain male villagers. Their role is not only entertainment, however; some masks, like the *kieze* mask (a) listed below, have judicial functions. The masks depict various animals and occasionally humans. While dances include characteristic movements of the creatures represented they usually go beyond simple mime into virtuoso performance.

a.
Mask (*kieze*), ca. 1900–1950
Guro people; Ivory Coast
wood, iron nails, fibers, pigments
27 × 6¾ × 8 (68.6 × 17.1 × 20.3)
AfA 79-16-33

Three *dye* masks are not used in the usual observances of the cult. Instead, they represent supernatural judicial figures who settle disputes among villagers. *Kieze*, the mask shown here, is one of these figures. He plays the role of prosecutor, pronouncing charges against defendants and menacing them with a wooden dagger.

b.
Mask, ca. 1900–1950
Guro people; Ivory Coast
wood, cloth, string, pigments
35 × 13½ × 8 (88.9 × 34.3 ×
20.3)
AfA 71-22-2

With its hornlike protrusions, this
dye mask probably represents an
imaginary animal.

c.
Mask, ca. 1900–1950
Guro people; Ivory Coast
wood, pigments
13 × 6¹³⁄₁₆ × 7⁵⁄₁₆ (30.3 × 17.4 ×
18.6)
AfA 75-31-4

Perhaps this mask is meant to depict a bat or some kind of cat,
either wild or domestic. It may just
as plausibly be the head of an imaginary creature.

256.
MASONS. Masons form the largest
fraternal organization in the world
today. The brotherhood describes
itself as "a system of morality
based on allegory and illustrated
symbols."

This fraternal organization
evolved from guilds of stoneworkers who built the cathedrals of Europe. When new construction of cathedrals waned in the mid-
seventeenth century, many stone-
working guilds gradually turned
into social fraternities that initiated honorary members to fill their
declining numbers. The modern
symbols developed in the seventeenth and eighteenth centuries as
members adopted rites and regalia
of ancient religious orders and chivalric brotherhoods.

Any male believing in the supreme being of any faith is eligible
to join the fraternal organization of
the Masons. Members are ranked
in three degrees, or levels—Entered
Apprentice, Fellow Craft, and Master Mason. These roughly correspond to the three grades of work-
men in a guild system—apprentice,
journeyman, and master. In the
United States, Masons may take
advanced degrees in the Scottish
Rite or the York Rite, or both.

Knights Templar is the highest
degree of the York Rite. To become
a Knight Templar a Mason must
also be a Christian.

Before modern Masonry existed,
the earliest known Knights Templar formed a brotherhood in A.D.
1118 during the period of the Cru-
sades. Under solemn oath they
pledged to defend pilgrims journey-
ing to and from the Holy Land.
During the first half of the eighteenth century, certain Masons
looked back to the Knights Templar of the Middle Ages as an embodiment of chivalric ideals. The
first recorded Knights Templar degree associated with modern Masonry was conferred to William
Davis in 1769 at Saint Andrew's
Royal Arch Lodge in Boston. Masonic teachings emphasize principles of brotherly love, equality,
mutual aid, morality, charity, and
obedience to the law of the land. A
set of symbols derived from architectural tools and principles, common objects, nature, and religion
aids in teaching the moral and social philosophy of the organization.

Although today not a political
movement in the United States,
American Freemasonry became a
vehicle for patriotic ideals during
the Revolutionary War of 1776.
Many Americans—and Europeans
as well during the century of the
Enlightenment—turned to Freemasonry after becoming disenchanted
with religion. Men seeking an advanced moral order were attracted
to a system symbolized by rational,
utilitarian building tools—the compass, square, and level—with God
as The Grand Architect.

Nine of the fifty-six signers of
the Declaration of Independence
and fourteen presidents have been
members of this fraternal organization.

a.
Knights Templar Regalia, before
1929
NMAH 61.1 b, d, e, g; Gift of the
Children of Richard Bland Lee
Fleming through Miss Roberta Lee
Fleming

Hat (Knights Templar Chapeau)
Philadelphia, Pennsylvania
simulated fur, cloth, feathers, ribbon, velvet
7 × 18 × 7 (17.8 × 45.7 × 17.8)

Gloves and Gauntlets
place of manufacture unknown
buckskin, velvet, metal thread
15 × 9 (38.1 × 22.9)

255 a

Apron
place of manufacture unknown
velvet, cloth backing, metal, metallic ribbon, fringe, cord, tassles
17 × 18 (43.2 × 45.7)

This Knights Templar regalia belonged to Richard Bland Lee Fleming (1848–1929), gentleman farmer of Plains, Fauquier County, Virginia, who attained to the degree of Masonic Grand Master in 1891.

Generally, Knights Templar wear ceremonial dress according to the dictates of their commandery for important meetings, parades, church services, and funerals. The Knights Templar uniform current in the United States evolved from the Civil War uniform worn by naval officers.

The Masonic apron is a bond of fellowship with fellow Masons that recalls the occupational dress of stoneworkers in the Middle Ages. The Knights Templar apron here has been decorated with several important symbols. The metal triangle represents the Holy Trinity (three divinities in one); the stars symbolize the original thirteen states of the union; and the cross and serpent recall Saint Paul's casting of a snake into a fire. This story is related to a symbolic Masonic rite. The skull and crossbones are emblems of the Knights Templar.

b.
Knights Templar Sword, 19th century
New York, New York
ivory, metal, nickle-plated scabbard
33¼ × 5½ (85.7 × 14)
NMAH 36512; Gift of Frank S. Zappulla, crafted by James Fuker

The sword forms part of the Knights Templar full dress regalia, worn on the same occasions as hat, gloves, gauntlets, and apron. Engraved on the scabbard is the Knights Templar motto: "In Hoc Signo Vinces," "By this sign you will conquer." Emblems of knighthood and chivalry decorating the sword symbolically link modern Knights Templar with the legends and ideals of the Middle Ages.

c.
Knights Templar Membership Certificate, 1865
Saratoga Springs, New York
ink on parchment
11⁷⁄₁₆ × 14⅝ (29.1 × 37.1)
NMAH CBA9002; Collection of Business Americana

This document certifies membership of George P. Hopkins in the fraternal organization of the Knights Templar. The two columns represent the two pillars of King Solomon's Temple. The gold seal of the grand commandery of the state of New York at the botton left depicts the All-Seeing Eye, another Masonic emblem that stands for the supreme being and watchfulness.

257.
Quilt, ca. 1861
Brooklyn, New York
cotton top, lining, batting
85 × 85 (215.9 × 215.9)
NMAH T15474; Gift of Mrs. Eva McNeill
Illustrated in color, p. 47

In addition to patriotic symbols, floral motifs, and a Christmas tree, Susan Rogers incorporated many Masonic emblems into her design for this quilt. At the time she was working on it during the Civil War era, Masonic symbols were as popular in the decorative arts as patriotic and religious motifs. American craftspeople familiar with the emblems of Freemasonry used them to decorate everyday items as well as the clothing and ceremonial objects associated exclusively with the fraternity.

The middle block in the top row of this quilt depicts several tools used by stonemasons. Most of them carry symbolic meaning for the Masonic organization. The square, for example, is the emblem of virtue, and the level symbolizes equality. Some of the other images in this block—the star, the columns, and the keys—are derived from everyday life, but to the Masons these images represent the moral and philosophical concepts upon which their fraternity is based. Elsewhere on the quilt a cross, anchor, and heart give traditional decorative representation of faith, hope, and charity.

258.
TORCHLIGHT PARADES. One hundred years ago, American political campaigns were celebrations in which entertaining the voter was as important as selling the candidate. Toward the latter part of the nineteenth century, torchlight parades became a common strategic feature of most political races. Campaign torches had been patented in 1837, but it was not until 1860 that the "Wide-Awakes," a Republican marching group that originated in Hartford, Connecticut, popularized the torchlight parade. Dressed in patriotic costume and carrying special kerosene torches, the Wide-Awakes marched through city streets in the North to advertise their candidate, Abraham Lincoln.

It was not long before additional groups formed to parade for other political aspirants. Some of these groups were made up of trained paraders skilled in marching techniques. Several campaigns hired marchers regardless of their experience or party loyalty just to fill out the ranks. Firemen were considered especially desirable paraders since they already had uniforms.

Torchlight parades lasted two to three hours and involved more than uniformed marchers with kerosene torches. Participants also sang political songs, shouted campaign slogans, and carried banners and pictorial transparencies. An 1892 issue of *Harper's Weekly* described the spectacle: " 'CAMPAIGN equipments' include . . . tin helmets and breastplates, wooden spears and battle axes with kerosene torches at their tops, and leggings, capes, and tunics in limitless variety of shape, material, and color."

a.
Broadside, 1868
Boston, Massachusetts
lithograph on paper
24½ × 19⅝ (62.2 × 49.8)
NMAH 227739.1868.F3; Ralph E. Becker Collection

This broadside announces the schedule of a torchlight parade held in 1868.

b.
Engraving, 1860
USA
engraving on paper
16¼ × 23 (41.3 × 58.4)
NMAH 227739.1860.G25; Ralph E.
Becker Collection

The Wide-Awakes parade in 1860
for Abraham Lincoln.

c.
Torch, before 1888
USA
tin
9 × 5 × 5 (22.9 × 12.7 × 12.7)
NMAH 227739.1888.H2; Ralph E.
Becker Collection

This torch was carried in political
campaign parades in 1888.

d.
Helmet Torch, before 1884
USA
chrome tin with cotton lining
12 × 11 × 8 (30.5 × 27.9 × 20.3)
NMAH 227739.1884.H2; Ralph E.
Becker Collection

In the campaign of 1884, the supporters of James G. Blaine wore
helmet torches like this one as part
of their plumed knight regalia.

e.
Torch, before 1860
USA
tin
10 × 7½ × 2 (25.4 × 19.1 × 5.1)
NMAH 227739.1860.H3; Ralph E.
Becker Collection

Abraham Lincoln's Wide-Awakes
used this type of torch in their parades during the presidential campaign of 1860. The ring around the
torch revolves and creates an oscil-
lating pattern of light.

f.
Torch, 19th century
USA
tin
12 × 9½ × 1¼ (30.5 × 24.2 ×
3.1)
NMAH 319005.1; Gift of Mrs. Mel-
inda Y. Frye

This star-shaped torch dates from
the nineteenth century.

g.
Torch, 1860
USA
tin
12 × 6 × 6 (30.5 × 15.2 × 15.2)
NMAH 245215.01; Gift of George
H. Watson

The double-swinging device on this
conical torch was practical for campaign parades because it held the
torch in an upright position and
prevented the oil from dripping.

h.
Campaign Lantern, 19th century
USA
tin, glass
17 × 5 × 5 (43.2 × 12.7 × 12.7)
NMAH 227739.1894.H1; Ralph E.
Becker Collection

This hurricane lamp was carried in
parades during the 1896 presidential campaign.

258 i

258 j

i.

Lantern, 19th century
USA
punched tin with wooden handle
12½ × 7¼ × 5¾ (31.8 × 18.4 ×
14.6)
NMAH 319892.05

Partisans of William McKinley in
the 1900 presidential campaign
called this a "full dinner pail" lantern.

j.

Paper Lantern, 19th century
USA
paper on wire frame
9½ × 5½ × 5½ (24.1 × 14 × 14)
NMAH 1979.0520.05

This lantern, which resembled a
balloon, was used in the presidential campaign of 1888.

k.

Lantern, 19th century
USA
glass, metal
12¾ × 6½ × 6½ (32.4 × 16.5 ×
16.5)
NMAH 305360.145; Gift of
Michael V. DeSalle

Lanterns like this one were carried
by Abraham Lincoln's supporters in
1864.

259.

Quilt, 1841
USA
silk, cotton
100 × 98 (254 × 248.9)
NMAH 34124; Elizabeth C. Beale
Accession

This quilt was made to commemorate the inauguration of President
William Henry Harrison on March

4, 1841. It contains colorful silk
ribbons collected from various inaugural festivities.

260.

FOURTH OF JULY. These posters
dating from the first decade of the
twentieth century advertise festivities for the Fourth of July—the
most widely celebrated patriotic
holiday in the United States.

July 4, 1776, was the day that the
Declaration of Independence
drafted by Thomas Jefferson was
approved by almost all representatives of the colonies.

It was actually on July 2, 1776,
that the representatives voted for
independence from Great Britain.
John Adams wrote to his wife Abi-
gail on July 3 that this event
"ought to be solemnized with
Pomp and Parade, with Shews,
Games, Sports, Guns, Bells, Bon-
fires, Illuminations from one End
of this Continent to the other from
this Time forward forever more."

In the late 1700s and early 1800s
Americans glorified Independence
Day with orations, pageants, displays, fireworks, and military
shows. The date of July 4 has often
been chosen to mark important national events, such as the granting
of nationhood to the Philippines;
for dedicating or opening buildings,
parks, and public works; and for
formally marking additions of
states to the union by the flying of
flags with new stars—most recently for Alaska and Hawaii.

The posters here make no mention of oratory. The events they
feature show a modern trend toward entertainment rather than in-
trospective patriotic reflection on
the origin and historical continuity
of the republic.

a.

Fourth of July Poster, ca. 1910
Barton Press, Farmington, Maine
lithograph on cardboard
21 × 14 (53.3 × 35.5)
NMAH CBA9001; Collection of
Business Americana

b.

Fourth of July Poster, 1910
Ohio
lithograph on paper
20⁹⁄₁₆ × 6¹¹⁄₁₆ (52.2 × 17)
NMAH CBA5972; Collection of
Business Americana

261.
Quilt, ca. 1863–98
Nashville, Tennessee
silk, cotton
70 × 80 (177.8 × 203.2)
NMAH T8900; Gift of Mrs. Mary
Alice Hughes Lord

During the Civil War, Mary Alice
Hughes carried this quilt through
Confederate lines from Tennessee
to Cincinnati and then back to
Tennessee after the fall of Fort
Donelson. The dates on the quilt
range from 1863 to 1898, and the
signatures on it include those of
Abraham Lincoln, Chester A.
Arthur, William McKinley, and
Theodore Roosevelt.

262.
APPAREL OF LEADERSHIP. In
Polynesia, items of apparel made
from rare, laboriously gathered or
manufactured materials were an in-
dex of social prestige. Only a prestigious leader could command suf-
ficient resources and manpower to
produce the finest garments and
adornments. A chief's costume ex-
alted him above his subjects—especially during public occasions—because of its visual impact and,
often, its conceptual complexity.

a.
Feather Cloak, date unknown
Maori people; New Zealand
flax, parrot feathers, wool
21 × 39¾ × 1½ (53.3 × 100.9 ×
3.7)
NMNH T11446

Maori society was organized according to aristocratic concepts,
but an individual could gain the respect of his peers through courage
and wisdom. A chief's personal
power, called *mana*, was extended
to his belongings, such as weapons,
amulets, and feather cloaks. Imbued with the *mana* of its original
owner, a feather cloak like this one
became a family heirloom and its
mana increased with the noble
deeds of heroic descendants.

b.
Ivory Pendant with Necklace (*lei
niho palaoa*), before 1838
Hawaii, East Polynesia
walrus tooth, human hair
11 × 6¾ × 3 (27.9 × 17.2 × 7.6)
NMNH 3565

Necklaces such as this one were
ornaments of the Hawaiian aristocracy. In pre-European times the
pendants were made of whale
ivory, but after Hawaii came in
contact with the West they were
frequently made of walrus ivory
traded from the northwest coast of
America.

c.
Whale Tooth (*tambua*), before 1923
Ngau Island, Fiji, West Polynesia
sperm-whale tooth
2½ × 8¼ × 4 (6.4 × 20.9 × 10.2)
NMNH 369325; Gift of Dr. Casey
Wood
Illustrated in color, p. 46

262 b

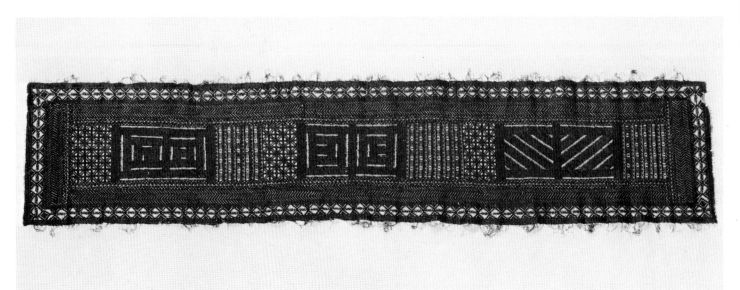

262 e

d.

Whale-Teeth Neck Ornament, before 1877
Levuka Island, Fiji, West Polynesia
sperm-whale teeth, vegetable fiber, red cotton cloth
4½ × 12¾ × 10 (11.5 × 32.4 × 25.4)
NMNH 23918

In Fiji, whale teeth are a token presented to mark important transactions, such as marriage, performance of a service by an expert, and formations of alliance. They may also be formally given prior to a statement of request. Exchange of whale teeth honor both donor and recipient, and if a request is made at the time of the exchange, it has to be regarded as a matter of great social weight. As symbols of a chief's power and corresponding responsibility, whale teeth are especially prominent in political ceremonies. As with bark cloth, the relative quantity of whale teeth is an indication of power.

e.

Loincloth, before 1900
Fiji, West Polynesia
bark cloth made from paper mulberry tree, pigments
110 × 22 (279.4 × 55.9)
NMNH 205111

In Fiji no material or object of special quality is reserved for leaders—unlike the custom in Hawaii, where the special feather cape exists solely for the leaders' pleasure or adornment. Instead, power and

status is indicated by a vast quantity of everyday things. The greatness of a chief, for example, can be judged by his wealth of bark cloth. Although any man could wear a bark-cloth loincloth, a chief's might be hundreds of feet long. In addition, a chief often owns huge bales of bark cloth that he presents to allies or distributes among his people during marriage and funeral ceremonies.

f.

Feather Cape (*'ahu 'ula*), before 1842
Hawaii, East Polynesia
bast, feathers from the *'i'iwi* (*Vestiaria coccinea*) and *'o'o* (*Maho nobilis*)
21¾ × 36¼ × ⅜ (55.2 × 92 × 0.9)
NMNH 3574
Illustrated in color, p. 46

In Hawaii important male chiefs could own and wear feather capes such as this. The size of a cape was an indication of the prestige of its wearer. Production of a single cape required the coordinated labor of several specialists. Bird trappers worked many hours to gather colorful feathers in the wild. Yellow feathers were scarce and difficult to accumulate, and the amount of yellow in a cape was also an indication of a chief's relative position in the hierarchy. The tightly meshed backing for the capes was fabricated from laboriously prepared natural fibers. High-ranking craftsmen-priests arranged the designs and attached the feathers.

263.

Chief's Staff (*kafunda ya kutembele*), ca. 1880
Luba people; Zaire
wood, copper, iron
62½ × 5 × 2½ (158.8 × 12.7 × 6.4)
NMNH 323052

The great staff symbolized formal leadership among the Luba. A chief took it with him on his voyages as an immediately recognizable sign of his royal status. In his own village, the chief planted the staff in the ground before a house to indicate his presence within. At occasions of state or in council, he planted it at his side. In a messenger's hands the staff was a royal assurance of trustworthiness and good faith.

264.

Ax, ca. 1850–1920
Luba people; Zaire
wood, iron, copper
13¼ × 2⅛ × 9¾ (33.7 × 5.4 × 24.8)
NMNH 322759

As part of a leader's insignia, ornamented implements like this ax attested to their owner's status. Generously decorated and sometimes structurally altered, everyday tools became symbols of prestige and power. The leader of a village or clan would carry an emblem such as this on official visits and ceremonial occasions.

In several African societies the ornamented ax was an integral part

A Fijian noble dressed in swaths of bark (tapa) cloth; drawing by Theodor Kleinschmidts, 1877. Courtesy, Herbert Tischner and Baessler Archive, Museum für Volkerkunde, Berlin, West Germany (see no. 262 e).

of certain traditional dances in which it aided its user in gesturing and punctuating the beat.

265.
Ax (*kpo*), ca. 1850–1900
Fon people; Republic of Benin
wood, iron
8¼ × 19½ × 1½ (20.9 × 49.4 × 3.7)
NMNH 249738

264

After commissioning a stylized ax of this kind, a king presented it to a trusted courtier. The courtier carried it with him to give validity and solemnity to his words when he delivered messages for the king. The courtier also used it to gesture and keep time in dances at court.

266.
Baton, ca. 1880
Mbundu people; Angola
brass tacks, wood
18¼ × 2½ × 2¾ (46.3 × 6.4 × 7)
NMNH 205403

Batons such as this one identify and protect chieftains among the Mbundu people. They are usually custom made for particular individuals, having been prescribed by diviners or soothsayers. To show his status and to insure supernatural protection, a chief carries his baton when sitting in the village council, when visiting, and when welcoming guests.

The motif of the young woman, seen here and on many carved batons, is thought to refer to the "guardian of the sacred fire," the girl who tends the fire that is lit for each new chief. She controls rainfall and fertility in her chief's domain and guards the insignia held by the successors of deceased leaders. The hairstyle with a loop in back is characteristic of traditional Mbundu women.

267.
Flywhisk, ca. 1850–1900
unspecified people; probably northern Congo Basin
elephant tail
24¼ × 9½ × 1½ (61.5 × 24.2 × 3.7)
NMNH 323386

The flywhisk serves a symbolic political function beyond its practical one of brushing away flies. To emphasize a point, a leader may brandish it or strike it into his palm while speaking. Although an elephant-tail whisk is too stiff to serve its practical purpose well, its association with the largest land animal makes it an appropriate symbol of power and leadership.

268.
Tableau, ca. 1900–1925
Fon people; Republic of Benin
brass, wood
4½ × 23 (11.5 × 58.4)
NMNH 349146

This tableau depicts a king being carried in a litter with his retinue before and behind him. The scene might be an important visit or a festive ceremony. Included among the retainers are porters, musicians, and umbrella bearers.

Commissioned by the king, tableaux like this one commemorated important events and recorded daily life among the Fon people. The king kept these brass figures in his palace or on the tombs of his ancestors. He also gave them as signs of favor to clan leaders, who were expected to treat them with the same respect. As colonization in Africa increased, brass figures in the traditional tableau style became popular trade items for Europeans.

269.
SYMBOLS OF OFFICE. When the Secretary of the Smithsonian Institution carries the mace on high ceremonial occasions and in academic processions, he also wears a badge of office affixed to a silk and velvet master's gown. Designed by Leslie Durbin of the Worshipful Company of Goldsmiths in London, these objects were first used during the 1965 bicentennial of James Smithson's birth.

a.

Smithsonian Secretary's Badge of Office, ca. 1965
Made in London, England; used at the Smithsonian Institution, Washington, D.C.
gold, ribbon
2¾ × 2¾ (7 × 7)
SI Office of the Secretary

On the obverse of the badge is the owl of Athena, a symbol of wisdom that has become an unofficial emblem of the Smithsonian. On the reverse of the badge Durbin engraved "a sun in his splendor," derived from the Smithson family's coat of arms, which relates both to the worldwide importance of the Smithsonian today and to Smithson's personal quest to light the darkness.

b.

Smithsonian Mace, ca. 1965
made in London, England; used at the Smithsonian Institution, Washington, D.C.
oxidized silver, gold, smithsonite, diamonds, spinel rubies
5¼ × 47 (13.3 × 119.5)
SI 73.188; Gift of Anonymous Friends of the Smithsonian

The Smithsonian Mace, carried in academic processions and on other formal occasions, represents and symbolizes the institution founded by James Smithson (1765–1829). The mace, like the Smithsonian Torch, stands for knowledge, freedom, and progress. The metal flames of the symbolic torch in the mace burn inside the hollow golden globe, an astrolabe, illuminating the world.

The demi-lion, from the Smithson family coat of arms, is set into smithsonite, the mineral identified in 1802 by James Smithson. The ruby-eyed lion holds a diamond-studded sun, which radiates the light of knowledge that illuminates the darkness of ignorance.

The motto of the Smithsonian, "For the Increase and Diffusion of Knowledge," taken from Smithson's will, encircles the globe. A golden ribbon spiraling down the staff contains the names of the Smithsonian Institution's eight secretaries.

269 b

270.
GUARANI CHIEFTAIN'S COSTUME. Native South Americans reserved elaborate costume and adornment, especially featherwork, for high ceremonial occasions. In daily life they went naked or nearly naked. Only when feasting, dancing, or asserting power over others did they wear outfits such as the one shown here. As for two other South American peoples in this exhibition—the Bororo (no. 173) and Jívaro Indians (no. 211)—the Guarani Indians used feathers as currency, and spectacular feathered ornaments were signs of wealth and prestige. The original owner of this costume must have had considerable status to have put together such an ensemble. Perhaps he was a chieftain or priest. In times of danger and of celebration a ritual leader depended upon such finery to emphasize his crucial role of focusing and heightening his community's response to threat or good fortune.

Chieftain's Costume, ca. 1900
NMNH 213621 a–j, 213622,
220415; Collected by Hon. J. N.
Ruffin
Illustrated in color, p. 48

From top:

Feathered Headdress
Guarani Indians; Paraguay or Mato
Grosso, Brazil
feathers, native twine
30 × 21¼ × 1½ (76.2 × 54 × 3.8)

Vertical Diadem
Guarani Indians; Paraguay or Mato
Grosso, Brazil
feathers, quills, native rope
8⅓ × 21½ × 1½ (21.3 × 54.6 × 3.8)

Feather Plume
Guarani Indians; Paraguay or Mato
Grosso, Brazil
feathers, wooden rod
12¾ × 3¾ × ⅛ (32.4 × 9.5 × 0.3)

Necklace
Guarani Indians; Paraguay or Mato
Grosso, Brazil
bamboo, seeds, beads, native twine,
metal button
10 × 8 × 2 (25.4 × 20.3 × 5.1)

Three Net Bags
Guarani Indians; Paraguay or Mato
Grosso, Brazil
native twine
largest: 22 × 5½ × ⅛ (55.9 × 14
× 0.3)

Two Feathered Armlets
Guarani Indians; Paraguay or Mato
Grosso, Brazil
feathers, native twine
largest: 13 × 7½ (33 × 19.1)

Two Feathered Wristlets
Guaicurú Indians; Paraguay
feathers, native-twine netting
each: 3½ × 24½ × 1 (8.9 × 62.2
× 2.5)

Feathered Dangle Ornaments
Guarani Indians; Paraguay or Mato
Grosso, Brazil
feathers, padded shaft, porcupine
tail
each: 18 × 6¾ × ¾ (45.7 × 17.2
× 1.8)

270 (three net bags)

Feathered Skirt
Guarani Indians; Paraguay or Mato
Grosso, Brazil
feathers, native cotton string
56 × 9⅛ × 1 (142.2 × 23.2 × 2.5)

Rattle
Guarani Indians; Paraguay or Mato
Grosso, Brazil
deer- or peccary-hoof points, native
twine, feathers, down, wire
18½ × 4¼ (47 × 11)

DATE DUE

This book was designed by Carol Hare,
typeset by FotoTypesetters, Inc.,
and printed by Wolk Press, Inc.,
on the occasion of the exhibition
Celebration: A World of Art and Ritual,
held at the Renwick Gallery,
March 17, 1982–June 26, 1983.

ISBN 0–87474–433–4